SAFE SURFING

A Family Guide to the Net

LIMITED WARRANTY AND DISCLAIMER OF LIABILITY

ACADEMIC PRESS, INC. ("AP") AND ANYONE ELSE WHO HAS BEEN INVOLVED IN THE CREATION OR PRODUCTION OF THE ACCOMPANYING CODE ("THE PRODUCT") CANNOT AND DO NOT WARRANT THE PERFORMANCE OR RESULTS THAT MAY BE OBTAINED BY USING THE PRODUCT. THE PRODUCT IS SOLD "AS IS" WITHOUT WARRANTY OF ANY KIND (EXCEPT AS HEREAFTER DESCRIBED), EITHER EXPRESSED OR IMPLIED, INCLUDING, BUT NOT LIMITED TO, ANY WARRANTY OF PERFORMANCE OR ANY IMPLIED WARRANTY OF MERCHANTABILITY OR FITNESS FOR ANY PARTICULAR PURPOSE. AP WARRANTS ONLY THAT THE MAGNETIC DISC(S) ON WHICH THE CODE IS RECORDED IS FREE FROM DEFECTS IN MATERIAL AND FAULTY WORKMANSHIP UNDER THE NORMAL USE AND SERVICE FOR A PERIOD OF NINETY (90) DAYS FROM THE DATE THE PRODUCT IS DELIVERED. THE PURCHASER'S SOLE AND EXCLUSIVE REMEDY IN THE EVENT OF A DEFECT IS EXPRESSLY LIMITED TO EITHER REPLACEMENT OF THE DISC(S) OR REFUND OF THE PURCHASE PRICE, AT AP'S SOLE DISCRETION.

IN NO EVENT, WHETHER AS A RESULT OF BREACH OF CONTRACT, WARRANTY OR TORT (INCLUDING NEGLIGENCE) WILL AP OR ANYONE WHO HAS BEEN INVOLVED IN THE CREATION OR PRODUCTION OF THE PRODUCT BE LIABLE TO PURCHASER FOR ANY DAMAGES, INCLUDING ANY LOST PROFITS, LOST SAVINGS OR OTHER INCIDENTAL OR CONSEQUENTIAL DAMAGES ARISING OUT OF THE USE OR INABILITY TO USE PRODUCT OR ANY MODIFICATIONS THEREOF, OR DUE TO THE CONTENTS OF THE CODE, EVEN IF AP HAS BEEN ADVISED OF THE POSSIBILITY OF SUCH DAMAGES, OR ANY CLAIM BY ANY OTHER PARTY.

Any request for replacement of a defective CD-ROM disc must be postage prepaid and must be accompanied by the original defective disc, your mailing address and telephone number, and proof of date of purchase and purchase price. Send such requests, stating the nature of the problem, to Academic Press Customer Service, 6277 Sea Harbor Drive, Orlando, FL 32887, 1-800-321-5068. APP shall have no obligation to refund the purchase price or to replace a disc based on the claims of defects in the nature or operation of the Product.

Some states do not allow limitation on how long an implied warranty lasts, nor exclusions or limitatiions of incidental or consequential damage, so the above limitations and exclusions may not apply to you. This Warranty gives you specific legal rights, and you may also have other rights which may vary from jurisdiction to jurisdiction.

THE RE-EXPORT OF UNITED STATES ORIGIN SOFTWARE IS SUBJECT TO THE UNITED STATES LAWS UNDER THE EXPORT ADMINISTRATION ACT OF 1969 AS AMENDED. ANY FURTHER SALE OF THE PRODUCT SHALL BE IN COMPLIANCE WITH THE UNITED STATES DEPARTMENT OF COMMERCE ADMINISTRATION REGULATIONS. COMPLIANCE WITH SUCH REGULATIONS IS YOUR RESPONSIBILITY AND NOT THE RESPONSIBILITY OF AP.

SAFE SURFING
A Family Guide to the Net

Julie McKeehan

AP PROFESSIONAL

AP PROFESSIONAL is a division of Academic Press, Inc.

Boston   San Diego   New York
London   Sydney   Tokyo   Toronto

Microsoft ® is a registered trademark and Microsoft Internet Explorer™ is a trademark of Microsoft.

Eudora Light ® is a registered trademark of QUALCOMM, Inc. The version included on the CD is NOT the fully-supported commercial version of the product.

Surfwatch™ is a trademark of Surfwatch Software, Inc. **SURF WATCH.**

Cyber Patrol, CyberNOT, the Cyber Patrol logo and the Microsystems Software logo are trademarks of Microsystems Software, Inc. To Surf and Protect is a service mark of Microsystems Software, Inc. All other names are trademarks of their respective companies.

This book is printed on acid-free paper ∞

Copyright © 1996 by Academic Press
All rights reserved.
No part of this publication may be reproduced or transmitted in any form or by any means, electronic or mechanical, including photocopy, recording, or any information storage and retrieval system, without permission in writing from the publisher.

All brand names and product names mentioned in this book are trademarks or registered trademarks of their respective companies.

AP PROFESSIONAL
1300 Boylston Street, Chestnut Hill, MA 02167

An imprint of ACADEMIC PRESS, INC.
A Division of HARCOURT BRACE & COMPANY

United Kingdom Edition published by
ACADEMIC PRESS LIMITED
24-28 Oval Road, London NW1 7DX

Library of Congress Cataloging-in-Publication Data

McKeehan, Julie.
    Safe Surfing : a family guide to the Net
        p.   cm.
      ISBN 0-12-484834-6 (alk. paper)
       1. Internet (Computer network) 2. Computers and family.
  I. Title.
TK5105.875.I57M3827   1996
025.04--dc20
                                      96-8193
                                         CIP

Printed in the United States of America
96 97 98 99 IP 9 8 7 6 5 4 3 2 1

For Neil,

*thank you for this book,
for 15 years, for everything.*

Contents

Contents vii

Foreword xi

Acknowledgments xiii

Online Rules of Behavior xv

Introduction to Safe Surfing 1
    Who Are You? 1
    What the Net Has to Offer 2
    What You Need to Get on the Net 4
    Is There Awful Stuff on the Net? 4
    What I Think You Want 8
    How I Cover the Material 9

Part One   Figuring Out the Net

Chapter 1   What Is the Net, Anyway? 13
    What Is the Net? 14
    Email 20
    Newsgroups 21
    Discussion/Chat Groups 28
    World Wide Web 30
    FTP Storage Sites 32

Contents

Understanding Internet Addresses 36
In Conclusion 38

Chapter 2 Choosing an Internet Service 39
Words You Need to Know 40
Is an Online Service for You? 49
Is an ISP for You? 51
Making the Right Choice 53

Chapter 3 Choosing an Online Service 55
Online Services in General 56
America Online 59
CompuServe 67
Prodigy 77
Microsoft Network (MSN) 87
What's the Right Choice 95

Chapter 4 Choosing a Service Provider 99
Getting a Service Provider 101
Being a Wise Consumer 106
Bess, a Family ISP 113

Part Two   Exploring the Net

Chapter 5 Starting Places 123
Take a Tour 124
Great Overall Places 125
Great Kid Sites 139
Quick Dip Spots 150
Yuppy Favorites 152

Contents ix

Chapter 6   *News, Weather, and Sports*....................**159**
    News...160
    Weather..164
    Sports 168

Chapter 7   *The Weird and Wonderful of the Net*.............**171**
    A Walk on the Weird Side 172
    The Wonderful Stuff..182

Chapter 8   *All Sorts of Stuff for Parents* **199**
    Advice..200
    Resources 206
    Family Home Pages 213

Chapter 9   *How to Find Things on the Net*.......................**217**
    Finding People..218
    Finding a Certain Topic 224
    Going to the Library...239

Part Three   Being Safe on the Net

Chapter 10   *Making the Net Safe* **247**
    Why the Net Is Not Safe 248
    Net Safety Rules..252
    Online Rules of Behavior...257
    Safe Web Sites for Kids 261

Chapter 11   *Security Software Compared*......................**265**

  Security Software 266
  My Recommendations 290
  Quick Feature Comparison Chart............................... 297

Chapter 12 *The Future of Net Safety* 299
  What's Ahead for Net Safety?..................................... 299
  Standards for the Net 302
  What Will Happen to Web Sites................................. 306
  What about Newsgroups?.. 310
  What about Chat Rooms? 311
  Can a Voluntary Effort Work? 311
  What Will Always Work.. 312

Glossary 313

Index 321

Foreword

Nestled next to the family computer rests an open box of well-worn crayons, a visible reminder that many children are as comfortable using one as the other. Unlike many parents, children often confidently "boot up" and "log on" with the same ease as coloring a barnyard scene. Did things somehow become more complex than our box of crayons, or did we, as adults, create this complexity in our minds?

When we were our children's age, we colored all kinds of pictures for no other reason than we loved the feeling of placing colored wax on paper. As time progressed and the focus slowly shifted to the result of our efforts instead of our joy of creation, we graduated from eight colors to a box of 64. Eventually, the crayons were abandoned to pastels, oils, airbrushes and other "more artistic" means, leaving behind the tattered box full of the wonder of our childhood.

We feel that Julie McKeehan does more than simply present the Internet in an easy to understand way. She actually rejuvenates in us the childlike joy and wonder of exploration that resided in that original box of crayons. We understand the intimidation that many adults feel when they start their exploration of the Internet, and it is not presented here as a cold technical world of interconnected computers, but as a fun and exciting, family-oriented experience.

We believe the Internet is one of the most wonderful learning tools our children have, and a brand new way of communicating with each other. Due to its interactive nature and abundance of information, children enjoy using it and learn at accelerated levels and all of us are brought closer together as we share our ideas, thoughts and dreams.

This book recognizes the individuals and companies which have lent their creativeness and support to families and children online. They have utilized the advances in technology to create products and services and publish Internet content which protects, educates and entertains families and children everywhere.

The Internet is not the dark and dangerous place that our society has been led to believe. There are areas which only adults should visit, but there is technology which enables us to make sure our children do not. We believe that the solutions to these issues, and many issues that affect our lives, lie in the technology and the Internet community itself. It is for those very beliefs that we started our organization, Safe Surf, and strive each day to make the Internet safe and open to all people—adults and children alike.

Discouraging the free flow of information closes the online world to all of us. The Internet is a technology in its infancy, struggling to grow to its full potential. We believe that you will find the online environment a wonderful place to be, and it is our hope that you will finish this book with a sense of a understanding and enlightenment about the Internet, and allow it to enhance your lives and the lives of your children.

Take the time to relive your childhood through the sparkle and wonder in your whiz kid's eyes as they sail across the World Wide Web. Enjoy this book *with* your child and *as* a child. Treasure the window you have to the entire world together.

SafeSurfing to you,

Wendy Simpson, President
Ray Soular, Chairman
SafeSurf
http://www.safesurf.com/

Acknowledgments

I wish you could live in my neighborhood. If you did, you would know that the only way I get anything written is with the help of my friends and family. They clean my house, mother my children, and run my errands while I am writing a book. Worst of all, I force them to slog through countless versions of each chapter helping me catch bad descriptions, fuzzy ideas, and other things I'm far too embarrassed to mention. Everybody knows when I am in the middle of a book and they all breathe a collective sigh of relief when I finish.

I took on this project because I wanted people to know how amazing and just plain fun the Internet can be. As a parent, I have a good sense of what most parents and children would find useful, helpful, or fun. As a long time user of the Internet, I also have a problem—too much knowledge. (If you know too much, you assume that your audience knows everything as well, and you don't explain things enough.) Once again, my neighborhood came to the rescue. These wonderful people, which include computer-challenged individuals, as well as parents and teachers, helped me put my words into readable English. This is what I call prose that will not put people to sleep and which actually describes something usefully. I may have written this book, but you have to thank my friends if it is understandable and helpful.

To Barbie, a wonderful friend and mother, thank you once again. Her ideas, parenting, and morals have contributed more than you can imagine to whatever is good about this book; she is its spiritual co-author. To Jean and Gina, fine teachers that don't like computers very much, thank you for being my guinea pigs. Their lack of knowledge about computers, but clear intelligence about other things, caught some of my worst assumptions. To my mom, Gloria, just because she is the world's greatest grandmother and without whom it would have taken two more months to complete this book. To Loring, thank you for your wonderful attention to detail. To Bruce, Peter, Chuck, and Victor just because you were willing to let me talk about this stuff all the time. To Mary, my mother-in-law, and Carolyn, my sister-in-law, for help adding some humor and clarity to my work.

Then, there are the people whom I met during the course of my research. First of all, I have to mention the kind and generous people at Safe Surf. I met Ray Soular and Wendy Simpson as a result of this book; they are extraordinarily fine individuals. They have helped me in more ways than I can mention. Ray, in particular, has assisted me with demo software, talked to me repeatedly about security and safety issues, and helped in countless other ways. I would rather trust the future of Internet safety to these two people alone, than to the entire government of the United States. Their Safe Surf Web site is one you will want to check out often, and their organization is one you should acquaint yourself with. There are also many people at the companies whose software I have put on the CD-ROM that I want to thank. They have been helpful and generous with their time and software.

Then, there are the people at AP Professional. While I miss my old editor, Chuck Glaser, the new team has done a good job of making sure that everything turned out right. A special thanks to Jeff Pepper, Mike Williams, and Peter Sullivan. I know that they get paid to take care of this stuff, but I am grateful all the same. For my agent, Carole, I thank you once again.

Last of all I must thank my husband and children. My three children, Nicholas, Alexander, and Nathaniel, show a lot of patience when I write a book. Most of all they warm my heart when they whine about how busy I am (it proves they actually miss me). It is always a cause of celebration around my house when I finish. To my husband, Neil, thank you for everything. You are the best husband and father I know.

—*Julie McKeehan*
April 1996
julie@pobox.com

Online Rules of Behavior

These are rules that children should promise to follow as a condition of using the Net.

My Promises

1. I promise I will never give out personal information about myself without my parents' permission.

    This personal information includes: my home address, telephone number, parents' work address or telephone number, name or location of school, town, last name.

Online Rules of Behavior

2. I promise I will never meet someone from the Net without getting my parents' permission first.

3. I promise I will never send someone on the Net a picture of myself (or anything else) without my parents' permission.

4. I promise I will only give out my email address according to my parents' rules.

5. I promise I will tell my parents immediately if someone scares me, or makes me feel uncomfortable or bad.

6. I promise I will follow my parents' rules for how I am supposed to use the Net.

7. I promise I will be polite to other Net users.

_____   _____
Child's signature   Date

Introduction to Safe Surfing

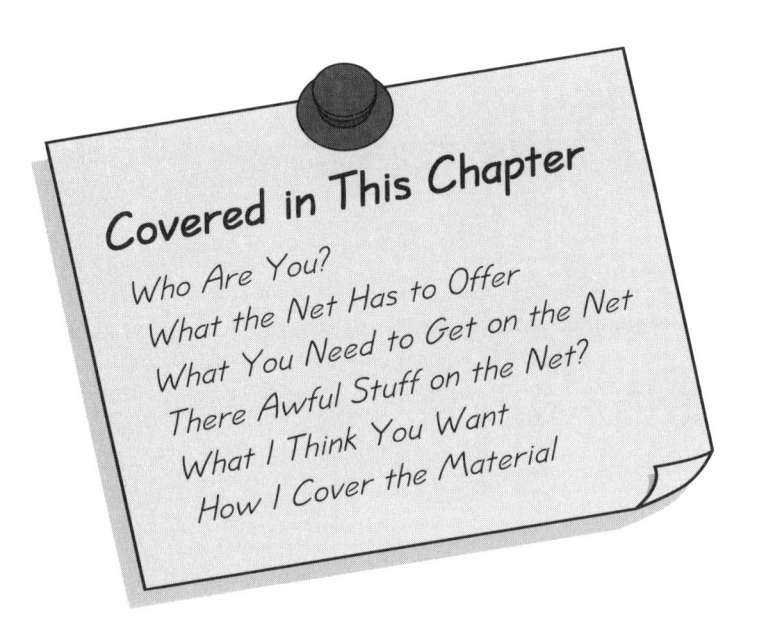

Covered in This Chapter

Who Are You?
What the Net Has to Offer
What You Need to Get on the Net
There Awful Stuff on the Net?
What I Think You Want
How I Cover the Material

Who Are You?

Since you picked up this book, I assume you are someone who *might* be interested in the Net. That, or someone has been nagging you about going online and you have finally succumbed. In either case, what you really want to know is what the Net has to offer you, and why you should you go to all the trouble of reading a book about this stuff. You are also concerned about your children. You have heard that the Internet is not a safe place for children and you want to know how to protect them. You probably want some advice on where you and your children can find good things to do online. If any of these descriptions fits, then this is the book for you.

What the Net Has to Offer

The Net is fun; it can also make your life easier. Besides that, it is great for helping you find out obscure stuff you always wanted to know. The Net also has a lot to offer families in general and children in particular. For now, let me show you what I mean by giving you just a taste of the Net.

I Like Going to the Movies

Typically, I don't plan to go to a movie ahead of time, but decide at the last minute. Before the Net came into my life, I would be forced to rummage around for an old newspaper or rustle through the phone book calling theaters to see what was playing. If this sounds familiar, then keep reading. These days, I saunter over to my computer and connect to the Net and the MovieLink Info page (see Figure 0.1) to see what is showing—far less work than dialing even one phone number. I can quickly scroll through the list of local movie theaters to see what is playing and the times. Neat, huh?

Figure 0.1 MovieLink Info Page.

Kids and Last-Minute Homework

Does this scenario sound familiar? It is 9:30 at night and the library is closed and the kid's homework is due tomorrow. Your daughter tells you that she has a report due the next day in her science class on the dietary habits of the *Microchiroptera*.

Well, if your daughter happens to be a fruit bat expert, okay, but it is more likely that she needs to do some research. Late at night (or any time of day) the Internet is an easy place to find out all she needs to know about these furry little creatures' eating habits. All of a sudden homework research is a snap any time of day.

What You Need to Get on the Net

I hope I have intrigued you enough to get you to read further. If that is the case, then you probably want to know exactly what you need to surf the Net. Here is short version of the list:

- A computer
- A modem (the faster the better)
- Some software (more on this later)
- A phone line

Later on, I will talk about the items in this list. I will give you enough pointers to help you decide exactly what kind of Net experience you want and what is the best way to get online. But first things first. What about the original reason you picked up this book. If you had a question something like, "What about all the foul stuff on the Net I hear so much about in the news?" I can help you figure out what to do.

Is There Awful Stuff on the Net?

Since everyone from the nightly television news to the floor of Congress has been talking about the Information Superhighway (that's the Net) and how important it is to clean it up, you probably have some sort of notion that the Net is littered with pornography. It is often portrayed as a dark and nasty place, full of predators waiting to snatch your children out of the warmth and safety of their home.

First off, I hope I don't need to spend much time convincing you that what you see in the news or how politicians portray things rarely resembles reality. That is no less true in this case. The Net is no more dangerous for your children than a typical park playground in an average town. Like a playground, the Net is a fun place to hang around and jump on things. But, just as the playground is not a place I would let small children go without my direct supervision, or older children go without knowing exactly where they were going and for how long, so I would treat the Net. Perhaps, it might help you to understand the Net better if you first realize who created it and who currently uses it.

Who Is on the Net—People Just like You

The Net was created by people a great deal like you. These are folks with families, hobbies, and bad and good habits. And every single person on the Net has a mother and a father, and many have children of their own.

For example, here are some of the hobbies that folks on the Net regularly like to talk about:

- Sports
- Children
- Politics
- Cooking
- Product reviews
- Movies
- Television
- Good vacation spots
- and, of course, computers

It is probably best to think of the Net as similar to any other ecological environment. It has its share of predators and prey, bad weather and good, nice places to look at a sunset, and, most importantly, lots of great places to explore. It is certainly a place you should not explore without first knowing the rules.

So, Is It full of Dark and Nasty Stuff?

Of course it is. Yes, there is pornography and other types of offensive material on the Net. Do you have to see or read it? Not if you don't want to. You can usually avoid anything that you think is inappropriate. Through what I will show you in this book, you can filter out all types of material you find offensive, thereby ensuring that neither you nor your children are exposed to such things.

Reasons Not to Avoid the Net

Avoiding the Net because there is some stuff there that you will not like makes as much sense as never reading any books because one book may contain some obscene words. Or as much sense as never watching television or seeing a movie because one movie may have a distasteful scene.

Reasons Not to Regulate the Net

Nor does turning some government loose to regulate the Net make any more sense. The Net is a wonderful place created out of the imaginations of people the world over. In its own haphazard and multi-dimensional way, it clearly shows what awe inspiring and marvelous things human beings are capable of making.

Attempting to regulate the Net will probably not work and will at best produce something even less useful than most Saturday morning cartoons. Regulating the Net makes as much sense as locking up libraries to avoid offending someone's sensibilities. Free speech is a treasure of great value, played out on the Net with extraordinary diversity and imagination.

Further, why would you imagine that a government (the United States government, for example) would be any better at regulating the Net than it is at balancing its budget?

What Should Be Done with the Net

So, should you just turn children loose on the Net with no supervision? Absolutely not! The whole point in being a parent or teacher is to thoughtfully govern what children are exposed to in their lives. It is absolutely our responsibility —each and every one of us—to know what our children are doing on the Net. And that is the best way to handle the Net as well: know exactly what material a child is exploring. In fact, it can be fun exploring the Net together, and it is certainly a more engaging way to spend time than watching television.

The Good News

The best news I have for you is that there are a lot of parents and other people who regularly use the Net, who write computer programs, who love children, and who are genuinely interested in making the Net a safe place to explore. Those people are busily writing all sorts of software that will let you control what your child sees. I will be talking about most of that software and helping you decide what the right program is for you and your family.

My Promise to You

I promise you that I will teach you enough so that you can oversee what your children do on the Net. I will help you find the good stuff, help you figure out how to do the supervision, and as an added benefit, give you a great new way to spend time with your children. I will also make sure you know exactly how to avoid areas of the Net you do not like, show you to what extent you can keep children out of them, and help you understand some basic rules of Net safety for both you and your children.

What I Think You Want

Here is what I think you want from this book:

- Some tips on the right sort of Net account for children and families
- Explanations in everyday language about what the Net has to offer
- Information on where the good stuff for children and families is on the Net
- Help learning to explore the Net
- Help finding the interesting stuff
- Help learning how to do research on the Net (perhaps for that homework that is due tomorrow)
- How to search for a particular subject

- Information on how to keep children (or yourself) away from inappropriate material

You are in luck because that is exactly what this book covers. I hope you can hardly wait to start the adventure.

What This Book Doesn't Give You

What this book does not give you is all the software you need to connect to the Net. Is also does not tell you all you may want to know about various ways to connect to the Internet. Relax. I will make sure to point you in the right direction for that material as well (there are a lot of great books that do this).

The problem is that until you decide a few basic issues about how you want to access the Net I won't know in which direction to point you. So first you will need to decide what kind of Net access you want; then I will point you in the right direction to get everything you need to get it. If you already have a Net account, we can proceed directly to the exploring.

I pick you up again after you have your Net account and teach you how to explore the Net and deal with security issues. Why not do everything here, you might ask? The simple answer is that would make this a huge book, and other writers have already covered getting connected to the Internet.

How I Cover the Material

This book is divided into three parts. If you are completely new to the Internet, you should read the book straight through. If you are already familiar with the Net, feel free to read the parts in any order you wish.

The First Part—Figuring Out the Net

The first part is a basic guide for people completely new to the Net. It covers everything you need to know about what the Internet is and how to get on it. I also help you decide what type of Internet account is right for your family. If you are on the Net and are comfortable with online terminology, you should feel free to skip this section.

The Second Part—Exploring the Net

In the second part, I talk about some of the exciting places on the Internet for children and adults. I show you how to use the Net to do homework and to find things of interest. The rest of the time is spent describing the marvelous and fun places your whole family can visit during your online adventures.

The Third Part—Being Safe on the Net

In the third part, I explain how to block Internet material you do not want your children to see. I talk about the steps you can take to make sure that your kids have a safe and fun Internet experience. I tell you what type of supervision children require on the Net and describe the software tools that can help you do this. I also mention some sites that are dedicated to providing safe and fun places for children to explore.

The CD-ROM

See "What's on the CD" to find out what is on the CD-ROM. It includes the access control software that allows you to block certain Internet sites and various other helpful files.

Part One

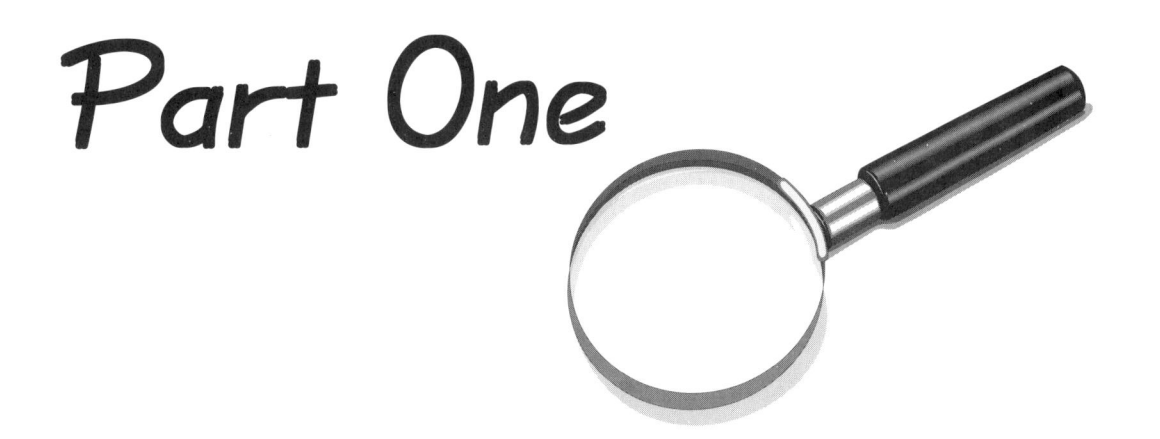

Figuring Out the Net

Location: http://www.dsiegel.com/vestibule/vestibule.html

| What's New? | What's Cool? | Handbook | Net Search | Net Directory | Newsgroups |

THE VESTIBULE

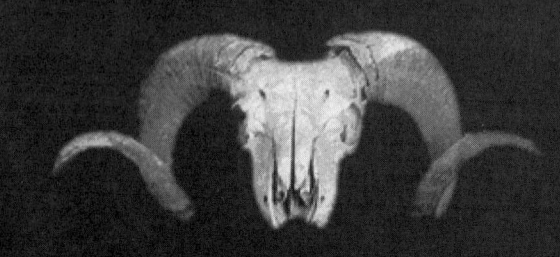

TEMPORARY SANITY

If you have just come from   This door takes you right to a   This takes you to my Home

Chapter 1
What Is the Net, Anyway?

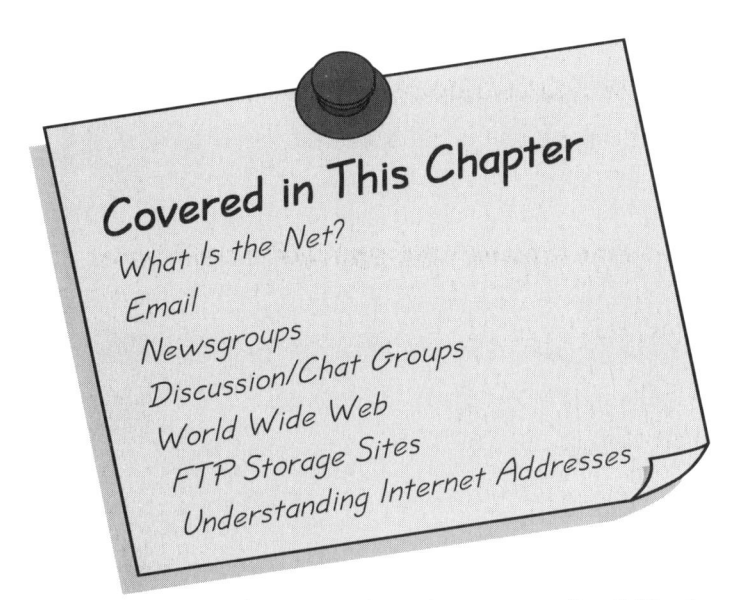

Covered in This Chapter
- What Is the Net?
- Email
- Newsgroups
- Discussion/Chat Groups
- World Wide Web
- FTP Storage Sites
- Understanding Internet Addresses

You know, of course, that this is a really difficult question to answer. It is hard because the Net is such a complex thing (actually it isn't just one thing). So bear with me while I give it a try…

CyberSpace   Virtual Reality   Surfing the Net   Internet
             The Net   Information Superhighway
                                                                World Wide Web
             Getting Wired   Going Online

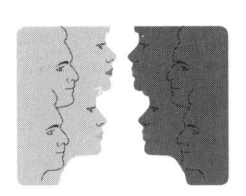

What Is the Net?

When I tell someone who does not use the Net about this book, I invariably get asked the question, "Just what is the Net, anyway?" When asked this question I usually grimace, pause a long time, and eventually answer something like this:

"A huge number of interconnected computers filled with interesting people and really useful stuff."

Just as routinely I have read descriptions of the Net (short for Internet) in books and magazines that are couched in terms of the Internet's origins or its exact physical makeup. They usually read something like:

"The Internet is a network of computers, all speaking the same Protocols that had as its backbone the ARPA (Advanced Research Projects Agency) network. ARPAnet was created by the U.S. government for experimental purposes."

Now that cleared things up, don't you think?

From this example, I expect that you will have already figured out the first thing I want you to know about the Net:

- Explaining to you how the Internet came into being or exactly how it works physically will not help you to understand what it means to use it.

But that is what you should have expected, because this is just as true of other complex, life-changing modern inventions. I could explain to you until I am blue in the face how metal conducts electricity and how to capture voice as packets of digital information. But I ask you, "Does that explain the telephone? Will that convey the enormous effects on and changes made to our daily lives by its presence in our homes and workplaces?" I don't think so. Well, neither will talking about the Internet in exact physical terms. If truth be told, I don't think it is important for most people to understand what the Internet is composed of or how it works. Just like the phone, people only need to know enough information about the Net to be able to use it.

Here Is a Physical Definition of the Net

So, let's start with the only part of the physical description you might profit from knowing. The Internet is just a bunch of computers connected together by phone wires, underground cables, and satellites. These connections are important, however, because they span the globe. There are computers sitting in Nairobi, London, Los Angeles, Washington, D.C., and Beijing that talk to each other all the time.

Because those computers are connected in an interlacing pattern (much like a real-life fishing net) they can all communicate with each other and share stuff. The "stuff," or contents, of these computers is what is interesting to us.

Note: When you think about these computers being connected together you might wish to visualize them in the same way you think of phones being connected (while not perfect, this is a good enough analogy). There is a phone in your house that is connected by a wire that runs from your house out somewhere (usually to a telephone pole) where all the other houses' phone wires go. All those wires meet together at a switching station.

So here is our first, working definition of the Internet:

- The Internet is a huge number of computers that are connected together and filled with stuff.

When I talk about one of these Internet computers, you should imagine that it may be either like or unlike the computers that you use at home, school, or the office. In fact, some of the computers that make up the Internet are exactly the same as the computer sitting on your desk right now. Other computers in this collection are really big, unlike any you have ever seen, and probably at some university or major research facility. These are very fast computers with huge amounts of storage space and special ways of communicating with other computers. There are also medium-sized computers that are bigger than what you have but smaller than the gigantic ones.

With that piece of information, we can refine our definition of the Internet a little bit more.

- The Internet is a huge number of big, medium, and small computers that are connected together and filled with interesting things.

Technical Aside: Most people do nicely using the phone without knowing much about the mechanics of phone calls. Likewise, people probably don't know much about telephone switching stations except that they take incoming phone calls, process them, and send them along their way. Same deal with these gigantic computers. They handle the majority of the Internet traffic.

That is all you need to know about how the Internet works physically. So let's move on to the next interesting part, which is where the interesting things come from and the special ways you can use it.

Just Where Does This Stuff Come From?

This stuff can be literally anything. Just as your own computer can have all sorts of things on it—anything from games, to paint programs, to word processors, to CD-ROMs full of great multimedia, just so with the Net. The programs on your computer, however, are different from the things on the Net in two very important ways:

- The contents of the Net are the result of the creative expression of millions of people.

- You can explore this stuff in any way you can imagine.

The Creative Expression of Millions of People

Let's take this first point about creative expression. Both the most marvelous and the most difficult thing about the Net is that it contains so much stuff. Imagine, if you will, having at your fingertips the creative expressions, opinions, mailboxes, and conversations of roughly every single person in Canada or the combined populations of Chile, Sweden, Iceland, and Malta. Current estimates of the number of users on the Net are at 24 million. For your own amusement, look at Figure 1.1 to see where the Net stands in comparison to the population of some countries.

And if that is not staggering enough, the population of the Internet is doubling quite quickly these days, making the statistics I just gave you inaccurate even before you read them. This virtual community is huge, creative, and marvelous to behold. When you enter it, you are entering what many people have called:

18 Chapter 1 What Is the Net, Anyway?

- CyberSpace
- The Information SuperHighway

Figure 1.1
Populations (in Millions) of Various Countries.

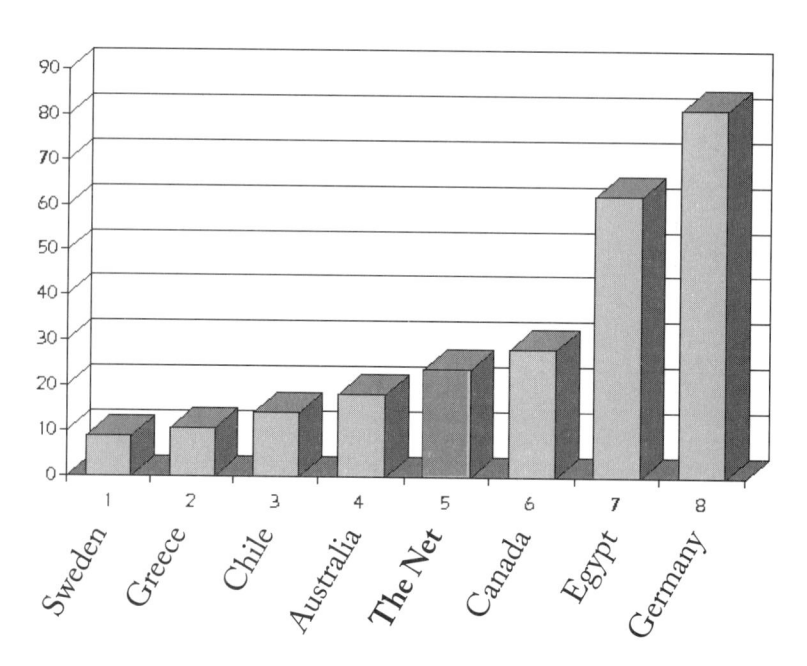

Bar chart showing populations in millions:
1. Sweden ~9
2. Greece ~11
3. Chile ~13
4. Australia ~17
5. The Net ~25
6. Canada ~28
7. Egypt ~60
8. Germany ~80

I hope by now that you have a pretty good idea why the Internet is filled with huge amounts of stuff. The best part of it all, however, is that you use it very differently than most other forms of communication. To explain that, we need to talk about how the Net differs from other things.

You Can Explore Net Stuff in Any Way Imaginable

Please bear with me for this part of the explanation of the Net, as it is one of the most difficult parts to describe to someone who has never used it before. Stop for a moment and think about how you daydream…

I know that when I allow myself to daydream, I think about tons of different things. I might start with what I need to do that day, wander to where I went on vacation last year, to the last time I went swimming, to countless other things. That is what daydreaming is like, and it bears a startling resemblance to what you can do when you surf the Net. ("Surfing the Net" just means navigating from one Net stop to another and another.)

> *Comment:* Many thanks to my high school English teacher for making me read James Joyce's *Portrait of the Artist as a Young Man*. This book comes the closest I know of any to trying to capture on paper the fluidity of thought that occurs in a young man's mind. It is also the book that I immediately thought of in my attempts to describe Net surfing. If you haven't read it, you might want to give this strange classic a try. You can find the text of Joyce's book at:
>
> http://www.datatext.co.uk/library/joyce/artist/chapters.htm

I will describe this notion of Net surfing in more detail in a little while. But first I want to go into more depth about Net stuff.

Just What Is Net Stuff, Anyway?

The Net is composed of five basic types of things:

- Email
- Newsgroups
- Discussion/chat groups
- World Wide Web
- FTP storage sites (anything from classic works of literature to downloadable software)

Each of these things is distinctive and useful in its own way, so let's go through them in order. You should know, however, that the most interesting material on the Net is usually found on the World Wide Web.

Email

Let's start with email, which is a big part of the everyday traffic on the Net. At its most basic level, an email message is just a bit of text sent to one person from another. A typical email message could well look like this message from a friend of mine that I haven't seen for a year (see Figure 1.2). I sent him a quick message just to see if he was still alive, and he zapped me back with this:

Figure 1.2
A typical Email Message.

```
From: gandreas@skypoint.com (Glenn Andreas)     My friend
Subject: Re: Geeting from Me
To: julie@pobox.com (Julie McKeehan)             Me
Date: Fri, 1 Mar 1996 18:36:00 -0600 (CST)
Mime-Version: 1.0
Status:                                          The > indicates my
                                                 original message.
>
> How did I know that a pin-head like you would have a home page by now.  How
> are you these days?  I hope this finds you well and happy in the middle of
> boring middle America.  We in the land of sunshine scoff at you.

What can I say - it keeps the riff-raff out.  Did you hear that I bought
a home?  And that there is a Home Depot openning BLOCKS from my house?
(I can actually see the peak of the orange roof from my front window when
the leaves are off the trees).  (yes, I actually have many trees in my
yard, including a pair of apple trees, and did I mention the fence around
the lot has grapes growing on it - as in real, edible grapes?)

Oh well, I'm assuming that I'll see all you people at WWDC, provided the
"big one" doesn't come first and dump the lot of you into the sea...

Glenn
```

This is his reply.

For lots of people on the Net, email is the best thing since sliced bread or the invention of paper clips. People all over the globe use email as a way to talk with each other *free of charge*. That's right, free. No stamps, no toll charges, just what ever you were already paying to use the Net. While lots of people have email at work, it gets used on the Net for personal reasons as well. Kids can correspond with grandparents and pen pals. People can find old friends whom they don't want to bug with a phone call but do want to say hello to now and again. (I talk about how to find lost friends in Chapter 9.)

Newsgroups

Newsgroups came into being to deal with people's desires to congregate in like-minded circles and talk about things of mutual interest. This took the notion of the email message one step further. People were no longer talking to each other on an individual basis but as a group of people all interested in the same topic.

Just to prove that people like to talk about all sorts of things, the range of Newsgroups topics is enormous. You can find anything from Disney fan clubs to topics of interest only to gardeners or programmers. If you look in Figure 1.3 you can see a small subset of newsgroups that deal just with K–12 education and schools.

You have access to over 14,000 of these newsgroups via the Internet, and you can find almost any topic of interest. To find a newsgroup just look at the list of groups and do a **Find** on a word that is interesting to you, like "cars" or "sports" (the more specific the better). If you have some time or a lot of patience, you can also just scroll through the list looking for interesting groups.

Free Advice:	One of the most frequently visited newsgroups is alt.sex. I suggest you look at it if you need any convincing that the Internet is not a place to leave children to wander about in alone.

Once you enter a newsgroup you should know that discussions take a certain form and are categorized under a certain title relating to the first person who brings that issue up for discussion. Figure 1.4 shows a sample of topics that can be found in a typical newsgroup.

Chapter 1 What Is the Net, Anyway?

Figure 1.3 Some Newsgroups.

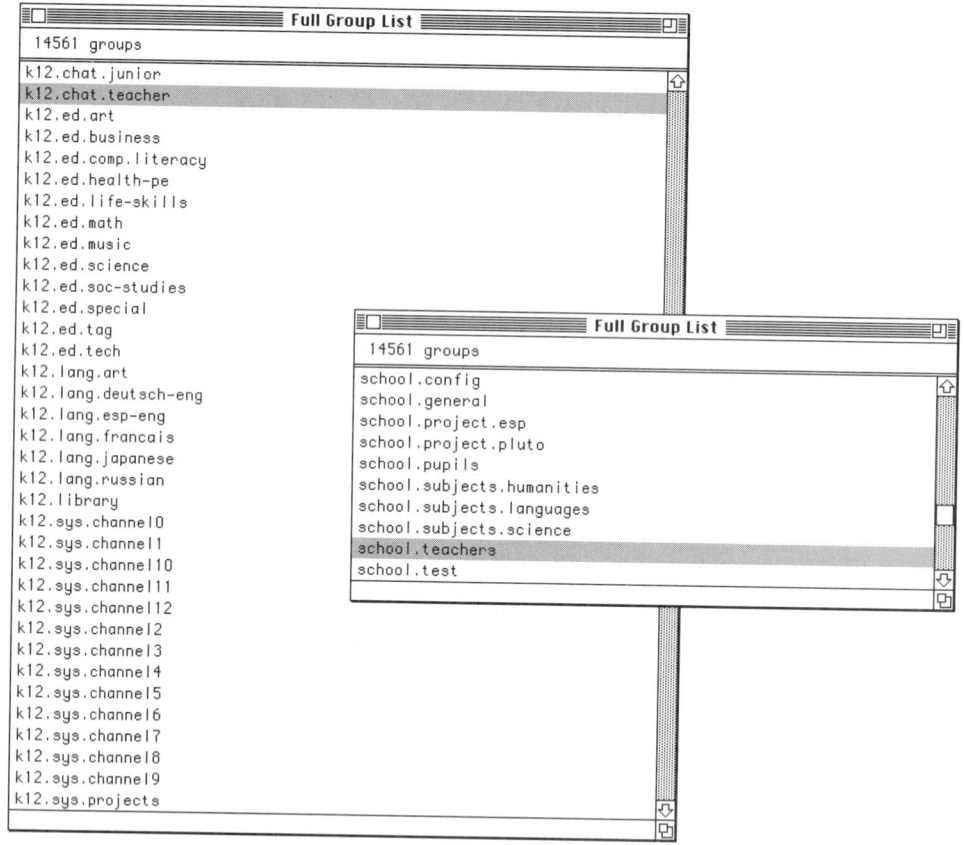

```
Full Group List
14561 groups
k12.chat.junior
k12.chat.teacher
k12.ed.art
k12.ed.business
k12.ed.comp.literacy
k12.ed.health-pe
k12.ed.life-skills
k12.ed.math
k12.ed.music
k12.ed.science
k12.ed.soc-studies
k12.ed.special
k12.ed.tag
k12.ed.tech
k12.lang.art
k12.lang.deutsch-eng
k12.lang.esp-eng
k12.lang.francais
k12.lang.japanese
k12.lang.russian
k12.library
k12.sys.channel0
k12.sys.channel1
k12.sys.channel10
k12.sys.channel11
k12.sys.channel12
k12.sys.channel2
k12.sys.channel3
k12.sys.channel4
k12.sys.channel5
k12.sys.channel6
k12.sys.channel7
k12.sys.channel8
k12.sys.channel9
k12.sys.projects
```

```
Full Group List
14561 groups
school.config
school.general
school.project.esp
school.project.pluto
school.pupils
school.subjects.humanities
school.subjects.languages
school.subjects.science
school.teachers
school.test
```

Figure 1.4 Sample Newsgroup, misc.kids.

```
misc.kids
400 articles, 400 unread
▷  2    Michelle Kalehz…   Re: father and daughter bathing
▷  3    Steve Holmes       Re: What to call Grandma
▷  2    catherine a. me…   Re: CTTS/D - almost 4 year old
▷  5    Paula Burch        Re: BBT - how do you take it, and why is mine all over the place??
▷  2    Cynbatt            Re: 2 year olds and Whining
-       Cynbatt            Re: Mongolian Patch/Birthmark on Butt
▷ 17    Michal Peri        Re: secular "carols"
▷  5    Ron Christian x…   Re: BIRACIAL CHILDREN
▷  6    Katie Healey       Re: What book is this?
▷  9    Maureen A. Edmo…   Re: The right way to spank- PLEASE READ
▷  2    Sandra Shepard     CT(I think)TS: 14 months
▷  2    naomi pardue       Re: Q:  Toys for 2 month old
▷  4    Karen Jonscher     Re: YK You're Tired When...
▷  5    Lynn Turriff       Re: consequences of physical punishment
▷  2    Michal Peri        Re: Mandatory child care classes in U.S. public schools?--You've got to be kid…
-       Deborah Conrad     Punishment v. Consequences (was Re:  The right way to spank)
▷  5    Ron & Sheila Ki…   Re: Formula cheapest at Walmart
▷  9    JCRASWE@america…   Re: What will it be like after baby is born
▷  3    Robyn Kozierok     Re: CTTD:  The Big Blankie Switch
▷  2    Cherie Machler     Where to Find Grant Money for Sign Language Training?
```

As you read these comments, you will see that a discussion takes this form:

1. Someone asks a question or makes a comment and posts it to the newsgroup. (Posting is the same as mailing.) Look at Figure 1.5 to see a typical post.

Figure 1.5
Someone Posts a Question/Comment.

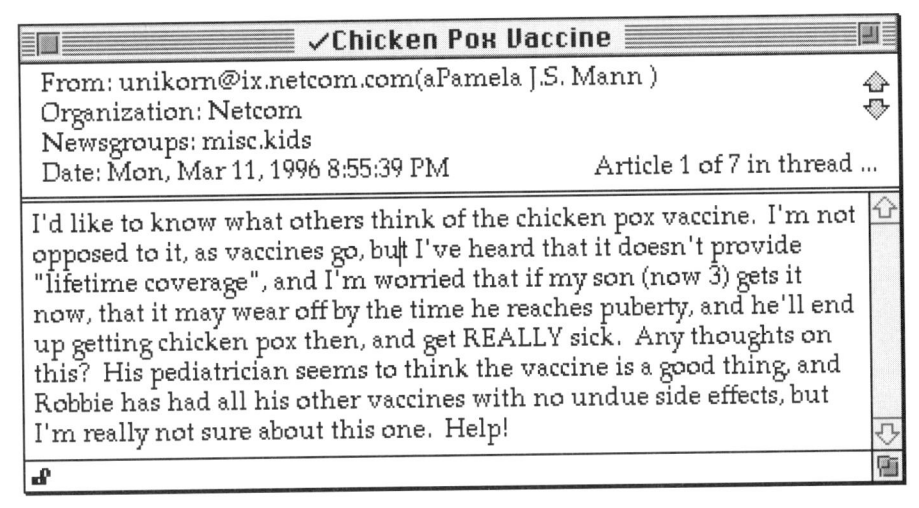

```
┌─────────────── ✓Chicken Pox Vaccine ───────────────┐
│ From: unikorn@ix.netcom.com(aPamela J.S. Mann)     │
│ Organization: Netcom                                │
│ Newsgroups: misc.kids                               │
│ Date: Mon, Mar 11, 1996 8:55:39 PM    Article 1 of 7 in thread ... │
├─────────────────────────────────────────────────────┤
│ I'd like to know what others think of the chicken pox vaccine. I'm not │
│ opposed to it, as vaccines go, but I've heard that it doesn't provide │
│ "lifetime coverage", and I'm worried that if my son (now 3) gets it │
│ now, that it may wear off by the time he reaches puberty, and he'll end │
│ up getting chicken pox then, and get REALLY sick. Any thoughts on │
│ this? His pediatrician seems to think the vaccine is a good thing, and │
│ Robbie has had all his other vaccines with no undue side effects, but │
│ I'm really not sure about this one. Help! │
└─────────────────────────────────────────────────────┘
```

2. Anywhere from a couple of hours to a couple of days later, responses to the question/comment show up in the newsgroup (see Figure 1.6) or are sent privately by email back to the original poster.

3. Some of the responses to the original comment can also generate their own responses, particularly if it is a heated or controversial discussion (see Figure 1.7).

4. And so on and so on, until nobody wants to talk about that particular thing again.

You will generally find that newsgroup topics are either very technical (such as those on programming or Danish cooking) or somewhat philosophical in nature (like politics or parenting). It is in these latter types of newsgroups that you will also find the most "energetic" discussions of topics and the most vehement of opinion holders.

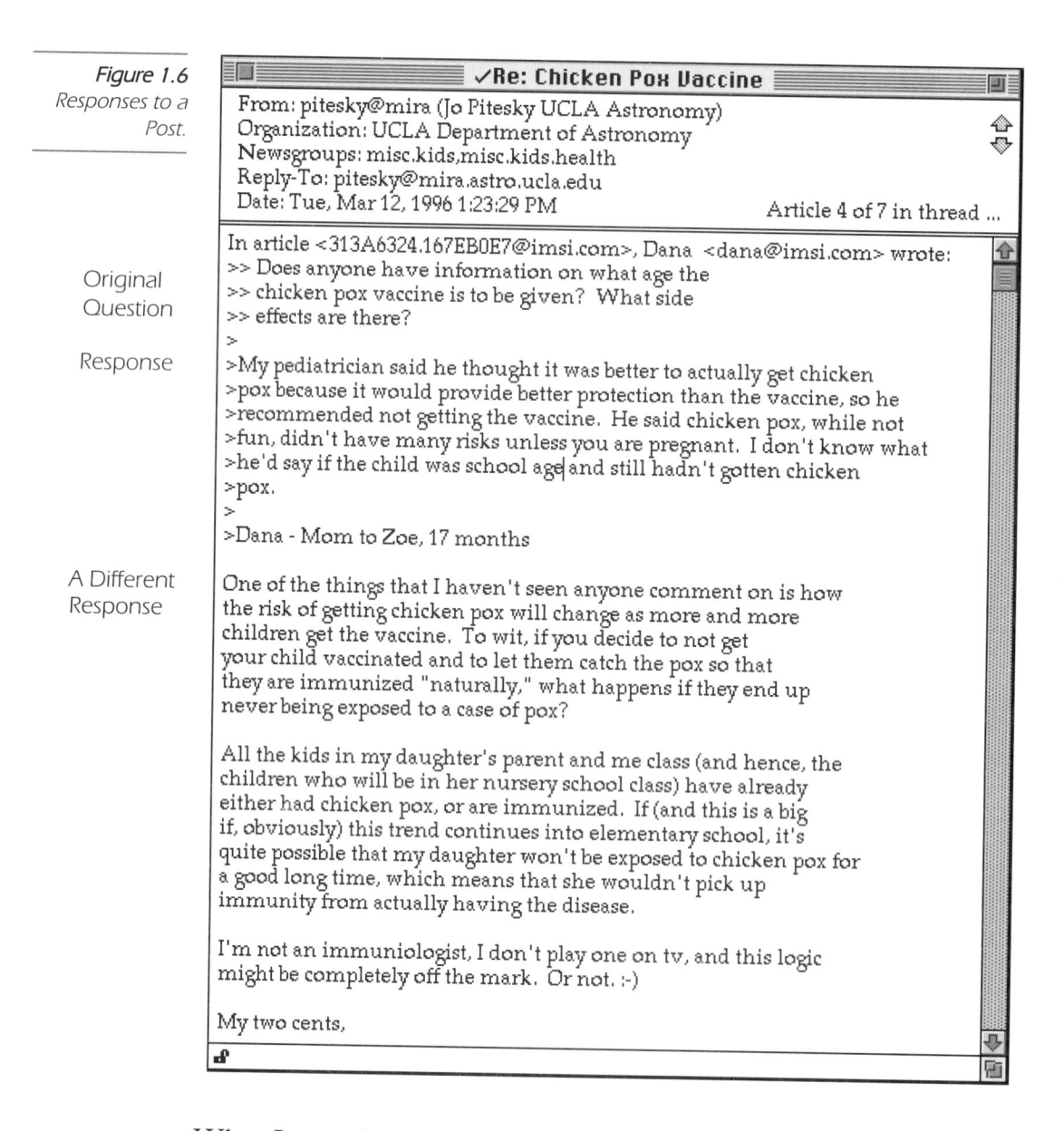

Figure 1.6 Responses to a Post.

Re: Chicken Pox Vaccine

From: pitesky@mira (Jo Pitesky UCLA Astronomy)
Organization: UCLA Department of Astronomy
Newsgroups: misc.kids,misc.kids.health
Reply-To: pitesky@mira.astro.ucla.edu
Date: Tue, Mar 12, 1996 1:23:29 PM   Article 4 of 7 in thread ...

Original Question

In article <313A6324.167EB0E7@imsi.com>, Dana <dana@imsi.com> wrote:
>> Does anyone have information on what age the
>> chicken pox vaccine is to be given? What side
>> effects are there?
>

Response

>My pediatrician said he thought it was better to actually get chicken
>pox because it would provide better protection than the vaccine, so he
>recommended not getting the vaccine. He said chicken pox, while not
>fun, didn't have many risks unless you are pregnant. I don't know what
>he'd say if the child was school age and still hadn't gotten chicken
>pox.
>
>Dana - Mom to Zoe, 17 months

A Different Response

One of the things that I haven't seen anyone comment on is how the risk of getting chicken pox will change as more and more children get the vaccine. To wit, if you decide to not get your child vaccinated and to let them catch the pox so that they are immunized "naturally," what happens if they end up never being exposed to a case of pox?

All the kids in my daughter's parent and me class (and hence, the children who will be in her nursery school class) have already either had chicken pox, or are immunized. If (and this is a big if, obviously) this trend continues into elementary school, it's quite possible that my daughter won't be exposed to chicken pox for a good long time, which means that she wouldn't pick up immunity from actually having the disease.

I'm not an immunologist, I don't play one on tv, and this logic might be completely off the mark. Or not. :-)

My two cents,

When I say vehement, it is quite possible that you have no idea how vehement I mean. Let's just say that it is an unfortunate side effect of the anonymity of the Net that many people lose what few manners they have in normal society. If you think people's discussions of politics, religion, and schooling get out of hand when they are talking face to face, they are mild in comparison to discussions on these same issues on the Net. There is really no other way to put this except to say that some people become frothing-at-the-mouth lunatics, lacking any notion of civility.

So, is she saying they are rude?

Figure 1.7 Responses to a Responder.

Re: Chicken Pox Vaccine

From: "T. Hulsey" <thulsey@vvm.com>
Organization: VVM, Inc.
Newsgroups: misc.kids,misc.kids.health
Date: Tue, Mar 12, 1996 5:02:40 PM   Article 5 of 7 in thread ...

Jo Pitesky UCLA Astronomy wrote:

Response to Question

> One of the things that I haven't seen anyone comment on is how
> the risk of getting chicken pox will change as more and more
> children get the vaccine. To wit, if you decide to not get
> your child vaccinated and to let them catch the pox so that
> they are immunized "naturally," what happens if they end up
> never being exposed to a case of pox?
>
> All the kids in my daughter's parent and me class (and hence, the
> children who will be in her nursery school class) have already
> either had chicken pox, or are immunized. If (and this is a big
> if, obviously) this trend continues into elementary school, it's
> quite possible that my daughter won't be exposed to chicken pox for
> a good long time, which means that she wouldn't pick up
> immunity from actually having the disease.
>
> I'm not an immuniologist, I don't play one on tv, and this logic
> might be completely off the mark. Or not. :-)

Response to Response

I've wondered the same thing. My boys are 4 and 5. When I worked, they went to the babysitter's, and never got them. Even though I stay home with them, about once a month, I still let them go there to stay the day. No pox yet.

--
Carla, Mommy to Shawn and Seth
~~~~~~~~~~~~~~~~~~~~~~~~~~~~~~~~~~~~~~
    The place is very well & quiet & the children
      only scream in a low voice. ~ Lord Byron

Newsgroup Rules for You

While you and I might wish that these folks would get off the Net and read a few books on manners, this is not likely to happen. So, to make sure you don't expose yourself or your family to any inappropriate things in newsgroups, I suggest you follow these three simple rules:

1. When you or your child finds a newsgroup that you are interested in reading regularly (called subscribing), spend a minimum of four weeks lurking before posting any question or comment yourself.

Subscribing just means that you move the newsgroup from the big list (of 14,000) to a small list of groups that you want to look at on a more regular basis. It doesn't mean that they know your email address.

Note: Lurking refers to the time-honored activity of reading what other folks write without joining in yourself. You sit quietly in the shadows, and the posters don't even know you are there.

2. Read the FAQ attached to the newsgroup.

Note: FAQ stands for Frequently Asked Questions, and it is a useful first stop for any new person. FAQs are attached to specific newsgroups and contain collections of questions and answers that commonly come up in that newsgroup.

For more general rules of behavior you can also read the rules of Net etiquette found in **news.announce.newusers**. If you don't want to go to all that trouble, I can sum them up for you in three points:

- Don't post to a group unless you know how to do so.

- Don't ask a question that belongs in another group.

- Show courtesy to other people in that newsgroup.

3. *This is the hard one.* If you do work up the courage to post something and someone flames you, then UNDER NO CIRCUMSTANCES respond to that person. (If everyone ignored these folks, they would either go away or control themselves better.)

Note: Ah, yes. I have used the expression "flames you." You are probably wondering what it means. Flaming refers to the act of sending an insulting, ill-mannered responses to a poster in a group.

Once upon a time, a long time ago, flaming was carried out in a very civilized fashion. There was a newsgroup called alt. flame. People could go to this newsgroup when they were mad and rant about anything that was bothering them. Airlines that canceled flights, stores that didn't give refunds, politicians who lied—you name it, anything was fair game for a flame.

Unfortunately, our tale ends rather badly, as the flamers multiplied and left the nest. They spread to other groups, and their act of flaming went with them. And to this very day we have flames spurting up all over the Net. Alas, not everything is wonderful in the land of the Net.

Remember, if all you subscribe to is rec.gardening and rec.gazebo.building then you will probably never see a flamer or believe that any of this is true. But if you check out the discussions in Figure 1.8, you will get a perfectly clear idea of what I mean by flaming. I must warn you that very few flames are as tame as the one I picked out. Indeed, I had to search for a while to find one that could be printed in this book.

28 Chapter 1 What Is the Net, Anyway?

Figure 1.8
Flames, Flames.

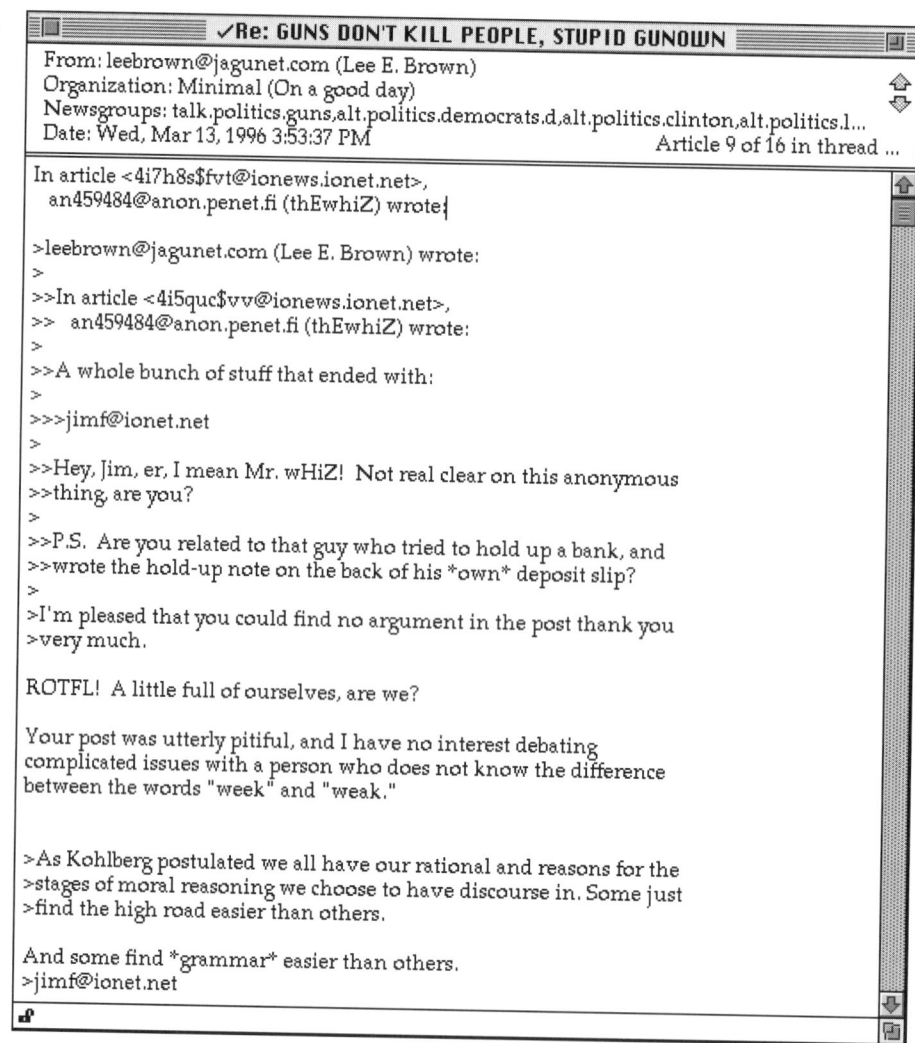

```
┌────────── ✓Re: GUNS DON'T KILL PEOPLE, STUPID GUNOWN ──────────┐
│ From: leebrown@jagunet.com (Lee E. Brown)                       │
│ Organization: Minimal (On a good day)                           │
│ Newsgroups: talk.politics.guns,alt.politics.democrats.d,alt.politics.clinton,alt.politics.l...
│ Date: Wed, Mar 13, 1996 3:53:37 PM        Article 9 of 16 in thread ...
│
│ In article <4i7h8s$fvt@ionews.ionet.net>,
│    an459484@anon.penet.fi (thEwhiZ) wrote:
│
│ >leebrown@jagunet.com (Lee E. Brown) wrote:
│ >
│ >>In article <4i5quc$vv@ionews.ionet.net>,
│ >>  an459484@anon.penet.fi (thEwhiZ) wrote:
│ >
│ >>A whole bunch of stuff that ended with:
│ >
│ >>>jimf@ionet.net
│ >
│ >>Hey, Jim, er, I mean Mr. wHiZ!  Not real clear on this anonymous
│ >>thing, are you?
│ >
│ >>P.S. Are you related to that guy who tried to hold up a bank, and
│ >>wrote the hold-up note on the back of his *own* deposit slip?
│ >
│ >I'm pleased that you could find no argument in the post thank you
│ >very much.
│
│ ROTFL! A little full of ourselves, are we?
│
│ Your post was utterly pitiful, and I have no interest debating
│ complicated issues with a person who does not know the difference
│ between the words "week" and "weak."
│
│ >As Kohlberg postulated we all have our rational and reasons for the
│ >stages of moral reasoning we choose to have discourse in. Some just
│ >find the high road easier than others.
│
│ And some find *grammar* easier than others.
│ >jimf@ionet.net
└─────────────────────────────────────────────────────────────────┘
```

Discussion/Chat Groups

For people who want real live people to talk to, there is an abundance of chat groups in which they can while away the hours. In these groups, you can meet other people who are online at the same time. Once you are in a chat group you can talk either to the whole group or to a particular individual. If you look at Figure 1.9, you will see a typical discussion/chat room with some people in it. I am not exactly sure what they are talking about, however.

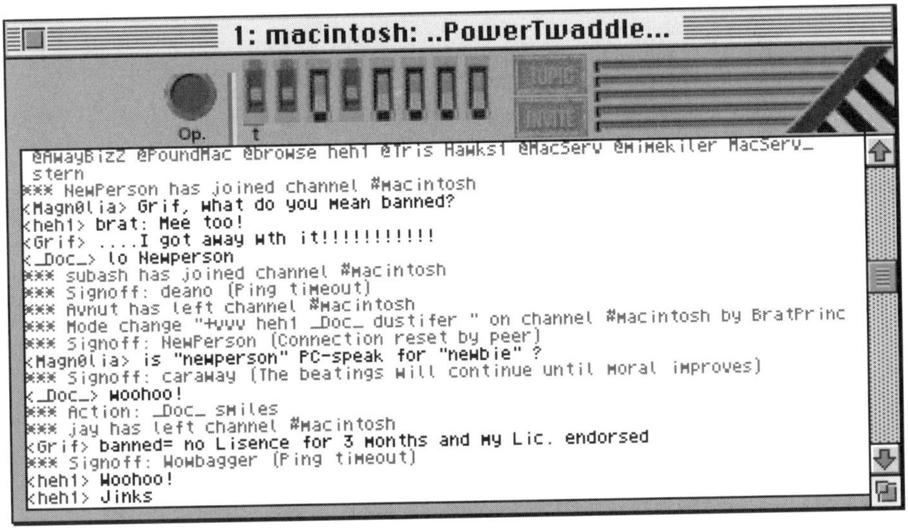

Figure 1.9 Chat Group.

My guess is that this whole way of interacting with people grew out of the old Internet capability called **Talk**. In **Talk**, you could call someone up on the Net and "talk" to them. Talking went like this, all of it via the keyboard and typing. When bored I used to look for someone on the system to "talk" to:

Looking for Neil, found Neil. Neil answering...

Me: Hi, what are you doing?

Neil: Nothing much, what are you doing?

Me: Working on a paper.

Neil: Finish it soon so we can go to the movies tonight.

Me: Okay, Bye.

30   Chapter 1 What Is the Net, Anyway?

World Wide Web

By far, the most popular stuff on the Net is the World Wide Web. In fact, when people talk about the Net they are probably referring to the World Wide Web because it is both graphical and hot (hot means you can click on parts of Web pages and that takes you to other Web pages, also called links. Let me show you an example (see Figure 1.10).

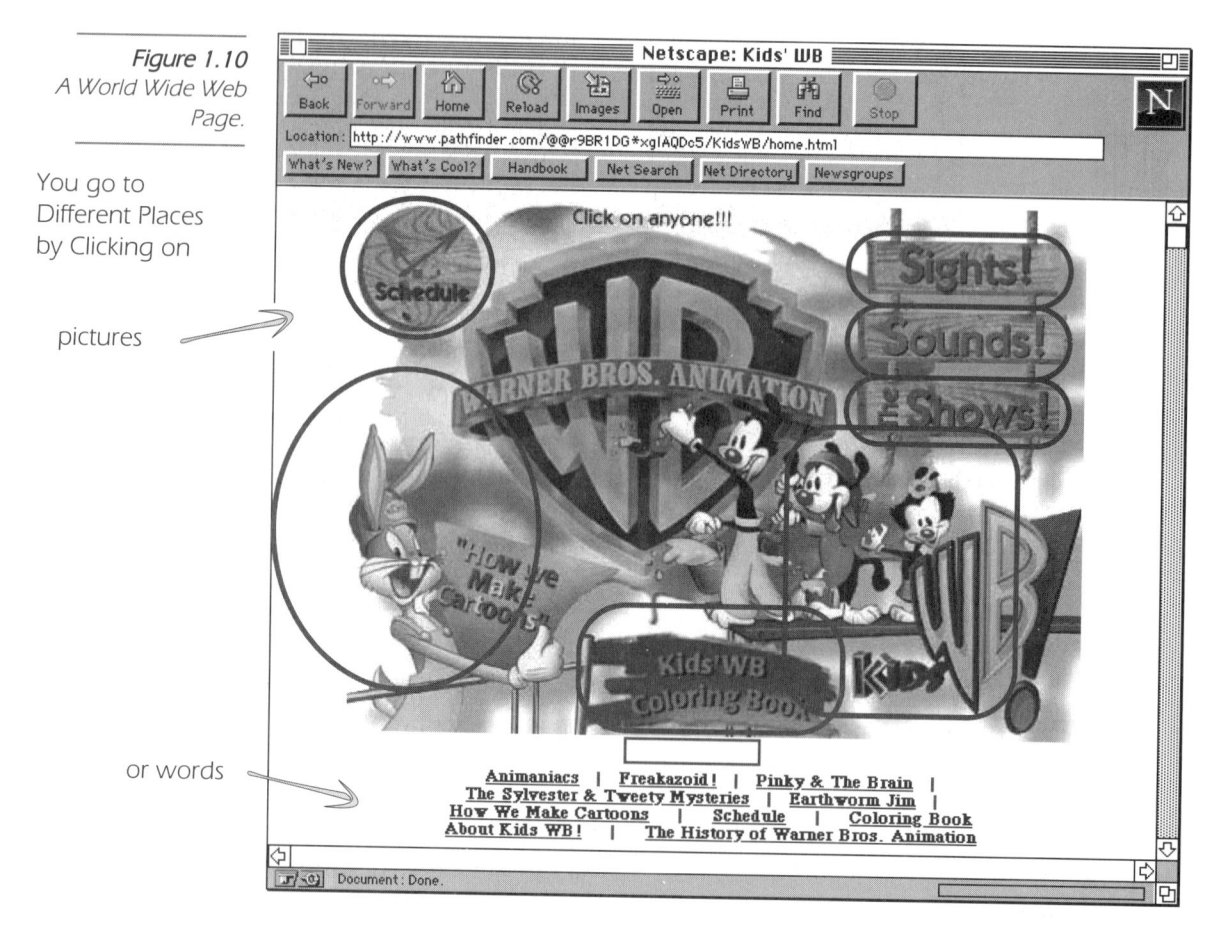

Figure 1.10
A World Wide Web Page.

You go to Different Places by Clicking on

pictures

or words

For example, if I click on **Animaniacs** as shown in Figure 1.10, I get transported to a different Web page that looks like the one in Figure 1.11.

World Wide Web   31

Figure 1.11
The Animaniacs
Web Page.

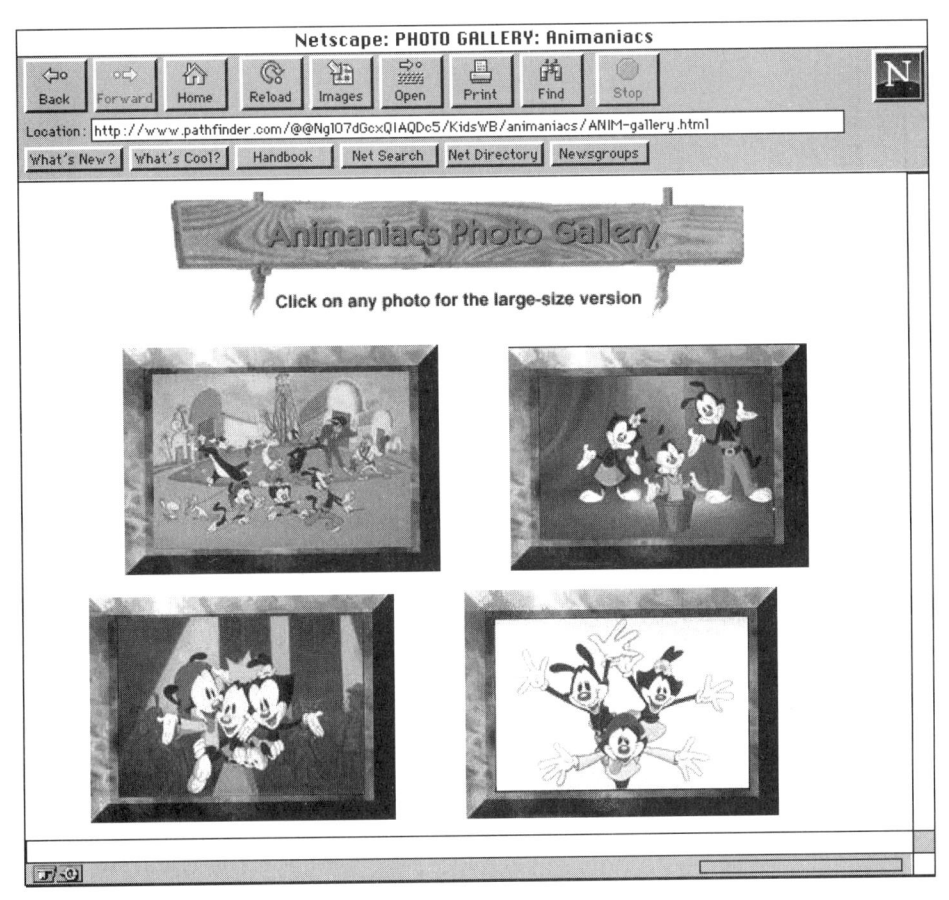

You can easily keep this up for hours, following one topic to another and to another. Which brings us back to the neat thing about the Net that I mentioned earlier when I was talking about daydreaming and Net surfing. This way of looking at stuff is very different from most any other thing you do.

For example, in reading this book you are limited to learning about stuff pretty much in the order I decide for you. Same deal with a movie: You learn about the story in the way the movie's director decided for you. Your only real choice is to watch/read in the way the thing was originally created. (Yes, I know you can use the remote control to forward or reverse, but the movie isn't intended to be watched that way.)

When you Net surf the World Wide Web (WWW for short) everything has been set up to give you a lot more flexibility in what you do. You decide how much of a Web page to read, when to jump to another spot, and so on and so on. This means that I could take two people, plop them down in front of the same moderately interesting Web page full of links, and 10 minutes later they would be looking at entirely different stuff. This brings me to one of the most important points in this chapter:

- The ability to Net Surf is one of the best and most evolutionary things about the Net.

The World Wide Web is also fun because it is so graphical (as in pretty to look at) and interesting because of the thousands of people creating Web pages. By having so many of the constraints on *how* you learn removed, the Net really has created a brand new way of interacting with information.

Because it is a brand-new thing it also very hard to describe to someone who has never experienced it before (that's you). I hope, however, that the unique newness of it is so enticing that you will want to try it out. One thing I can promise is that 10 minutes on the WWW will do more to explain Net surfing than any number of pages of me talking about it.

FTP Storage Sites

The last big piece that I need to explain is the archival material you can get from the Net. This stored material is mostly of two types:

- Text files

- Software and related material

Archival material is kept at certain types of Net sites called FTP sites.

> *Note:* FTP stands for File Transfer Protocol (just remember FTP). It is the main way that you take files off the Internet and download it to your own computer.

FTP sites store information that you can put on your own computer. In much the same way as you take information off a floppy disk and store it on your hard drive, you go to an FTP site to find what you want and download it to your own computer.

Let's look at some of the stuff you can get from these FTP sites.

Text Files

People have been putting works of literature on the Net for a very long time. The good news is that by this point you have access to many of the greatest works of literature of Western and Eastern civilization. The resources of the whole world become your library.

Let me name just one of the more important collections and show you some of its contents.

Project Gutenberg

This is a great collection of electronic works of literature. As volunteers, these folks have put more than 10,000 works online in Project Gutenberg. Some of these works include:

- The Complete Works of Shakespeare
- The Complete Alice in Wonderland
- The Wizard of Oz

- Anne of Green Gables
- Tarzan of the Apes, and more

Truly, the most amazing thing about this effort is the reason these people do it. Asking them produces this answer:

- Giving people books to read is our part in getting rid of illiteracy and helping democracy to flourish.

That's really why they do it.

Software and Related Material

You can get tons of software on the Net—some of it silly, some of it harmful (with bugs in it), and some of it very useful. At FTP sites you find:

- Freeware (that's right, free software)
- Shareware (pay-by-the-honor-system software)
- Demos of commercial products

The types of software can be just about anything you can imagine, including such stuff as:

- Internet Software, including some useful stuff that you are going to want (see Figure 1.12)
- Games
- System utilities (Windows, DOS, Macintosh, and more)

FTP Storage Sites   35

- Software updates (both system software and commercial products)

- Video and sound software

- Communication software

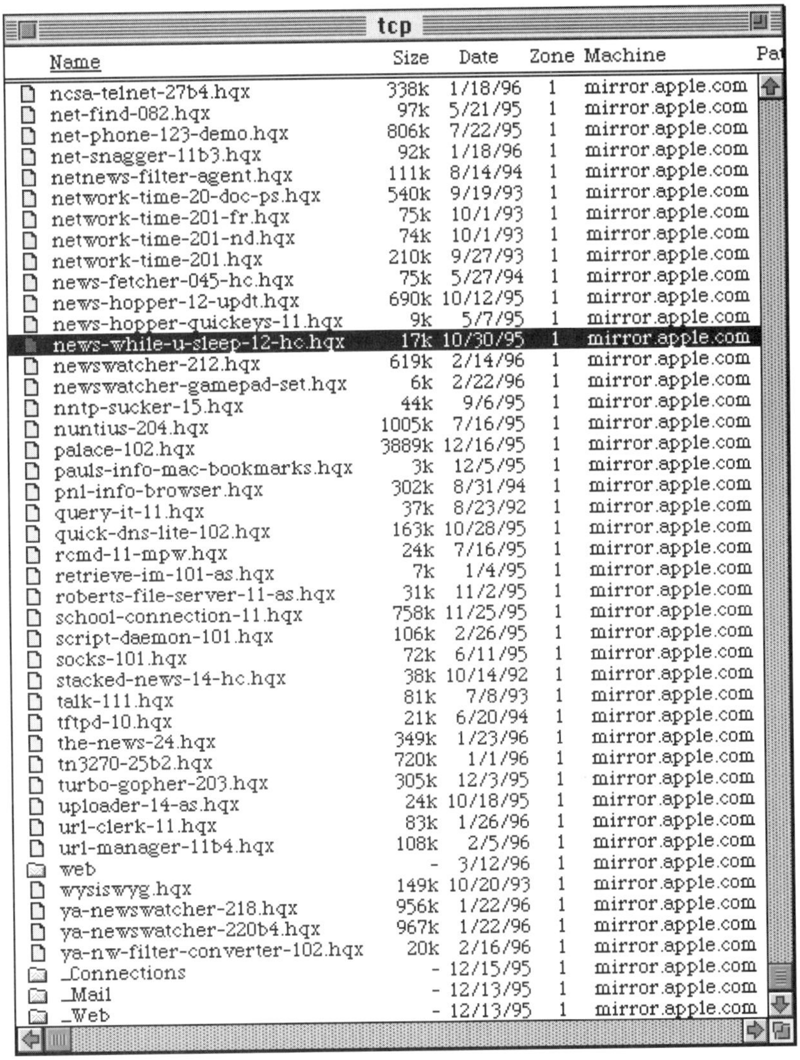

Figure 1.12
Internet Software Available at an FTP site.

Name	Size	Date	Zone	Machine
ncsa-telnet-27b4.hqx	338k	1/18/96	1	mirror.apple.com
net-find-082.hqx	97k	5/21/95	1	mirror.apple.com
net-phone-123-demo.hqx	806k	7/22/95	1	mirror.apple.com
net-snagger-11b3.hqx	92k	1/18/96	1	mirror.apple.com
netnews-filter-agent.hqx	111k	8/14/94	1	mirror.apple.com
network-time-20-doc-ps.hqx	540k	9/19/93	1	mirror.apple.com
network-time-201-fr.hqx	75k	10/1/93	1	mirror.apple.com
network-time-201-nd.hqx	74k	10/1/93	1	mirror.apple.com
network-time-201.hqx	210k	9/27/93	1	mirror.apple.com
news-fetcher-045-hc.hqx	75k	5/27/94	1	mirror.apple.com
news-hopper-12-updt.hqx	690k	10/12/95	1	mirror.apple.com
news-hopper-quickeys-11.hqx	9k	5/7/95	1	mirror.apple.com
news-while-u-sleep-12-hc.hqx	17k	10/30/95	1	mirror.apple.com
newswatcher-212.hqx	619k	2/14/96	1	mirror.apple.com
newswatcher-gamepad-set.hqx	6k	2/22/96	1	mirror.apple.com
nntp-sucker-15.hqx	44k	9/6/95	1	mirror.apple.com
nuntius-204.hqx	1005k	7/16/95	1	mirror.apple.com
palace-102.hqx	3889k	12/16/95	1	mirror.apple.com
pauls-info-mac-bookmarks.hqx	3k	12/5/95	1	mirror.apple.com
pn1-info-browser.hqx	302k	8/31/94	1	mirror.apple.com
query-it-11.hqx	37k	8/23/92	1	mirror.apple.com
quick-dns-lite-102.hqx	163k	10/28/95	1	mirror.apple.com
rcmd-11-mpw.hqx	24k	7/16/95	1	mirror.apple.com
retrieve-im-101-as.hqx	7k	1/4/95	1	mirror.apple.com
roberts-file-server-11-as.hqx	31k	11/2/95	1	mirror.apple.com
school-connection-11.hqx	758k	11/25/95	1	mirror.apple.com
script-daemon-101.hqx	106k	2/26/95	1	mirror.apple.com
socks-101.hqx	72k	6/11/95	1	mirror.apple.com
stacked-news-14-hc.hqx	38k	10/14/92	1	mirror.apple.com
talk-111.hqx	81k	7/8/93	1	mirror.apple.com
tftpd-10.hqx	21k	6/20/94	1	mirror.apple.com
the-news-24.hqx	349k	1/23/96	1	mirror.apple.com
tn3270-25b2.hqx	720k	1/1/96	1	mirror.apple.com
turbo-gopher-203.hqx	305k	12/3/95	1	mirror.apple.com
uploader-14-as.hqx	24k	10/18/95	1	mirror.apple.com
url-clerk-11.hqx	83k	1/26/96	1	mirror.apple.com
url-manager-11b4.hqx	108k	2/5/96	1	mirror.apple.com
web	-	3/12/96	1	mirror.apple.com
wysiswyg.hqx	149k	10/20/93	1	mirror.apple.com
ya-newswatcher-218.hqx	956k	1/22/96	1	mirror.apple.com
ya-newswatcher-220b4.hqx	967k	1/22/96	1	mirror.apple.com
ya-nw-filter-converter-102.hqx	20k	2/16/96	1	mirror.apple.com
_Connections	-	12/15/95	1	mirror.apple.com
_Mail	-	12/13/95	1	mirror.apple.com
_Web	-	12/13/95	1	mirror.apple.com

36   Chapter 1   What Is the Net, Anyway?

Much of this software is also available at WWW sites—simply click on a hot link. Sometimes, however, Web pages have a link to the FTP site that holds the particular software in question. If you look at Figure 1.13 you will see a Web site that lets you do this.

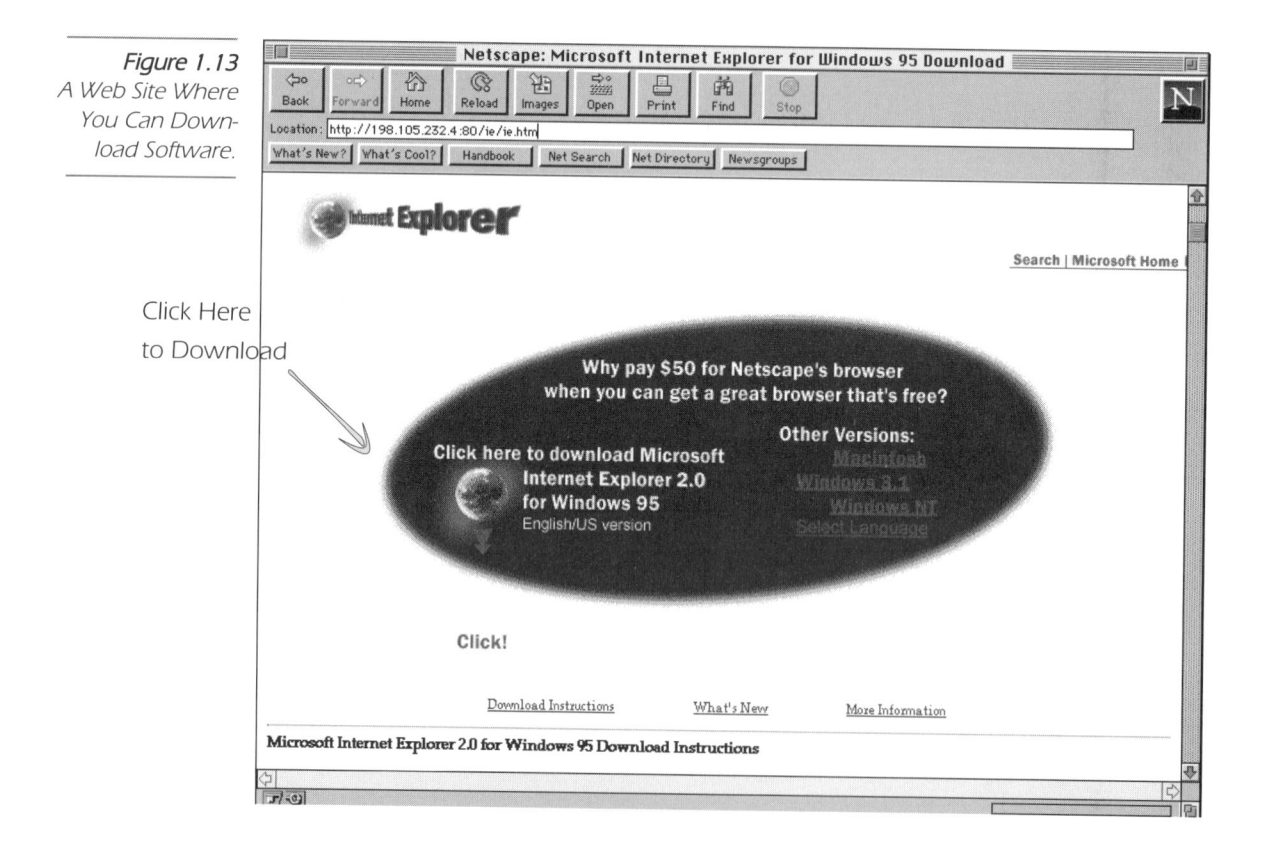

Figure 1.13
A Web Site Where You Can Download Software.

Understanding Internet Addresses

The last thing we have to cover about the Net is how addresses work. As you've seen, there are many different things to be found. And in order to find them, you need an address. Just as your home has a unique address and your phone has its own number, just so each and every site on the Internet has its own address. Getting to places on the Internet is no different than directing someone to your home. Whether it is mail, the WWW, or news, every place has an address and it is called a URL.

Understanding URLs

If she keeps talking like this I'm going to fall asleep.

URL stands for Uniform Resource Locator. URLs are the standardized forms used to identify a location of something on the WWW or other such servers. You do not need to know what each abbreviation stands for, but you do need to remember the address exactly (with all the dots and slashes) if you want to reach it again.

Here are some sample URLs:

> http://www.yahoo.com
> http://www.exploratorium.edu
> http://policy.net/capweb/Senate/Senate.html
> mailto:julie@pobox.com
> ftp://ftp.share.com/pub/peterlewis/
> news:comp.sys.mac.comm

One important thing about a URL is that the letters in front of the colon (:) indicate what type of site it is. This is what they stand for:

http	Web sites
ftp	A file (or directory of files)
mailto	An email address
news	A newsgroup (or article from a newsgroup)

In general, you will find that URLs are a real pain to use and type exactly right. It is not clear, however, what a better alternative would be. One good point is that you don't usually arrive at a site by typing in a URL. You are most likely to get there via another Web page or from a search for a specific subject.

In Conclusion

Having told you all of this, I hope that you have a better idea of just what the Net is and some understanding of why I ended up defining it like this:

- A huge number of connected computers filled with interesting people and really useful stuff.

No matter what, you will at least have familiarity with some of the more common terms used in discussions of the Net. And now that you know a little bit about the Net, it is time to help you figure out how to get connected. Then you can do some exploring on your own.

Chapter 2
Choosing an Internet Service

Covered in This Chapter
Words You Need to Know
Is an Online Service for You?
Is an ISP for You?
Making the Right Choice

Okay, you've decided to surf the Net. So let's figure out the right way for you to do that. Yes, more than one road leads to the land of the Net. Some roads were built for folks who are very happy not knowing how to set the clocks on their VCRs, and some roads were built for pinhead, techno-loving nerds. Because ending up on the wrong road could ruin the whole trip, let's find the right road for you. For that, I need to do two things:

Chapter 2 Choosing an Internet Service

- Explain some things to you
- Ask you some questions

Based upon the way you answer my questions, I will be able to point you in the direction of the Internet service that will best meet your needs. As you might have expected, several factors will influence you. Once made, your decision will lead you to either Chapter 3 or Chapter 4.

But that is jumping ahead of ourselves. First, it is time to learn some of the lingo of the Net.

Words You Need to Know

There are several terms whose meanings are not immediately obvious. You will need to understand them in order to make a decision. While I will talk in more detail about some later on, here is a quick list of terms:

- Access Time
- Commercial Online Services
- Internet Service Providers (ISPs)
- Chat Groups
- Software/Hardware Tools

Access Time

When you connect to the Net you do so via a phone line and a computer modem. Your computer dials out, just as you do when making a phone call.

Obviously, then, your computer needs to have a working phone jack. Once you have supplied that, you can plug your computer modem into that jack and your computer can dial out to the Net. You also need special software on your computer that lets it make the phone call.

The length of time your computer stays connected over the phone line is called "access time." When you pay for an Internet service you are paying for that access time. Most services offer one of the following plans:

- A flat fee for a certain number of hours of access time per month (for example, 5 hours). You pay an hourly rate for additional hours.

- A flat fee for an unlimited number of access hours.

- Free—that is for those of you lucky enough to be connected to some type of school or university. In such cases, you can usually get Net access for free.

Access time is tricky because it raises another very important issue.

Do you need more than one phone line?

If you are surfing the Net, then that means that no one can call you on that phone line. So suddenly you have the problem of all your friends and family whining about how your phone is always busy. Also, imagine if every time you want to make a phone call, you first have to check to see if someone else is on the Net. For some people, it is not worth the additional expense of another phone line; for others, the reduced hassle makes another line a real godsend.

Commercial Online Services

Commercial Online Services are most people's first exposure to the Net. The biggest services are almost household words in themselves. Indeed, many people have heard of *America Online*, *Prodigy*, or *CompuServe*, even if they don't exactly know what they are.

What is a Commercial Online Service, Anyway?

Think of a commercial online service as a miniature version of the Internet. Each service is its own little world that provides things that are like parts of the Net. Each service offers:

- Email
- Discussion groups or forums (similar to newsgroups)
- Chat rooms
- Graphic areas (a little bit like the WWW)
- Places to download stuff from (similar to FTP sites, these are areas where users go to get all sorts of downloadable files)

You connect to an online service via computer modem and have software files that help you do that. For all of this, online service users usually pay a minimum amount for a certain number of hours of access time per month and a fixed rate per hour above that.

Trapdoor Access to the Internet

These days, the online services offer access to most parts of the Internet, including the World Wide Web. Think of this as "trapdoor" access with a key. The online service user can get into to the Internet, but Internet users cannot get into the online service (except to send email).

Now, wasn't that a dry description! Let's try an explanation with pictures instead (see Figure 2.1):

Figure 2.1
Online Service Collage.

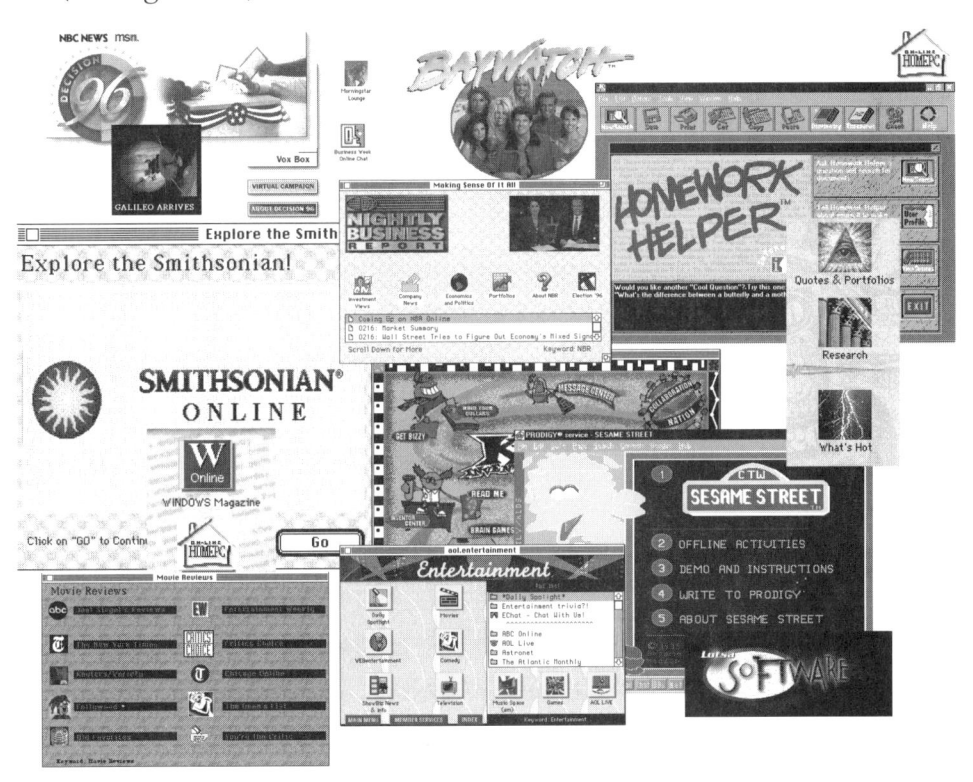

Differences between the Net and Online Services

One of the differences between most online services and the Internet is that of size and breadth of content. You can find and do anything imaginable on the

Internet. An online service, on the other hand, trims this material down to fewer subjects. Further, finding and weeding through this material is much easier. A practical example of this might be the subject of cooking. If you want to know how to make cheese, an online service can be a great resource. If you want to know how to turn camel's milk into a decent Swiss, then the Internet is the place for you.

Online services do offer distinctive features not available on the Net:

- Specialized homework help for students

- Special sites for interacting with famous people (like Bill Clinton, Rush Limbaugh, or Oprah Winfrey)

- Movie reviews by favorite critics (like Roger Ebert)

I will give detailed information on each of the online services in Chapter 3. For now, let's turn to a discussion of another phrase you need to understand which is, "Internet Service Providers."

Internet Service Providers

An Internet Service Provider (ISP) can be anyone or any company with a computer running 24 hours a day (for most of the year) and a bunch of incoming phone lines.

You, the computer user, call (using your computer modem) the ISP's computer using one of the phone numbers the ISP provides to you, and you have access to the Internet via that computer and its connections.

The ISP gives you this Internet access in exchange for a monthly fee. That amount can be for a set number of hours per month or for all the time in the universe.

Chat Groups and Forums

One of the biggest attractions that online services offer are rooms that people can enter to discuss topics of mutual interest. Imagine if you will, one big party line. I can talk from my computer to someone else via his or her computer. Further all of this is *live*. This is just like the telephone—anyone can listen in and talk about whatever is on her or his mind.

Each of the online services has specialized chat rooms where adults (see Figure 2.2) can talk about topics of mutual interest. Likewise, they have chat rooms where kids can talk with each other (see Figure 2.3).

Figure 2.2 Chat Rooms for Adults.

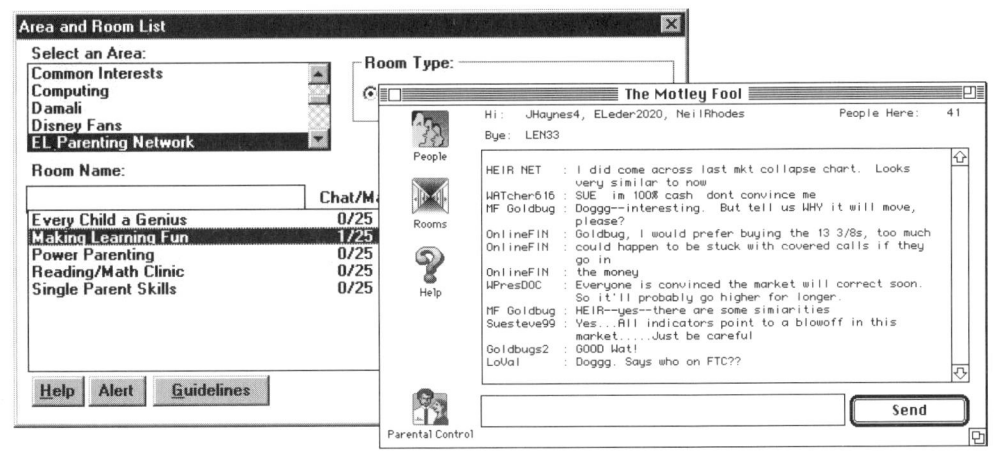

These chat rooms can be both a blessing and a curse. Kids can talk with other kids about hobbies of mutual interest, get homework help, or simply get to know someone who lives halfway across the world. They can be a curse, however, because you have absolutely no way of knowing whether your child is talking with another 10-year-old about horses or 40-year-old pedophile pretending to be a kid.

Comment: The virtue of the Net is that people can be anything they want to be. The curse of the Net is that people can be anything they want to be.

Figure 2.3
Chat Rooms for Kids.

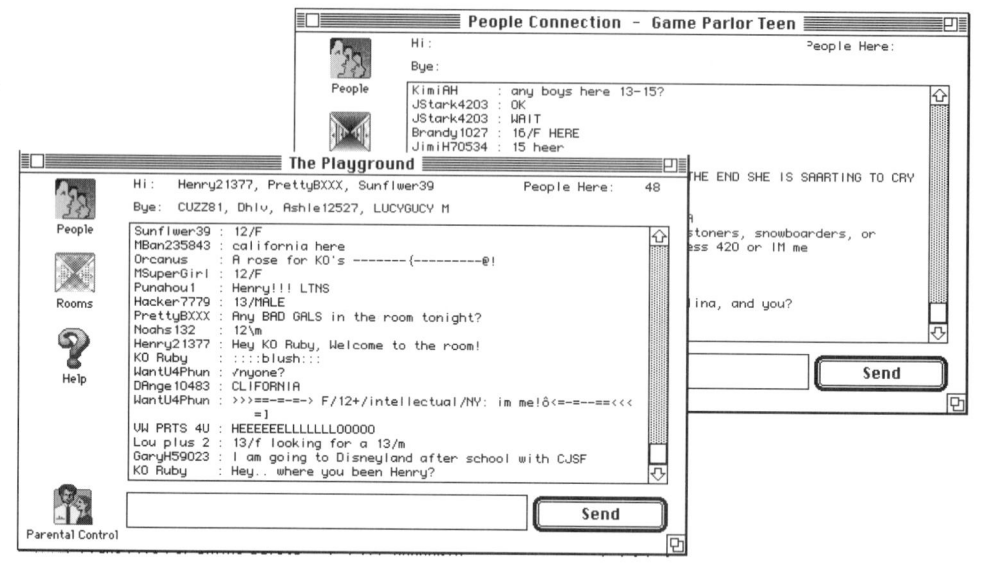

Hardware/Software Tools

To connect to the Internet, you need some hardware and some software. Here is the short list:

- A Computer
- A Modem
- A phone number to call *(the tricky part)*
- Some software

I am giving you a general idea of what's involved because it has bearing upon whether you will want to use an online service or get an ISP. Let's start with the easy stuff.

A Computer

Any of these computers will do:

- One running DOS/Windows 3.1
- One running Windows 95
- One running the Macintosh OS

A Modem

You also need a modem. Many computers come with an internal modem. If yours does not have one, you will need to buy one.

Free Advice: Buy the fastest modem you can find. I don't care if your computer is a slug, but if your modem is slow then you should forget about the Internet. Even if you ignore everything else I tell you in this book, please don't ignore this.

Modems come in different speeds with the faster ones being more expensive. They can be purchased in computer stores or by mail order.

You'll Be Sorry	2400 Bps Modem (About $65 US)
Okay	14.400 Kbps Modem (About $100 US)
Best	28.8 Kbps Modem (About $180 US)

> *Note:* "Bps" and "Kbps" are just terms that stand for how fast the modem can transfer data over the phone line to or from your computer. As you might already know, Bps stands for bits per second and Kbps stands for kilobits per second (1000 times as fast).

A Phone Number

Getting on the Internet is still a relatively new thing to do. For most people, the hardest part is acquiring a phone number to call, because that depends on where they live. Since there is no listing in the Yellow Pages under "Internet Service" most people will be at a loss for how to find the service in their local community. The commercial online services and ISPs handle this problem differently.

Commercial Online Services

If you decide to use a commercial online service (like *America Online*, *CompuServe*, *Prodigy*, or *Microsoft Network*), then all you need is:

- An 800 online service phone number

The online service will send you the software that you need.

ISP

If you decide to use an ISP, then your first job is to find one and that's a tricky task. Since you can't look in a phone book, my best advice is that you ask all your friends if they have an ISP you can use. If you have no friends on the Net, then you should read "Getting a Service Provider" on page 101. You also need some special software which you can acquire all by yourself or possibly from an ISP. You will need at least three pieces of software.

- TCP/IP

    Communication software that lets data be carried back and forth between your computer and the Net.

- A Dialer

    Software to connect you with the service provider.

- A Net Browser

    Software that allows you to view the contents and navigate around the Net and WWW.

> *Note:* I provide a Net browser and other software on the CD-ROM at the back of the book. I'll discuss this in detail in "What's on the CD" on page 321.

Is an Online Service for You?

Now that you know some of what is involved in getting yourself on the Net, it is time to make that crucial decision about which road to take. First, we are going to look at whether you are someone who should go with an online service. There are two quizzes to help figure this out.

The first quiz will help you figure out if an online service is your cup of tea. While the test is meant to be lighthearted, you should remember to answer the questions based upon your *true* feelings about this stuff. Remember, the great virtue of anonymous quizzes is that no one has to know your score. Following the quiz is the score section. Depending on the score you give yourself, you will be directed down the right road to the Net.

Chapter 2 Choosing an Internet Service

Answers	1	2	3	4	5
	Strongly Disagree	Disagree	In the Middle	Agree	Strongly Agree

1 2 3 4 5   I long for the days when using the Net meant I was about to catch a fish. I don't know what the Net is, why I should want it, or what to do with it once I have it.

1 2 3 4 5   Things just disappear on my computer. They reappear when I talk to a technical support person on the phone and disappear again when I hang up.

1 2 3 4 5   If I tried to do something new on my computer, I would most likely erase everything on my hard drive.

1 2 3 4 5   Word processing is okay, but don't talk to me about anything else.

1 2 3 4 5   Computer manuals are not written in English.

1 2 3 4 5   I'd rather clean the bathroom than discuss the virtues of a computer program.

1 2 3 4 5   My computer is filled with all sorts of stuff. I'm sure other people put it there, so why don't they clean it up?

1 2 3 4 5   A mouse is something that a cat eats.

1 2 3 4 5   The only reason for getting on the Net is so people will stop bugging me about it.

1 2 3 4 5   Memory is the recollection of an event from my past, RAM is a male sheep, hardware belongs in the garage, and space is something I don't have enough of in my closets.

Add up your score.

Rate Yourself

50 - 40 You most definitely want to use an online service to connect to the Net. Read Chapter 3 to find out which of the services is best for you.

40 - 30 You should probably start out with an online service and then move to an ISP once you have gotten your feet wet. You may find that the online service provides you with more than enough to keep you happy.

30 - 20 You are a person who can go either way; if the expense of an online service gives you pause then go with an ISP. Read Chapter 3 to find out if you are interested in an online service. Read Chapter 4 to find out about ISPs. I would recommend that you choose an ISP that will send you the software you need and give you technical support to help you get started.

20 - 10 Try out an online service for free if you want to, but you are someone who should connect directly to the Net via an ISP. Read Chapter 4 to find out which provider will work out best for you. If you check around, you can find some really great deals (small monthly fee and unlimited hours).

Is an ISP for You?

Here is an easy quiz to help you figure out if you are the type of hardy adventurer who likes to go it alone and would do best with an ISP.

Chapter 2 Choosing an Internet Service

Answers	1	2	3	4	5
	Strongly Disagree	Disagree	In the Middle	Agree	Strongly Agree

1 2 3 4 5   You've always been a little sad that you never got to solder a chip onto a computer's mother board.

1 2 3 4 5   As soon as you hear that your computer has a newer version of the operating system available, you install it.

1 2 3 4 5   Autoexec.bat is a not the sports equipment of a robot in middle management, a GIG drive is not a musical band on the road, and an bug is not a insect scuttling across the floor.

1 2 3 4 5   Mail order is the only way to go when buying software.

1 2 3 4 5   Computer manuals are for wimps.

1 2 3 4 5   You have been severely chastised for only talking about computers at parties and social gatherings.

1 2 3 4 5   There is nothing finer than learning a new program or tracking down squirmy little problems that cause your computer to reboot.

1 2 3 4 5   A day without email is like a day without sunshine.

1 2 3 4 5   You can never have a big enough hard drive, enough memory, or a fast enough processor.

1 2 3 4 5   When you discover a neat little trick or shortcut for something on your computer, you really can't be happy until you show it to somebody.

Add up your score.

50 - 40   Heck, I'm surprised you are not already on the Net. Read Chapter 4 to find out which ISP will work out best for you. You should only get an online service if it offers something you can't get on the Net.

40 - 30   You can go either way, but will probably do just fine with an ISP. I would stick with a reasonably sized one. Read Chapter 3 only if you want to learn about online services. Read Chapter 4 to find your ISP. I recommend that you choose an ISP that will send you the software you need and offers good technical support to help you set up your connection.

30 - 20   You should probably start out with an online service. If you've got your heart set on an ISP then find someone who has gotten on the Net using an ISP and talk with her or him about that experience. You may find that the online service provides you enough Net time to keep you contented. It will also help you by culling some of the better material from the Net and presenting it to you in an easy- to- use format.

20 - 10   You will want to use an online service to connect to the Net. Read Chapter 3 to find out which of the services is best for you. Stay away from an ISP unless you have a good friend to set it up on your computer and to deal with problems if you need help.

Making the Right Choice

What is the right choice for you? Should it be an online service or an ISP? Here are some of the more important questions to ask yourself.

Is there something special I want that is only on an online service?

For example, Prodigy's *Homework Helper* is a great resource for a kid who has to research and prepare a report on a subject. Likewise, some of the forums on CompuServe and America Online may be of special interest to you.

Is the cost of the service something that is important to me?

Online services are very expensive if you use them a great deal (bills of hundreds of dollars for one month aren't unknown). If you'll be using many hours a month, you'll probably want to stick with an ISP.

Am I worried about my kids being exposed to inappropriate conversations and people in chat rooms?

If you get an online service, your child might want to use the chat rooms. If you are concerned about the content and people in those rooms (as you should be) then it might be better not to have the service in the first place. (You can also turn off access to chat rooms for your children.) It is also important to remember that the online services are much more interactive and they are structured to encourage their members to talk to each other. Interactions are very important for you as a parent to monitor. The Net and WWW are not as interactive and in that sense much safer places for children to be.

Am I willing to put up with the greater amount of work involved in choosing an ISP and setting up my connection?

An online service is more expensive, but easier to use. Choosing an ISP is only the first step of many. You should determine if this sounds like your idea of fun or a nightmare.

Do I want to use the safest solution?

If the most important thing is that your children not be exposed to inappropriate material and you don't want to have to supervise everything they do, I recommend you use an ISP called *Bess*. Read more about Bess in "Bess, a Family ISP" on page 113. The security software that you can use to limit what your children see is very good, but not absolutely tamper-proof. If you are willing to sacrifice some content for having only childsafe material, then Bess is the way to go.

Chapter 3
Choosing an Online Service

Covered in This Chapter
Online Services in General
America Online
CompuServe
Prodigy
Microsoft Network
What's the Right Choice

If you are reading this chapter, you have probably decided that an online service's ease of use is right for you. If that is the case, or if you are just curious, then read on. At the end of the chapter, I will also give you a checklist of each service's good and bad points and make my recommendations. If you can't stand the suspense, just jump to the end.

Online Services in General

Commercial online services cover a wide range of topics and are great for a few specialized things:

- Sending and receiving email.
- Offering hookup numbers when you are traveling or away from home.
- Interactive chats or discussion forums (live talking via computer with other people about topics of mutual interest).
- Getting help with such things as homework.
- Offering trapdoor access to the Net and WWW.
- Offering free software for your favorite computer.
- Getting information on hobbies and areas of interest.

The Net versus an Online Service

The Internet, on the other hand, offers a much wider range of things to do, a richer graphic environment (the WWW), a global base of users, and access to information on any topic, no matter how unusual or esoteric.

Online services can save you time and give you access to the Net, but there is a trade-off for getting your access in this way:

- Online services are much more expensive

If you are the type of person who wants a smooth, easy path to Net access, an online service is clearly for you. On the other hand, if you are more interested in using the cheapest alternative, then you should use an ISP. Don't be too quick, however, to underestimate the value of ease of use. Before exploring what the online services have to offer you, let's look at what they cost.

The Monthly Cost of an Online Service

Here are the typical *monthly* costs you could expect to pay for using an online service for its own goodies and as your road to the Net:

$4.95 the absolute minimum you can spend

$54.00 by just blinking your eyes

$100.00 an easy amount to spend

The Monthly Cost of the Net Only

ISPs offer all sorts of plans:

$19.95 per month for as many hours as you want

$50.00 for a bunch of time (say about 100 hours)

$100.00 some plans charge by the hour

For more information on service providers and the various plans they offer, read Chapter 4.

Which Online Service Is for You?

If you think that an online service might be right for you, you need to know a little more about what each has to offer. I will discuss each service in light of these points:

- Its general features.

- What it offers for families and children.

- What types of parental control it offers.

- What kind of Internet access it offers.

- How to get the service and what it will cost.

- Where you can get more information and help on using that online service.

Free Advice: The online services frequently run ads in magazines (like *Family PC*) and on television and radio offering free sign-ups and some number of hours of free use. Such deals can be great for you. You get to explore the Internet and an online service for no money. What could be better than that—something that's both free and fun?

The service makes money from such deals from people who don't cancel the service and continue on as a paying customer. If you don't like the service, remember to cancel.

After I discuss all of the services I will give you a couple of evaluation charts (see Table 3.1 and Table 3.2 on page 97). These charts will compare the services in terms of cost and quality and make it easier for you to do an overall evaluation.

The Current Online Services

Here is a list of the biggest online services. They work with Macintosh, OS/2, DOS and Windows computers.

- America Online
- CompuServe
- Prodigy

The Windows 95 computer specific service is:

- Microsoft Network

With some recent legislation (the Telecom Bill), you should expect to see a variety of phone, cable, and television companies jumping into the fray. These companies will be offering new options over the coming months ahead.

America Online

America Online (AOL) is easy to use, and offers a range of material that will appeal to families and children. The main menu of AOL offers an attractive and simple point and click interface to its topics (see Figure 3.1). Plus, setting up an AOL account is no harder than calling an 800 number, ordering a free installation disk, and walking through the easy setup process when the disk arrives in the mail.

Once you have set up an account you have access to this main screen that launches you into the AOL world.

Figure 3.1
AOL Main Menu.

Email Services

You have full email support in AOL. You can send and receive email messages not only with AOL users but with anybody that has an Internet address. Figure 3.2 shows you what you what an typical AOL mailbox looks like.

Figure 3.2
Typical AOL Email Message Center.

News and Magazines

Adults and children will find that the news services and magazines available on AOL are vast. The news coverage extends to national and world news and other standard topics such as sports, entertainment, and business (see Figure 3.3).

*Figure 3.3
AOL News and Magazines.*

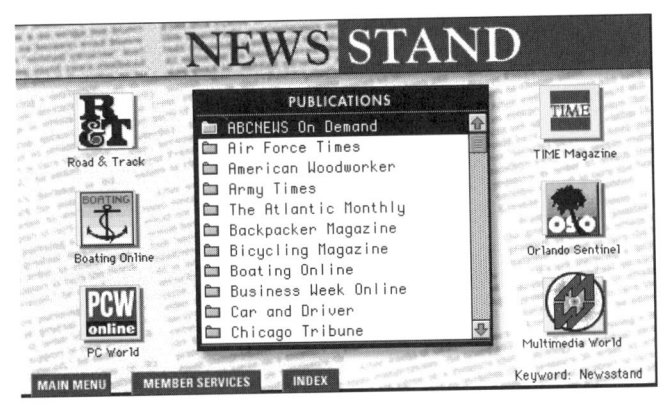

Other Areas

AOL offers topics in a wider range of areas. Here is a list of some of them:

- Business and personal finance areas
- Legal services
- Chat forums on numerous topics
- Travel
- Entertainment
- Personal web pages
- Computer information and software

For Families and Children

Kids' Areas

AOL has devised an area just for kids called Kids Only Online (KOOL). This area is available to all children in the 5–14 age range and is lightly supervised by adults. KOOL offers six areas of interest (see Figure 3.4) as well as a chat room where kids can go to talk to each other about all sorts of topics.

Family/Parent Information

A wealth of information is available to the AOL user on family topics. Everything from online versions of *FamilyPC* (a nice magazine for families dealing with computer issues) to information on vacation places.

There are also several discussion areas where parents can go to discuss everything from how to get kids to do their homework to what to do about ear infections.

Figure 3.4
KOOL Sites for Kids.

Educational Areas

AOL offers its users numerous types of educational information. Everything from chat areas for parents on educational issues to homework helpers for kids. You can also read book reviews, plug into a teachers network, and look at Internet sites. Inside Homework Help, kids get a choice between four different types of help.

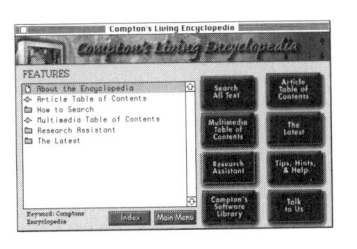

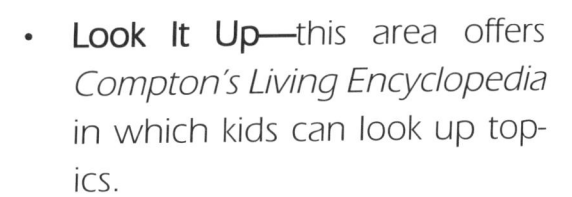

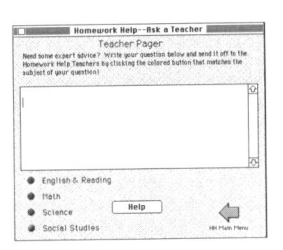

- **Look It Up**—this area offers *Compton's Living Encyclopedia* in which kids can look up topics.

- **Ask a Teacher**—this is a one-on-one email tutoring system. Children send questions to a teacher and receive email answers.

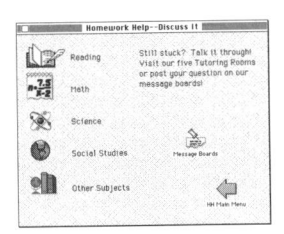

- **Discuss It**—this is an area where academic assistance classrooms offer help to students.

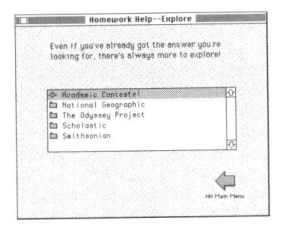

- **Explore**—this place gives kids access to lots of reference material on a wide variety of subjects.

Security and Parental Controls

AOL offers parents the ability to block access to certain parts of the online world (search for "Parental Controls"). Parents can block access to chat rooms, newsgroups, and instant messages. Very importantly, they can also block access to downloadable Internet images (see Figure 3.5).

Figure 3.5
AOL Parental Controls Center.

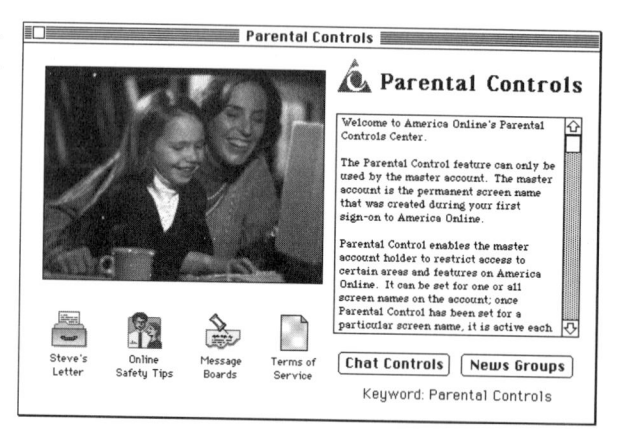

These controls are very general and of limited value. While it is good to be able to block access to chat rooms, that means all chat rooms (even education help areas) are blocked to your child. It would be better to have controls with greater flexibility—for example, ones that block particular rooms.

You can block all access to certain parts of the Internet (that is, newsgroups) or you can just block images. You cannot limit access to sites based on any type of keyword phrase such as "Power Rangers," and you cannot limit access to the World Wide Web. AOL has plans to offer more controls in the future.

Internet Access

America Online offers full Internet access for both Windows and Macintosh users. Access to the Net is no more difficult in AOL than using any of its other areas.

How to Get It and What It Costs

How to Get It

To order America Online anywhere in the United States you can call:

(800) 827-6364

What it Costs

Of course, as you might have imagined America Online, while easy to get, can be very expensive. It costs something like this per month (at $2.95 per hour above 5 hours):

5 hours	$9.95
10 hours	$24.70
20 hours	$54.20
30 hours	$83.70

AOL has been considering a plan with a higher monthly fee and more hours, so you might see one show up in the future. Above 20 hours per month, AOL is more than twice as expensive as most of the other online services. For some people, the extra cost will be clearly worth it; for other folks, one of the other online services might be a better solution.

Assistance to Users

Everybody needs a helping hand at one time or another in life. So AOL has provided its users with a wide variety of online help areas, including information about computers and software. AOL also offers a forum just for families called Family Computing (keyword "FC"), which is a special area on how to use a computer in a family setting.

America Online and Its Critics

Any organization with as many members as AOL has people who have been unhappy with the service. As a good consumer you should consider checking out the criticisms to see whether or not the issues are important to you. Among the most frequently mentioned complaints are:

- The long phone waits required to speak with someone about the service (I have found the wait to be about 10 minutes).

- The cost of the service.

- The slowness of the graphic interface, particularly the one used to interface to the World Wide Web.

- The policy of removing material it considers to be objectionable (including remarks critical of AOL).

Obviously many AOL users do not agree with these criticisms (or they would cancel their service). You should simply realize that no online service is perfect and make your decision only after being fully informed.

If you want to read more concerning criticisms, simply do a search on "America Online" from a Web site or go to Yahoo's WWW site:

> http://www.yahoo.com/Business_and_Economy/Companies/Computers/Networking/Online_Services/America_Online/Anti_AOL_Sites/

What is Yahoo you might ask? See page 126 for a description.

More Information

If you decide that you want America Online as your online service provider and as your access to the Net, you might want to consider getting one of the following books on this subject:

Books

John Kaufeld, *America Online For Dummies*, (2nd edition), IDG Books, ISBN 1-56884-933-8, $19.99 US, $26.99 Canada.
WWW site: http://db.www.idgbooks.com
Believe it or not, these books can be great if you can get past the annoying titles.

Gene Steinberg, *Using America Online* (2nd edition), QUE, ISBN 0-7897-0078-6, $19.99.
WWW site http://www.mcp.com/general/pr.html

CompuServe

CompuServe has been around the longest and offers a cartload of material. While CompuServe is not as easy to use as America Online or Prodigy, its

68 Chapter 3 Choosing an Online Service

strengths may make up for its slightly less easy interface. Some of its best features are:

- Setting up an account is easy.

- It has good parental controls.

- It has a huge number of public discussion areas (called "forums) where members can go to talk about their favorite subjects.

- It has a strong international presence. You can use it from more than 150 countries worldwide.

Once you have set up an account you have access to the main screen shown in Figure 3.6. There is also a tool bar that offers quick access to common actions.

*Figure 3.6
CompuServe Main Menu.*

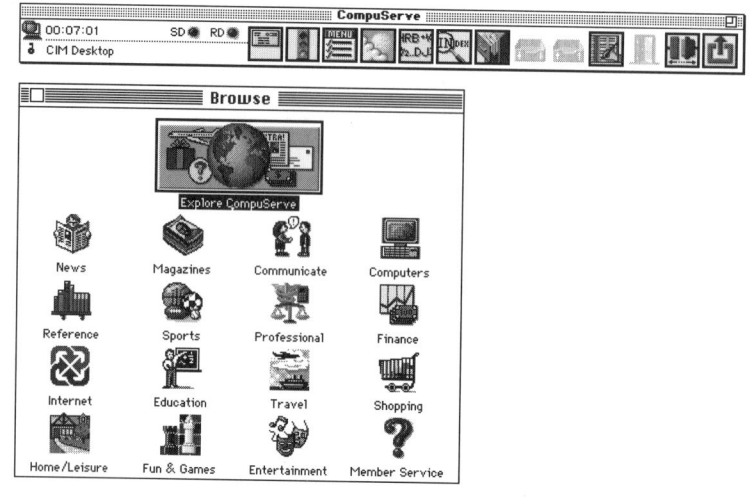

General Features

CompuServe's Browser menu serves as launch point to each of the topics shown there. When you access "Explore CompuServe" you see the menu shown in Figure 3.7. This menu offers a variety of services including information about the Internet and parental controls.

Figure 3.7
CompuServe's Explore Menu.

Email Services

You have full email support in CompuServe. You can send and receive email messages not only with CompuServe users but with anybody that has an Internet address.

News and Magazines

CompuServe's news services and magazines are the equal or better of any of the online services. Among other things, users have access to the Associated

Press wire service. You get news from here that may be only minutes old. Other standard topics such as sports, entertainment, and business are covered both in forums and in various publications.

Other Areas

CompuServe covers a wide range of topics. Here is a list of some of the ones it does best:

- Business and Personal Finance
- Computers
- Educational Forums
- Professional Forums
- Entertainment
- Games

For Families and Children

CompuServe offers older children and families a lot of nice options. It's kid material is less exciting than its other material, so if you want an online service exclusively for younger children (younger than 12 or so), you would do better with one of the other services. If you want a site that has strengths for the adults in the family, then CompuServe is one of the best.

Family/Parent Information

A wealth of information is available to the CompuServe users in the Home and Leisure section (Figure 3.8). Members can explore new hobbies, kids can get involved in activities just for them, and parents can go to forums to discuss their interests.

Figure 3.8 Home & Leisure Section.

Figure 3.9 shows you one such forum. It is for people to discuss Attention Deficit Disorder.

Figure 3.9 Attention Deficit Disorder Forum.

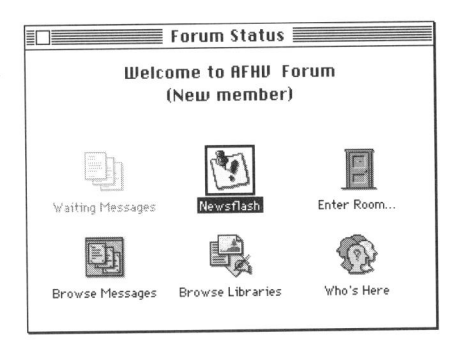

Educational Areas

There is some good material available for older children in CompuServe's Teens and Student's Forum. There is also a really neat area where you can select colleges based on certain criteria (see Figure 3.10). This area, Peterson's College Database, lets you select for location, type of scholastic aid, and so on.

Figure 3.10 CompuServe's Peterson's College Database.

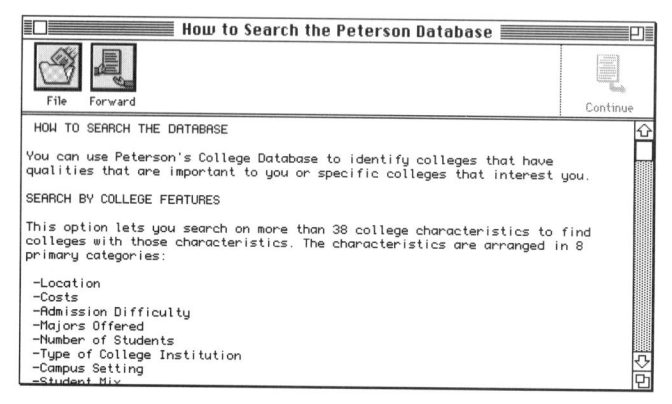

Resources for Teachers

CompuServe has great resources for teachers. In professional and training forums, teachers can pick up information on everything from computers to learning techniques.

Security and Parental Controls

CompuServe has great controls for parents. It uses Microsystems Software's *Cyber Patrol* filtering software (see Figure 3.11). While this software only works with CompuServe, it is identical in all respects to the Cyber Patrol demo included on the CD-ROM at the back of this book. To become familiar with this program see "Cyber Patrol" on page 266 where I discuss it.

With the integration of *Cyber Patrol*, CompuServe has excellent security controls that are easy to use. You can do all of the following with them:

- Specify certain times of day when a child can and cannot use CompuServe.

- Limit access per day or for a total amount per week.

- Restrict which sites a child can use based on type (such as chat rooms) or keywords (such as "penthouse").

Figure 3.11
CompuServe's Parental Controls Center.

Internet Access

CompuServe only offers Internet access for Windows computers. Macintosh users have been told to expect access some time in the coming year.

How to Get It and What It Costs

How to Get It

To order CompuServe anywhere in the United States call:

(800) 848-8199

What it Costs—The Standard Plan

CompuServe offers two packages. The basic package rate is $9.95 per month for 5 hours. Each hour above 5 is billed at a rate of $2.95:

5 hours	$9.95
10 hours	$24.70
20 hours	$54.20
30 hours	$83.70

What it Costs—The Frequent User Plan

CompuServe also offers a Frequent User plan. The monthly rate is $24.95 per month for 20 hours. Each hour above 20 is billed at a rate of $1.95:

20 hours	$24.95
30 hours	$44.45

What it Costs—The Internet-Only Plan

CompuServe has launched a new program called SPRYNET. This is an all-in-one, direct Internet service (Internet and WWW content only) with three pricing schedules:

unlimited time	$19.95	
3 hours	$4.95	($1.95 for each additional hour)
7 hours	$9.95	($1.95 for each additional hour)

SPRYNET also incorporates *Cyber Patrol*, making this a great choice if you want an Internet-only service.

Assistance to Users

CompuServe provides its users with a wide variety of online help areas, including information about computers and software.

CompuServe and Its Critics

CompuServe also has its critics. Just as with the other online services, you should consider checking out the criticisms made against CompuServe. The most frequently mentioned complaints are:

- It is not as easy to use as some of the other services.

- The cost of the service.

- The text-based interface is not as easy to use as a more graphic interface.

- It lacks Internet access for Macintosh users.

If you want to read more concerning criticisms simply do a search on "CompuServe" from any Web searching site or go to Yahoo's WWW site:

http://www.yahoo.com/Business_and_Economy/Companies/Computers/Networking/Online_Services/CompuServe/

More Information

If you decide that you want to use CompuServe as your online service provider, here are some books you might find useful.

Books

Wallace Wang, *CompuServe for Dummies*, (2nd edition), IDG Books, ISBN 1-56884-937-0, $19.99 US, $26.99 Canada.
WWW site: http://db.www.idgbooks.com

Richard Wagner, *Inside CompuServe* (3rd edition), NRP, ISBN 1-56205-455-4.
WWW site: http://www.mcp.com/general/pr.html

Prodigy

Prodigy is the smallest of the big three online services. Even so, it has much to offer and it has been greatly improved of late. One of the oldest complaints about Prodigy is that its interface is clunky, but that is not as true as it once was. It is replacing the clunky areas with much more stylish ones. The best parts of this online service include:

- Setting up an account is easy.

- It has a decent number of news and information sources, so you can get up-to-the-minute news from around the world.

- It has a great homework service and some fun things for little children.

Once you have set up a Prodigy account you have access to the main screen shown in Figure 3.12.

General Features

Prodigy offers the same general features as the other online services. Many hobby and chat forums are available on a wide variety of subjects. Likewise, there are areas on business, finance, entertainment, and educational resources for the whole family.

78   Chapter 3 Choosing an Online Service

Figure 3.12
Prodigy Main Menu.

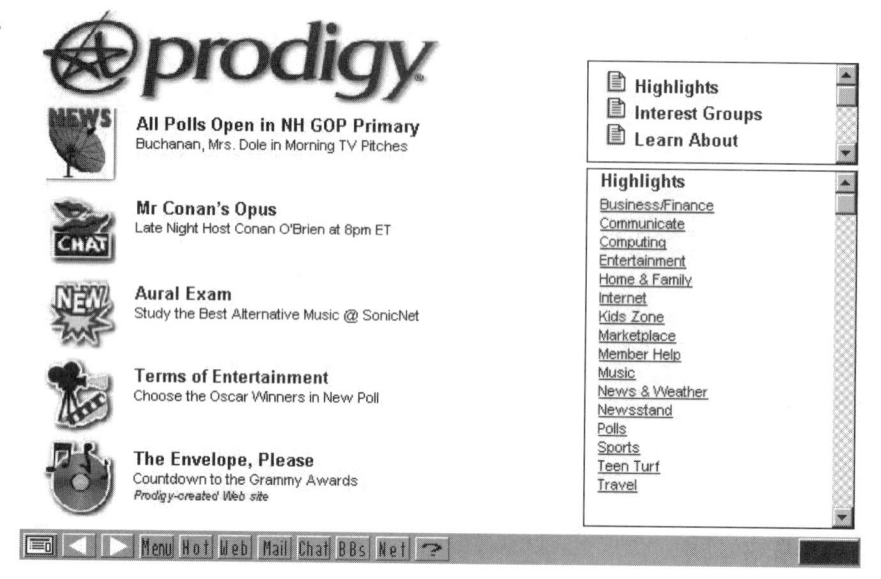

Email services

You have full email support both within Prodigy and on the Internet. Here is what your mailbox looks like (see Figure 3.13). Prodigy is the only online service that offers you individual mailboxes for each member of the family.

Figure 3.13
Typical Prodigy Email Message Center.

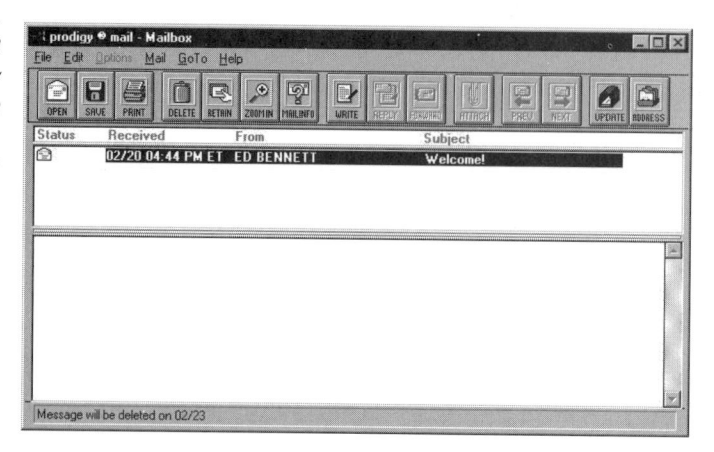

News and Magazines

Prodigy's news services and magazines are reasonable and offer members very good sports coverage (see Figure 3.14).

Figure 3.14 Prodigy Sports Services.

Other Areas

Prodigy covers topics in a wide range of areas, though its coverage lacks the depth of CompuServe or America Online. Areas that I have explored that seem well done are:

- Sports and News
- Financial and Business information
- Homework help for kids (excellent!)
- Good kid areas with distinctive features
- Members can have their own Web pages

For Families and Children

Prodigy has nice resources for all members in the family. It is especially noteworthy that it has the best homework help and nice areas for young children.

Kids Areas

Prodigy's **kids zone** offers children a lot of different things. Kids can go to the area shown in Figure 3.15 and can select activities ranging from music to pet care to the Internet. One of my favorite sites is Sesame Street, which is quite nice for very young children (see Figure 3.16).

Figure 3.15
Kids Area in Prodigy.

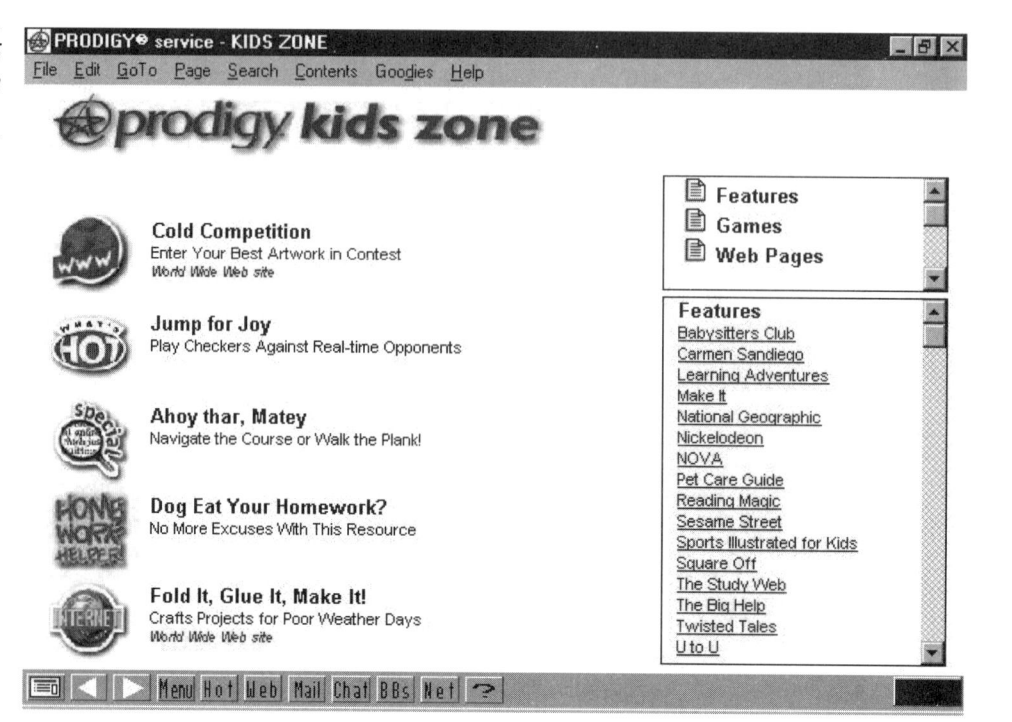

Figure 3.16 Prodigy's Sesame Street Activity Site.

Family/Parent Information

Prodigy offers access to online publications such as *Consumer Reports*. If you need to buy a stereo or car, you no longer have to rifle through your back issues. Instead, you can go directly to the latest review of that product online (see Figure 3.17).

Figure 3.17 Prodigy Consumer Reports Publication.

Educational Areas

You can see Homework Helper in Figure 3.18. This is a great service and, in my opinion, certainly worth the surcharge (other online services homework areas charge as well). It gives help on just about any subject. Best of all it allows questions to be asked in plain English. To try it out I typed in a question:

- "Who invented chess?"

Figure 3.18 Prodigy's Homework Helper.

I got back articles with relevant portions of text highlighted in color (Figure 3.19). Kids can also look for pictures and maps and cut and paste them into reports they are preparing (Figure 3.20).

Homework helper offers two payment plans. You can either pay $6.00 per hour or get a monthly plan for $9.95 that gives you 50 hours of time (each hour after that is $2.95).

Figure 3.19 Looking at Answers to a Question in Homework Helper.

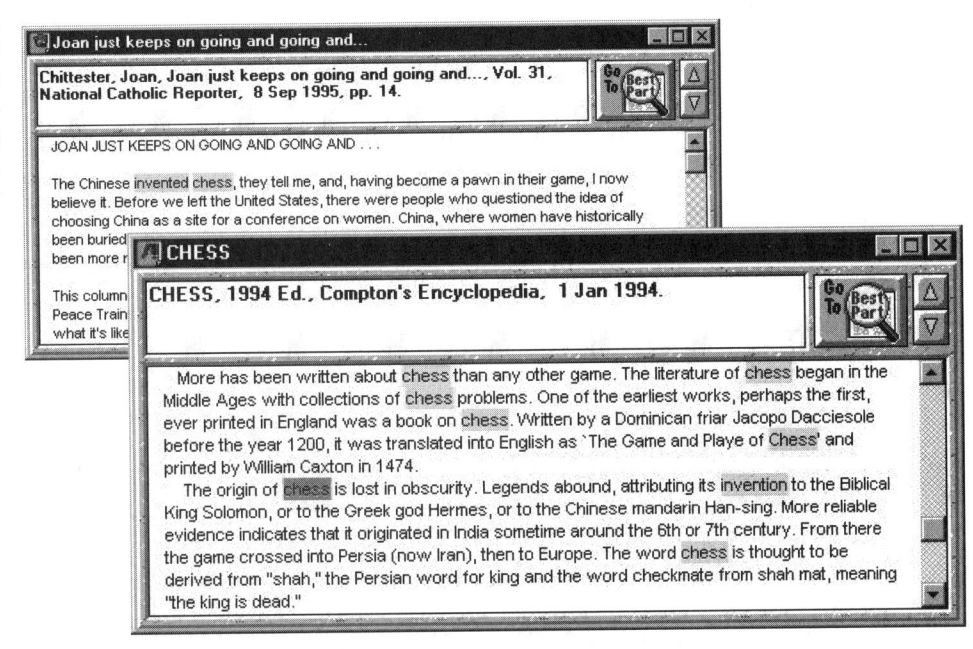

Figure 3.20 Getting Pictures of Ayers Rock in Homework Helper.

Security and Parental Controls

Prodigy offers some general types of controls to parents and has recently announced that they are also offering *Cyber Patrol* to their members. You can block newsgroups, chat rooms, specific bulletin boards, and the WWW. To look at these controls, you do a "jump Help" in Prodigy. Figure 3.21 shows you what they look like. With the use of *Cyber Patrol*, Prodigy's controls are just are good as CompuServe's and better than AOL's.

Figure 3.21 Prodigy's Control Options.

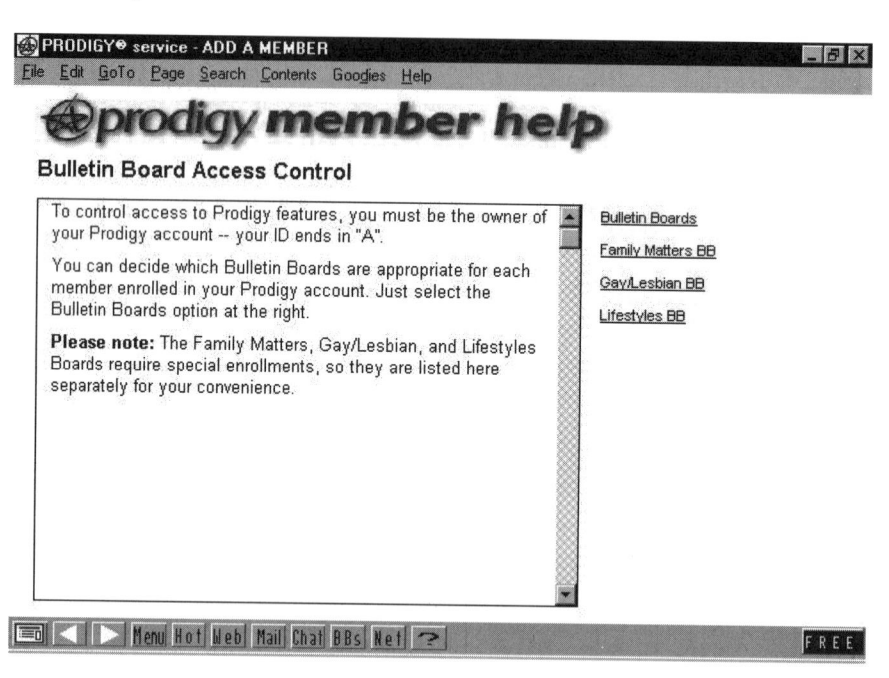

Internet Access

Prodigy offers full Internet access for both Windows and Macintosh users. Its interface to the Web also allows its users to maintain their own web sites. This last point alone is one that may convince people. Everyone wants a web site these days.

How to Get It and What It Costs

How to Get It

To order Prodigy anywhere in the United States call:

(800) 776-3449

What it Costs—The Standard Plan

Prodigy offers two monthly packages. The standard plan rate is $9.95 per month. Each hour above 5 is billed at a rate of $2.95:

5 hours	$9.95
10 hours	$24.70
20 hours	$54.20
30 hours	$83.70

What it Costs—The Frequent User Plan

Prodigy also offers a frequent user plan. The monthly rate is:

30 hours $29.95 (each additional hour is $2.95)

Assistance to Users

Prodigy provides its users with a wide variety of online help areas. To get help on a subject the user has only to type in "jump help" and is given a list of options.

Prodigy and Its Critics

Prodigy, like the other two services, has its critics. Among the most frequently mentioned complaints are:

- It offers far less content than other online services in such areas as business, news, and computer information.

- It has no support for Net access at high speeds.

- Some parts are clunky and difficult to use.

If you want to read more concerning criticisms do a search on "Prodigy," or go to Yahoo's WWW site:

> http://www.yahoo.com/Business_and_Economy/Companies/Computers/Networking/Online_Services/Prodigy/

More Information

Here are some other resources you might want to use if you decide to go with Prodigy.

Books

Dummies Press, *Prodigy for Dummies*, IDG Books, ISBN 1-56884-937-0, $19.99 US, $26.99 Canada.
WWW site: http://db.www.idgbooks.com

Michael Miller, *Using Prodigy*, QUE, ISBN 0-7897-0323-8.
WWW site: http://www.mcp.com/general/pr.html

Microsoft Network (MSN)

The newest online service to enter the fray is Microsoft Network. It is bundled with every Windows 95 computer, and to date Microsoft is still offering unlimited time for users for a modest monthly fee. MSN is a lot like other Microsoft software—it has a beautiful professional look and is very easy to use (see Figure 3.22).

It is also incredibly slow. Where the other services make you pay the time price for initial downloads of artwork, MSN works like a Web browser. That means that every new site you visit takes a long time before it is readable (the site loads in chunks thereby bringing the screen slowly into resolution). In theory, this should work as well as it does with web browsers, but in reality, it is much, much slower. The end result is that it always takes a long time to load a

Chapter 3 Choosing an Online Service

Figure 3.22
MSN Main page.

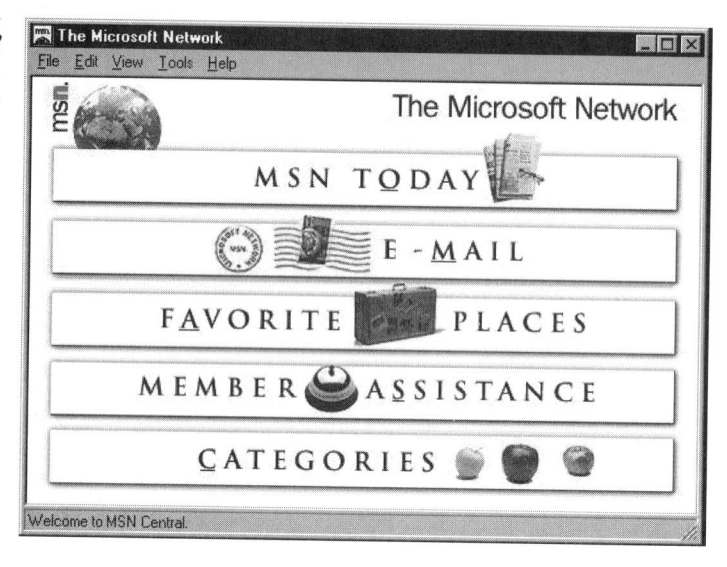

page. The good point to this interface choice, however, is that you don't have to wait for the whole page to finish before going to a link within it; you just click and go.

General Features

MSN offers content and discussion groups in all of its areas. Members can enter chat rooms or participate in scheduled sessions in any of the subject areas MSN covers:

- Front Page
- Arts & Entertainment
- Computers & Software
- Business & Finance
- More Events

*Figure 3.23
Computers and
Software.*

Front Page contains a variety of topics, including current national news and world events. Arts and Entertainment covers movies, fun, and games. Computers & Software, the best stocked area, offers information about other Microsoft software and various useful shareware and freeware products (see Figure 3.23). Business & Finance offers topics related to the business world, including chats with business leaders and access to such things as CNBC's money page. Each of these areas also offers a guidebook which is a very useful resource area to help you find things (see Figure 3.24).

*Figure 3.24
MSN Guidebooks
Page.*

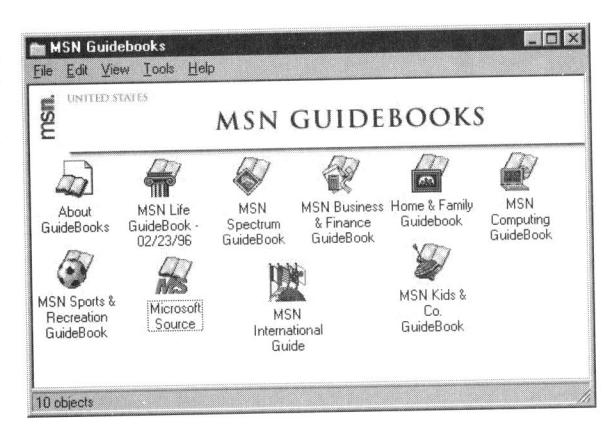

For Families and Children

MSN's offerings for families and children are the Home & Family and Kids & Co. sections.

Figure 3.25
The MSN Home & Family Area.

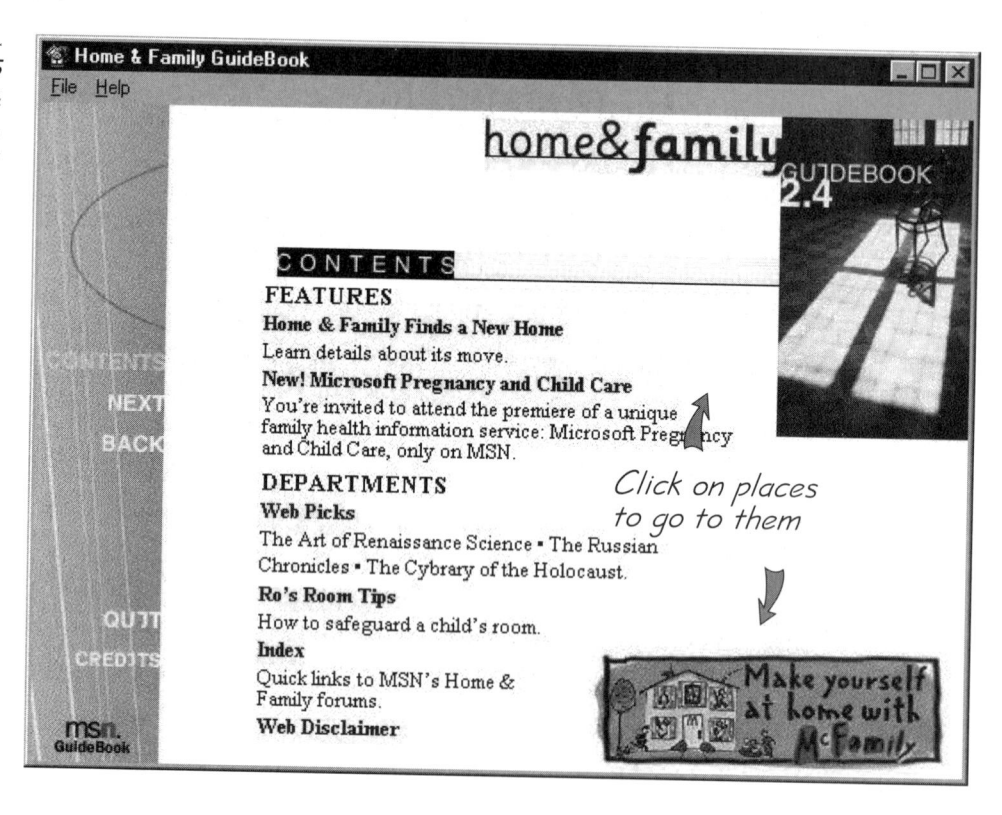

For Families

The Home & Family area contains a parent bulletin board where you can get advice on parenting issues and discuss pregnancy and childcare (see Figure 3.25).

For Children

Children have several discussion areas, including chat rooms for teens and younger children. There are also a few activities for kids, including Kids & Co. where they can guess riddles, read stories, and join in the ocean adventures of John Oman (Figure 3.26).

Figure 3.26
John Oman's Big Ocean Adventure.

A Word about MSN's Content

There is not much to this online service except for the few discussion forums and chat rooms in each area. Currently, MSN is relying heavily on the Net for content. As it is still offering unlimited time for a low monthly fee, the lack of content is certainly tolerable. You should, however, look for more content to appear as MSN moves from infancy into childhood. Everything points to this service having a bright future; it just isn't there yet.

Chapter 3 Choosing an Online Service

Security and Parental Controls

MSN offers the barest minimum of controls (see Figure 3.27). You can use email to deny your child access to particular forums or chat rooms. You can also turn off Internet access all together, but there is no password protection to ensure it stays off. You can also deny access to the Net newsgroups, but kids can thwart that too (see Figure 3.28).

Figure 3.27 MSN's Parental Info Area.

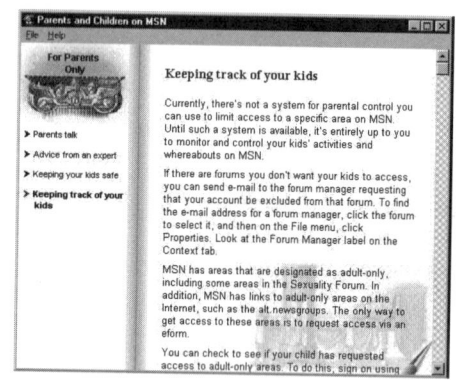

When discussing parental controls, MSN does say one thing that I agree with:

- It is the parents' responsibility to supervise what their children do, and not MSN's.

Figure 3.28 MSN Newsgroups Access Controls.

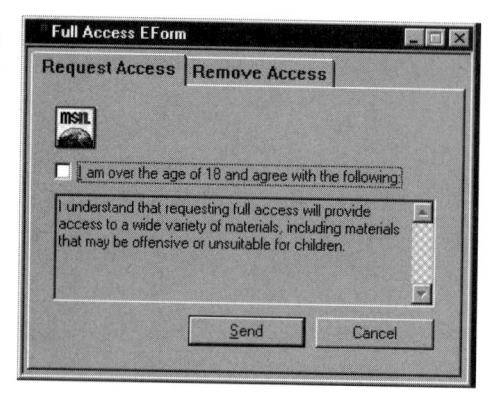

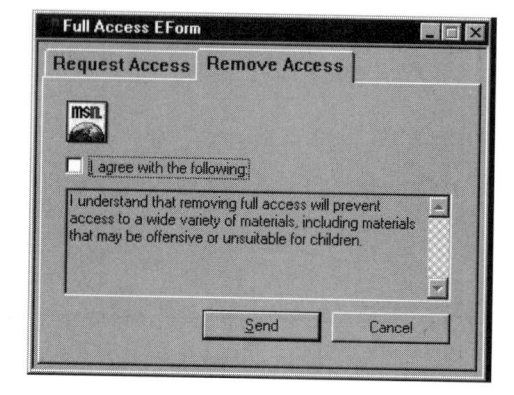

Microsoft Network (MSN) 93

In line with that belief, this service lets parents know that the only monitoring that is done is by them.

Internet Access

MSN offers full Internet access to its Windows users, including lots of nice tools, and a excellent Web browser, Microsoft's Internet Explorer (see Figure 3.29).

Figure 3.29 Internet Stuff on MSN.

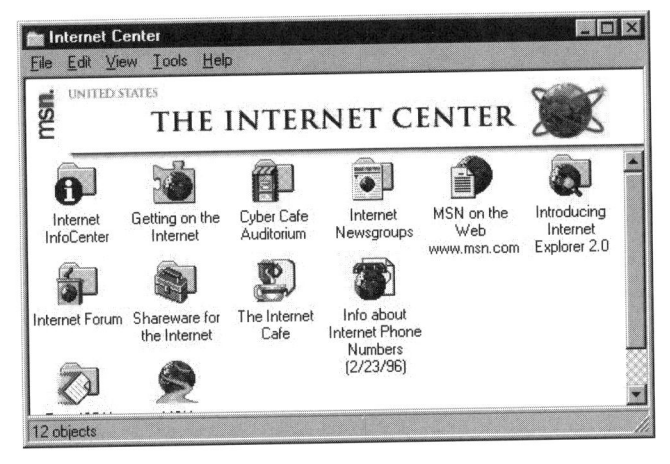

How to Get It and What It Costs

I would certainly recommend that you try MSN if you have a Windows 95 computer. It is worth your time as long as it offers unlimited hours.

How to Get It

To order MSN anywhere in the United States call:

(800) 386-5550

What it Costs—The Standard Plan

Microsoft offers a few different plans from which to choose. At the time this book went to press, Microsoft was still allowing unlimited hours. They have every intention of changing this policy, however. MSN plans to have the following costs in the future.

MSN offers a standard monthly package for a low initial price:

3 hours $4.95 (each additional hour is $2.50)

What it Costs—The Frequent User Plan

MSN also offers a frequent user package:

20 hours $19.95 (each additional hour is $2.00)

MSN has introduced an annual plan as well. For a yearly fee of $39.95 the user gets 3 hours of use a month and every additional hour costs $2.50.

MSN and Its Critics

The nice thing about being new is that you don't have many critics. Eventually, though, criticisms will show up. To find out what they are, do a search or go to Yahoo's WWW site:

http://www.yahoo.com/Business_and_Economy/Companies/Computers/Networking/Online_Services/Microsoft Network/

My own observations of the service is that it is beautiful, but unbearably slow. If MSN can speed up, it will be a pleasure to look at and use. Then all that will remain is filling up the subject areas.

More Information

Books

Doug Lowe, Microsoft Network for Dummies, IDG Books, ISBN 1-56884-921-4, $19.99 US, $26.99 Canada.
WWW site: http://db.www.idgbooks.com

What's the Right Choice

Now it is time to put all of this information together into some charts and recommendations.

My Guarded Recommendation

Of all the online services, I would recommend CompuServe the most highly. That recommendation is based primarily upon three factors:

- It has reasonable parental controls.

- It is the service with the widest international presence.
- The content of its subject areas is very good for parents and older children.

Quite honestly, the first factor alone would be enough for me. Neither the Net nor an online service is a place to leave children unsupervised around inappropriate material. By giving parents the controls available via *Cyber Patrol*, CompuServe is acting in everyone's best interests. Adults who use the service are not penalized by having what they look at regulated, and parents are given reasonable ability to control what their children see. Everybody wins!

If you intend the service to be primarily for your children, then I recommend you consider Prodigy instead. It has activities for younger kids that CompuServe lacks and it has nice homework help. Lastly, it has the same good parent controls.

The Services Compared

Even though I would choose CompuServe over the other online services, that does not mean that the others are not worth considering. In fact, if you look at Table 3.1 and Table 3.2, you can see that each service has its own strengths. Indeed, if you want a service that helps with homework, then Prodigy is clearly for you. If you want a service that is very graphic and easy to use then AOL is worth your time. You might consider trying out all three, if you are still unsure.

A Word About Free Time

Each of the services offers a get acquainted plan. You get a set number of free hours for one month to help you decide if you want to be a full time member. BE WARNED! Half of that time will be spent downloading art and other material the service needs in order to set up your screens. You have to be patient through this process. Just realize that in the beginning there will be long waits between activities (10–30 minutes) as material is downloaded.

The Online Services — Monthly Costs

	America Online	CompuServe	Prodigy	Microsoft Network
	1(800)827-6364	1(800)848-8199	1(800)776-3449	1(800)386-5550
Type of Plan	Standard	Standard/Frequent	Standard/Frequent	Standard/Frequent
3 hours	$9.95	$9.95	$9.95	$3.33/$4.95
5 hours	$9.95	$9.95	$9.95	$8.33/$9.95
10 hours	$24.70	$24.70	$24.70	$20.83/$22.45
20 hours	$54.20	$54.20/**$24.95**	$54.20/$29.95	$47.45/**$19.95**
30 hours	$83.70	$83.70/$44.45	$83.70/**$29.95**	$72.45/$39.95
40 hours	$113.20	$113.20/$63.95	$113.20/$59.45	$97.45/$59.95

Table 3.1   Comparison of Costs of Online Services.

As you can see in Table 3.1, the cost of an online service depends a great deal upon how much you are going to use it and which type of plan you have. Some of the figures in Table 3.1 are bold—this represents the best deal per hour for that online service. Note that America Online's rate is the same regardless of how many hours you use it. There is no frequent user plan. If you intend on using the online service for more than 10 hours per month it will usually make more sense to get a frequent user rather than a standard plan.

Online Services
Subject Area & Quality Ratings

	America Online	*Compu-Serve*	*Prodigy*	*Microsoft Network*
Parental Controls	C	A	A	D
Stuff for 2–7-yr-olds	B	C	A	D
Stuff for 7–12-yr-olds	B+	B	A	D
Stuff for 12–17-yr-olds	B	A-	A	C
Educational areas	A	A	B-	C
Homework help	B+	C	A	D
Hobbies	B	A	B-	C-
News & stuff	A	A-	B	C-
Sports	B	B	A	B-
Internet access	A-	C-	B	A+
Easy to use	A	B-	B	A

Table 3.2   Online Services Compared.

Chapter 4
Choosing a Service Provider

Covered in This Chapter
Getting a Service Provider
Being a Wise Consumer
Bess, a Family ISP

If you're reading this chapter, you are considering an ISP as your Net provider. You probably know that finding and using an ISP takes more patience, but you're ready for the challenge, right?

Now, it is time to tell you that you are in a bit of a pickle. Your pickle of a problem is that you want to get on the Net but the best way to do that is from the Net. You can't yet just open the phone book and look up "ISP."

That problem is further complicated by the fact that there is stuff you don't know and need to know.

Okay, let me explain this problem to you by using a useful analogy that will, I hope, begin to make the issues clear...

A Useful Analogy

A healthy-looking guy with a chimp walks up to you and says, "Hello, my name is Tarzan. I am lord of all the jungle, but do not understand the ways of your civilization." Looking very sincerely at you, he says, "Please, I need your help."

You reply, "Sure, what can I do for you?"

Tarzan asks you, "What is a grocery store? I've heard all sorts of good things about them. I want to try one and I've heard that you can help me find all of the good things in one."

You want to be as helpful as possible, so you ask a few questions. "Do you want a large grocery store chain or a small mom-and-pop store?" You also remember to ask, "Or do you want to go to a discount chain where you will need a special membership, but the prices are cheaper?"

Tarzan frowns at you for a moment—he is wondering if you are making fun of him. He decides to give you the benefit of the doubt and says, "What is a grocery store chain? Is that something I swing on to get to the grocery store?" He further asks, "And what is a mom and pop? I have heard of a 'popsicle.' Is that what you mean?"

(The narrator interrupts the story here to ask if you are getting an idea of the problem. The story continues...)

You pause for a moment. You then back up and start with some very simple questions. "Do you care if the grocery store has a lot of choices? Do you want one that carries specialty foods from your native country? Or do you want one that will deliver your groceries to where you live?"

Tarzan, sensing that you are really trying to be helpful, says, "Which is the best one? I just want to go to that one."

You reply, "Well, that really depends…"

He is getting impatient by now and so interrupts you by saying, "Okay, just point me in the right direction, and I will go to the grocery store by myself."

Seeing the situation dissolving into a horrible mess, you suddenly get a bright idea and say, "Look, Tarzan, I know this guy who has helped hundreds of people just like you learn about grocery stores. He can explain all about grocery stores—how to use them, what the difference is between a local and a national chain, and so on. Once you know all of those things, you come back to me and I'll show you just where all the good things are in the grocery store of your choice." Then you walk Tarzan down the street and introduce him to…Adam Engst, the writer of the *Internet Starter Kit* book series.

In a week or two, a very satisfied and happy Tarzan returns to you and says, "I would like a local provider who can offer me a full PPP account and support for my 28.8k modem. I have that account, and I want to go surf the Net with you."

You and Tarzan walk happily off into a virtual sunset past the white cliffs of Dover and into the Net…

Getting a Service Provider

The fact of the matter, is you only have a couple of choices in how you go about doing this. There is a whole lot of stuff you need to understand, and some software you need to get, in order to successfully set up an Internet account. You have three choices:

- Buy a book that comes with some software.

- Buy some software that comes with a book (that is, a manual).

- Go it on your own.

Let me introduce you to my recommended solutions. I have included a variety of approaches to accommodate different learning styles. You can buy another book, buy some software, or go it on your own. Any of the choices will get you to the same place, which is the Net.

The Internet Starter Kit

This is a book series that includes everything you need to know about Internet connections, helps you find just the right service provider for you, helps you figure out how to properly connect to the service, and in all other respects, helps you become a well prepared adventurer who is ready for the Net. The *Internet Starter Kit* is well worth your time and is an excellent resource.

Mac users should get the first book, Windows users the second, and Windows 95 users the third.

Internet Starter Kit for Macintosh, 3rd ed., by Adam C. Engst, Hayden Books. ISBN: 1-56830-197-9, $35 US.

Internet Starter Kit for Windows, 2nd ed., by Adam C. Engst, Corwin S. Low, and Stanley K. Orchard, Hayden Books. ISBN: 1-56830-177-4, $30 US.

Internet Starter Kit for Windows 95, by Adam C. Engst, Corwin S. Low, and Stanley K. Orchard, Hayden Books. ISBN: 1-56830-260-6, $35 US.

Each book supplies the software; you supply the computer, modem, and reading time.

Another Pretty Good Solution

If buying another book doesn't appeal to you, and you think you know enough about Internet connection issues, you can buy some software that comes with a manual. The software package also gives you a reasonable national service provider solution.

Macintosh Users

If you are a Macintosh user, you can buy Apple Computer's:

> Apple Internet Connection Kit. Apple Computer. Cost: around $50 US.

This software package includes Netscape Navigator (a great Web browser) and all the other software you need to connect to the Internet.

Note: Two mail order companies where you can purchase this software are:
MacConnection: (800) 800-1111
MacZone: (800) 248-0800

Windows 3.1 and 95 Users

If you are a Windows user, you can purchase a great piece of software:

> *Internet in a Box 2.0.* Publisher: CompuServe/SpryNet. Cost: around $35 US.

This software package includes everything you need to connect to the Internet. The service provider is SPRYNET, CompuServe's new all-in-one, direct Internet service (Internet and WWW content only).

Access Time Monthly Cost Choices:

unlimited time	$19.95 (a great deal!)
3 hours	$4.95 ($1.95 for each additional hour)
7 hours	$9.95 ($1.95 for each additional hour)

SPRYNET also incorporates *CyberPatrol's* Internet filtering software, making this a great choice for an entirely different reason.

Note: Mail order companies where you can purchase this software are:
PC Connection: (800) 800-1111
The PC Zone: (800) 258-2088

A Solution for Frugal People

If you are one of those people whose day is made when you find a really great deal, and you want to try this adventure on your own (none of the hand holding you get from a manual or book), then you can order everything you need directly from Sprynet:

(800) SPRYNET

Some fine salesperson will take your name and address and send you a disk with all of the software you need to connect to the Internet, free of charge. You will have the same hourly costs as the SPRYNET users who use *Internet in a Box*.

> *Note:* Unfortunately, Sprynet does not currently have software for Macintosh computers. The good news is that it is in the works, and hopefully by the time you read this book it will be available. Make sure to call 1-800-SPRYNET to check on availability.

The Totally Cheapo Solution

Though I don't recommend it for the faint of heart, you can also do something that is just a tiny bit wicked. Call one of the commercial online services, *America Online*, *CompuServe*, or *Prodigy* and get one of their trial-offer disks of free software and 10 free hours of access time.

- America Online: (800) 827-6364
- CompuServe: (800) 848-8199
- Prodigy: (800) 776-3449

Using that account you can get to the Internet and go to the sections I discuss in "Where to Get Yourself an Education" on page 107. Then you have three things to do:

- Read the articles on connecting to the Internet.
- Download the software you need to connect from your computer.
- Choose an ISP from "Where to Find a List of Local ISP's" on page 111.

You can do all of this during the free trial period for a total cost of zero dollars. With whatever free time you have remaining, you can explore the online service. You might find that you like it enough to continue your membership.

Being a Wise Consumer

Once you are on the Net you might find, for one reason or another, that you are unhappy with your service provider. Or you might be perfectly happy, but want a better deal. Where do you find the names of candidates, and what are the questions you should be asking them?

Before you can ask these questions intelligently, you need to know about the things covered in the *Internet Starter Kit* or educate yourself on the Net.

Warning:	I am going to talk about things in this section that you might not completely understand until you have done some research. I will point you to a place on the Net where you can read up on these issues, and provide you with a path to service providers, but I am not going to talk about those things in detail.
	Only the most stubborn of adventurers should attempt this path, as the dangers are many and the easy spots are few.

Where to Get Yourself an Education

If you want to learn about connecting to the Net, how it all works, and what each piece of software you use is responsible for, then you should look at the following sites.

Frank Hecker's Site

ftp://ftp.digex.net/pub/access/hecker/internet/slip-ppp.txt

The entire text of this first site is a very good article written by Frank Hecker. It is also on the CD-ROM at the back of the book.

The Charm Net Site

http://www.charm.net/pip.html

This second site, Charm Net as shown in Figure 4.1 is a great collection of sites. It contains links to every type of site you will need—from FAQs to sites where you can download all the Internet software necessary for either a Windows or Macintosh computer. This also includes all the accessory software, such as an emailer and a newsreader, that makes Net surfing much more fun. This is a wonderful place to get what you need.

Figure 4.1 Charm Net Web site.

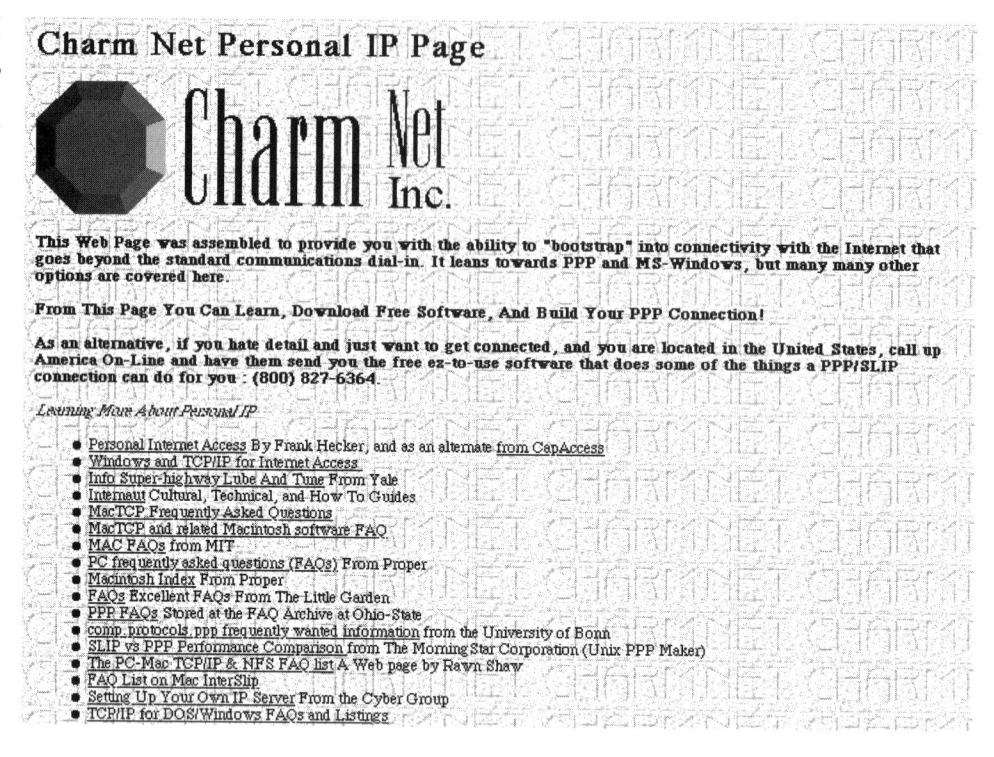

Yahoo's Collection

A final site worth your time is **Yahoo's** collection on connectivity (see Figure 4.2). There is also some good information in **Yahoo's** Internet section.

http://www.yahoo.com/Computers_and_Internet/Internet/Connectivity/

If you read though all of this information, you should have a fairly clear idea of what is involved in setting up your Internet connection.

Figure 4.2
Yahoo's Internet Connectivity Collection.

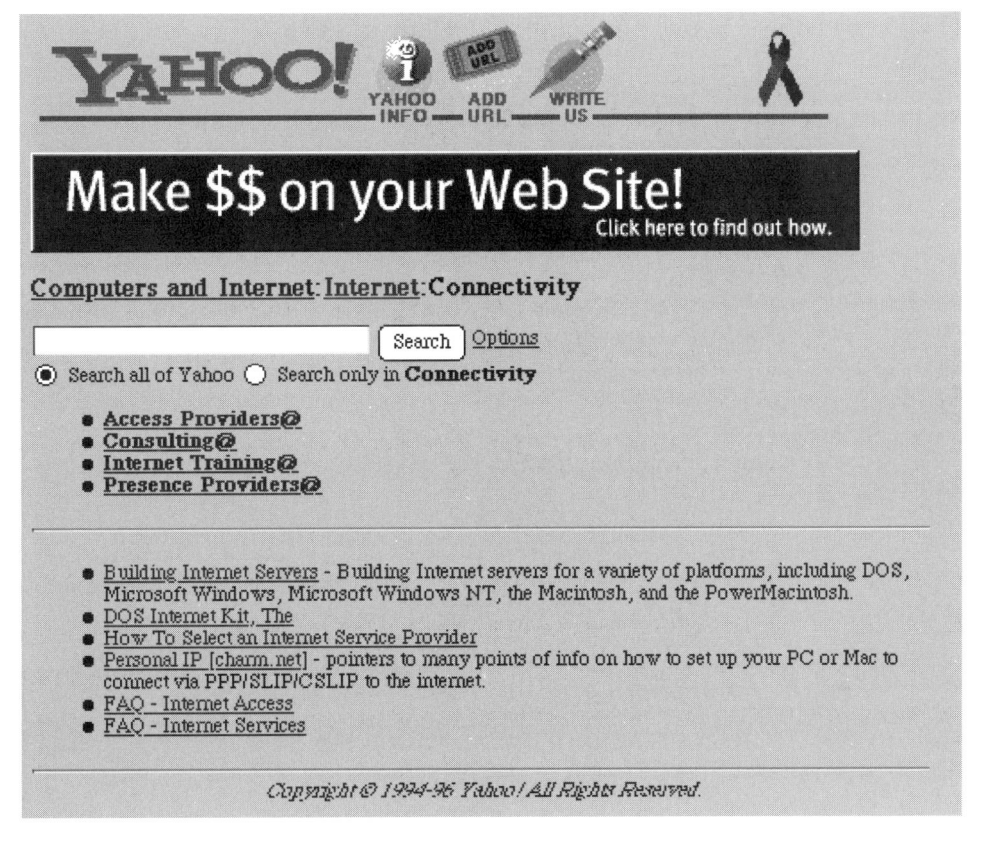

What Is a Local ISP?

A local ISP is a company in the same area code, ideally in the same city or town in which you live. This company keeps a large computer running 24 hours a day (for most of the year) and has a bunch of incoming phone lines and modems. You connect to the Net via this local ISP using the phone number they provide. Because the ISP has a bunch of phone lines (all attached to the same phone number) and a bunch of modems, a bunch of people can call up at once.

Free Advice: It takes one line and one modem for each user who calls up. If you select an ISP with 500 lines and 500 modems, and you are the 501st person to call that number you get an annoying busy signal.

Obviously, then, you should ask your prospective ISPs how many lines and modems they have.

You pay the ISP some amount of money each month, and they give you:

- This dial-up access to the Internet

- An email address where you can get mail

- Software to read news, send email, and browse the WWW (note that some ISPs do not provide this)

The amount of money you pay will vary a *huge* amount from ISP to ISP. It will also depend upon where you live. If you live in a remote region where your closest neighbor is 600 miles away, you will have less choice than someone who lives in New York City and is lucky to live 600 feet away from an ISP. The folks in New York have traffic and smog but lots of ISPs. The folks in the country have cows, nights filled with stars, and one or two ISPs at best.

Typically, you should expect to pay:

- between $20 and $100 dollars a month for Internet access.

Each ISPs pricing structure will vary. Be careful, however, as some ISPs base their prices upon strange formulas purposefully designed to confuse you. If you are lucky you will get one that allows you a large or unlimited number of hours (say 100) and a set monthly fee of about $20.

Where to Find a List of Local ISPs

To get a list of ISPs for your area, what better place could you imagine going to than **Yahoo**. If you look at Figure 4.3, you will see that Yahoo has made it easy to search by country or region to find an ISP in your home town.

http://www.yahoo.com/Business_and_Economy/Companies/Internet_Services/Internet_Access_Providers/

Figure 4.3
Yahoo's ISP Collection.

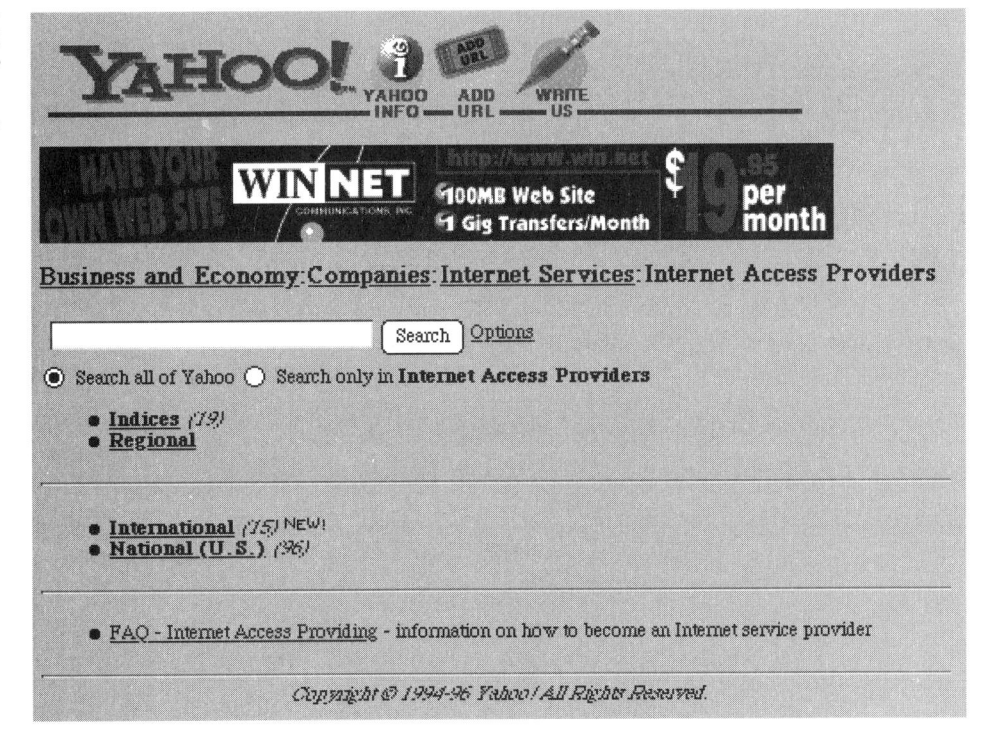

Yahoo will undoubtedly maintain this list in this place for some time to come. Given how quickly this information changes, it is much better to send you to **Yahoo** than to try and provide a list of ISPs here. Besides, it would have to be a huge list.

> *Note:* Recently, several of the big telecommunication giants (like MCI and AT&T) announced Internet access plans. By the time you read this, I expect the choices will have increased tremendously. The presence of such giants will bring lots of competition to this market and that is good for you, the consumer. It is always worth checking back with Yahoo occasionally to see what the current access rates are.

Questions to Ask an ISP

When you are out shopping for an ISP, here are a number of questions you should ask:

1. **How much does it cost?**
   This is a tricky question. You have to find out the number of hours per month and at what times you can use the service. Some ISPs only sell off-peak hours (for example, 9 P.M.– 6 A.M.) cheaply and other hours cost an arm and a leg. You also have to consider the per-hour charge for additional hours you use above your base allowance.

2. **Do they have a local phone number to dial up to?**
   If you don't get a local phone number, then you have to pay toll charges for all the time you are connected. Or you have to pay a surcharge to use their toll-free number. *That can get expensive.* This is probably one of the most important things to consider.

3. **What type of account will it be?**
   You want a PPP or SLIP account; not a shell account.

4. **What type of help do they provide?**
   Here are two important things to ask: Will they help you get your connection up and running or are you on your own? Do they provide you with newsreading software (like News-Watcher), a browser (like Internet Explorer) and email software (like Eudora)?

5. **What types of modems do they support?**
   You want to make sure that the service can support modems of your speed. You should also find out how many of those types of modems they have. If most of their modems are slower speeds, then you will end up with a slow connection most of the time.

Bess, a Family ISP

If you are worried about what your children see and you want the easiest possible solution, then you should get Bess—an ISP specifically designed for kids, families, and schools. It protects children from inappropriate material on the Net by not allowing access (called filtering) to that material in several important ways:

- Most Newsgroups and open chat areas are not accessible.

- Certain places on the Net known to contain large amounts of inappropriate material are blocked completely.

- Some sites that are otherwise good but have

profanity in them have the profanity smudged out.

- *Email is not delivered if it contains inappropriate language.*

Peter Nickerson and Holly Hill started this company with their own two kids in mind. "Bess," besides being the name of the service, is also the name of the family's retriever.

This is an ISP that not only does all the work for you, but also provides a nice home page filled with some great resources for kids (Figure 4.4). Some of the subjects they cover are entertainment, government, sports, news, and science and nature (see Figure 4.5).

Figure 4.4
Bess Home Page.

Figure 4.5
Bess Entertainment, News & Weather, and Government Pages.

How Bess Works

When children try to access a site that is completely inappropriate, Bess shows them the screen in Figure 4.6 instead.

When a site is mostly okay, but has one of the seven bad words in it (*use your imagination about what those words are*), Bess allows access but smudges out the bad word with "XXXX" as shown in Figure 4.7.

116   Chapter 4   Choosing a Service Provider

Figure 4.6
Bess Blocked Site Screen.

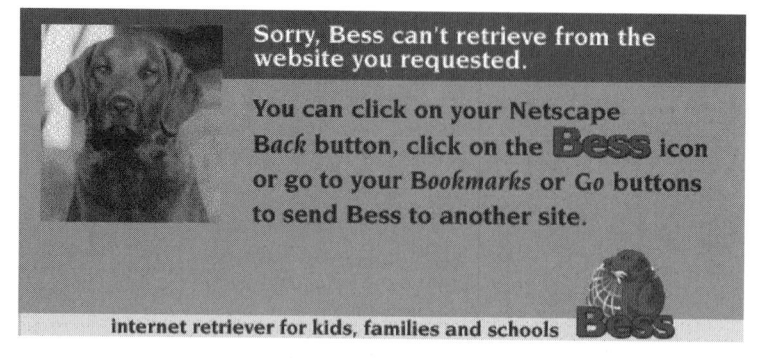

Figure 4.7
Site with Smudged-Out Words.

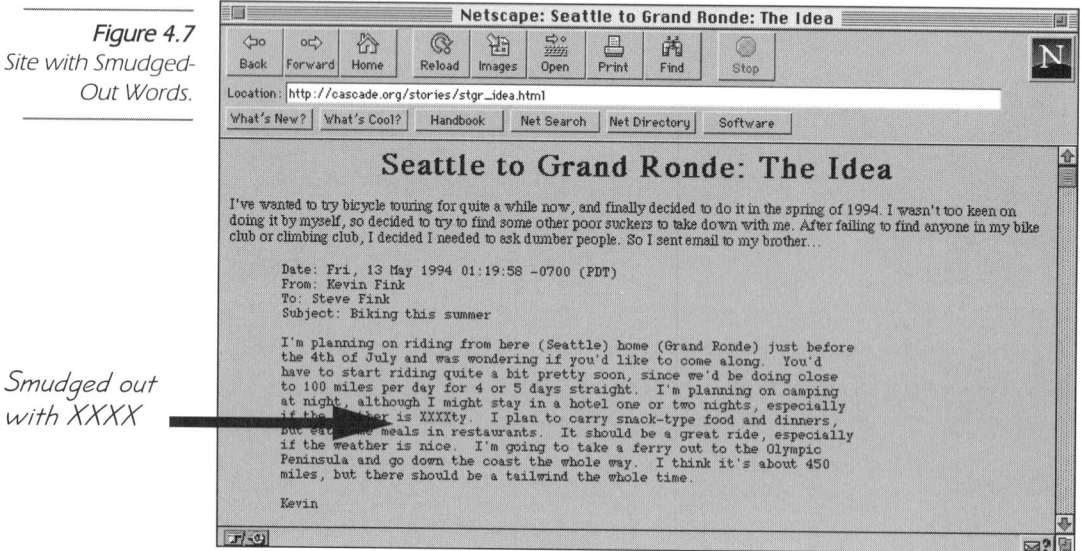

Smudged out with XXXX

What Does Bess Cost?

So, how much does such a wonderful service cost? Less than you might think. While Bess is not as dirt-cheap as many other services, it is worth remembering when you are making your decision that they are doing more work for their fees than a standard ISP.

Monthly Cost for Using Bess as Your Local ISP

By way of comparison, I would still place Bess' pricing plan on the inexpensive side of what most ISPs are currently charging.

- $29.95 for 50 hours.
- $.99 for each additional hour.
- A one-time $30 activation fee.

The Total Cost of Bess and Another ISP

If you are not fortunate enough to live in the area where Bess resides, then you are going to be dealing with two companies, your local ISP and Bess.

Remember, you need a local ISP to give you a local phone number you can use to access the Internet. This local ISP will charge you their standard fee for access. On top of that you will have to pay a small additional charge to take advantage of Bess and its Internet filtering. This extra amount will be approximately:

- $3–$5 Additional monthly charge

So, Who Can Get Bess?

Where is this wonderful ISP? It happens to be located in the United States in the area of Seattle, Washington. If you live in either the 206 or 360 area codes, you can probably just call Bess up and use it as your local ISP. If you don't live in those areas, then all is not lost. Here is what you do:

- Call Bess up and they will help you find an ISP where you live.

Bess will work out an arrangement with that company to provide you with their filtered service. If you already have an ISP, then you can ask the people at Bess if they can work with that company. *If your ISP is unwilling to work out an arrangement with Bess, I recommend you switch providers.*

Here is their phone number:

(206) 971-1400

Or you can email them at:

- bess@bess.net

Note: On the CD-ROM at the back of the book you will also find a demonstration set of Bess pages. Flipping through these with the Web browser on the CD will give you an idea of how Bess works as a service.

My Recommendation

If the cost of this service does not seem to be too much for your family, then I recommend that you use Bess as your Internet filter. Here is why:

- It is the easiest solution for protecting kids.
- It is far more foolproof than using another type of blocking solution (such as CyberPatrol or SurfWatch).
- You can also get an unblocked adult account.
- The people at Bess are very responsive to customer questions and requests about sites. They pride themselves on their service.

A Word of Caution

If you are looking for an ISP who will recreate the world of **Leave it to Beaver** and the **Brady Bunch** on the Internet for you, that is not Bess. In other words, not everyone will like the choices that Bess makes (though the folks at Bess encourage comments and listen seriously to concerns about sites). Some people might find that some of the sites Bess allows are ones that they would not want their children to see. Other people might find sites are blocked that they would like their children to see.

As you might have figured out, the problem doesn't occur with sites that contain explicit pornographic material—they are always blocked. Rather, it is with sites that contain material or images that some people believe children should see and other people believe children should not see. To get an idea of just such a page look at the site in Figure 4.8.

Figure 4.8
A Page that Bess Does Not Block.

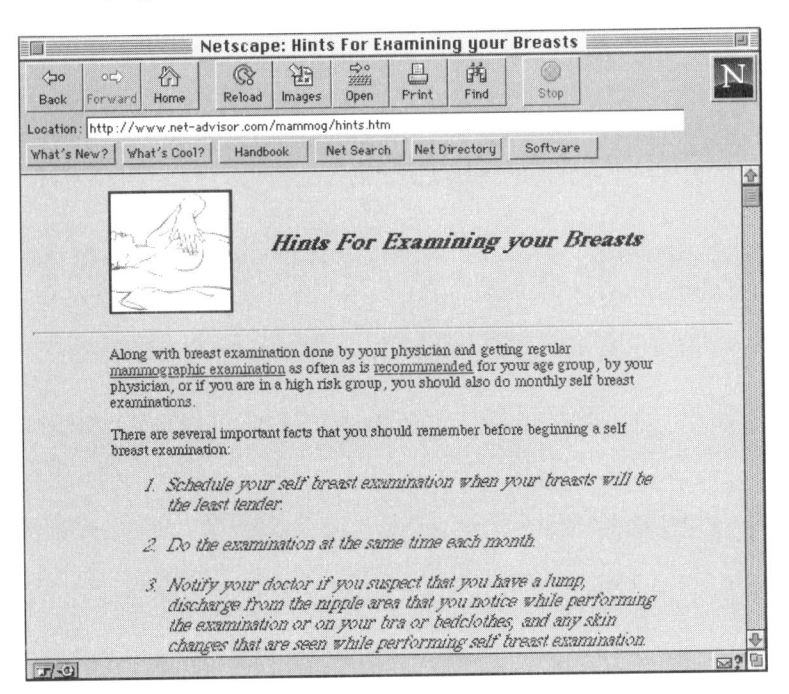

Obviously, some people will not mind this material and others will.

- My own opinion is that they do a very good job of choosing.

I like the material they leave in and usually agree with what they block. I have also found that if I ask them about particular sites, they are more than happy to talk with me and reevaluate the site if necessary.

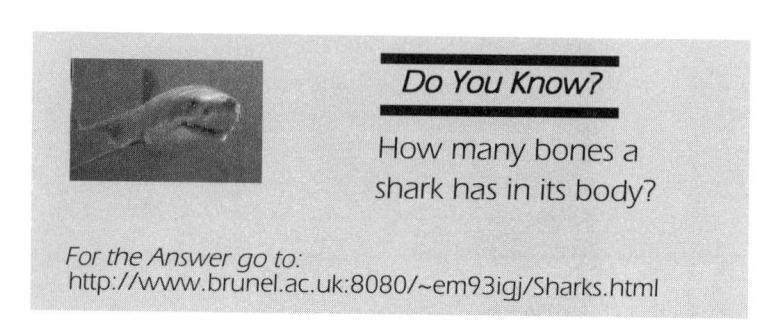

Do You Know?

How many bones a shark has in its body?

For the Answer go to:
http://www.brunel.ac.uk:8080/~em93igj/Sharks.html

Part Two

Exploring the Net

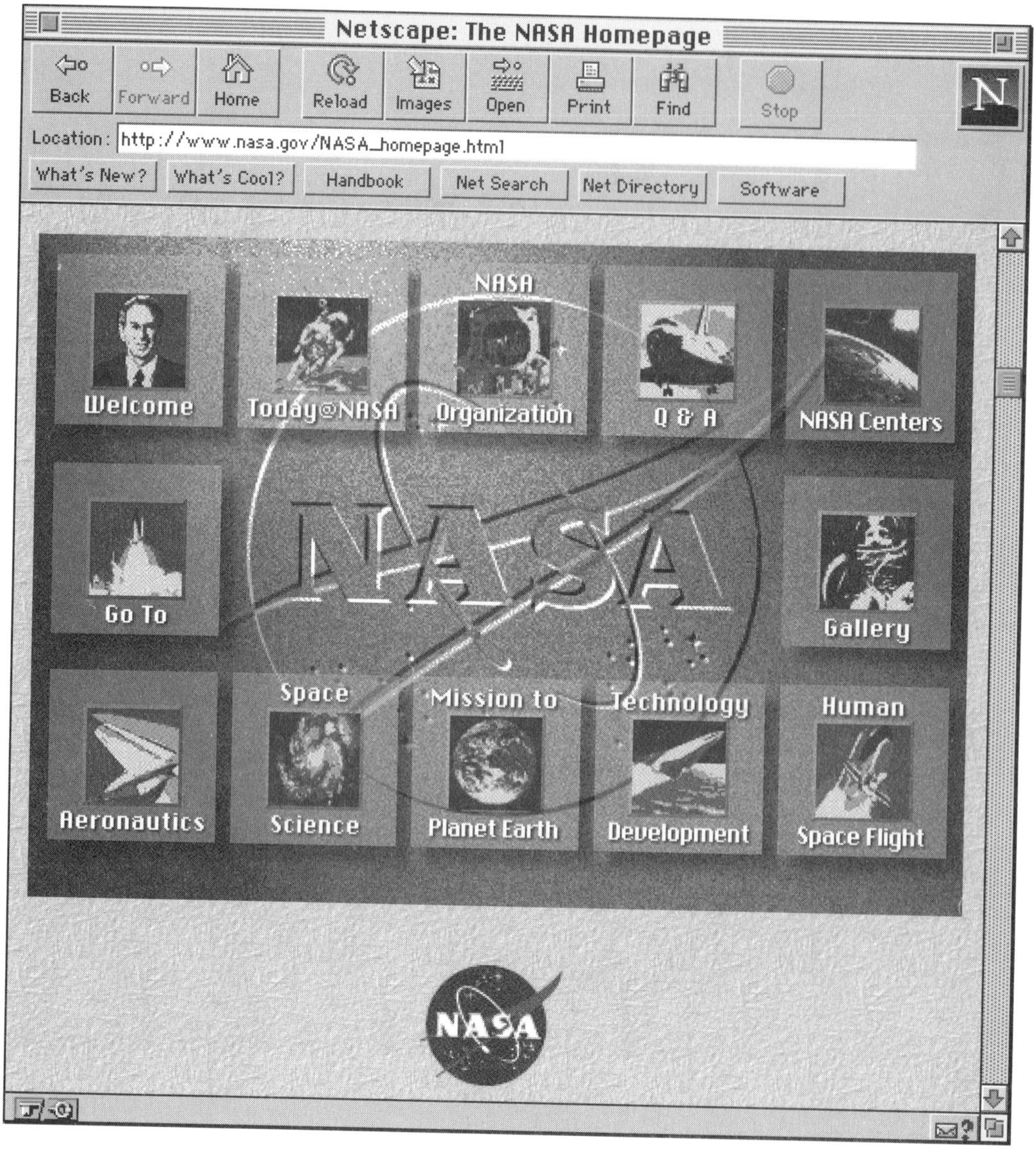

Netscape: The NASA Homepage
Back
Forward
Home
Reload
Images
Open
Print
Find
Stop
Location: http://www.nasa.gov/NASA_homepage.html
What's New?
What's Cool?
Handbook
Net Search
Net Directory
Software
Welcome
Today@NASA
NASA Organization
Q & A
NASA Centers
Go To
NASA
Gallery
Aeronautics
Space Science
Mission to Planet Earth
Technology Development
Human Space Flight
NASA

Chapter 5

Starting Places

Covered in This Chapter
Take a Tour
Great Overall Places
Great Kid Spots
Quick Dip Spots
Yuppie Favorites

Hello and congratulations! You should have decided by now on the type of Internet service you want and hopefully are up and running. Now is when the fun really begins for you and your family. Right away you have a difficult question to face:

"Where to start?"

Chapter 5 Starting Places

This is difficult to answer because of the abundance of choices. So, let me trim down the size of the problem by giving you some suggestions on good places to begin.

Our first stop is with a tour guide.

Take a Tour

http://www.globalcenter.net/gcweb/tour.html

Figure 5.1
Global Village's Tour of the Net.

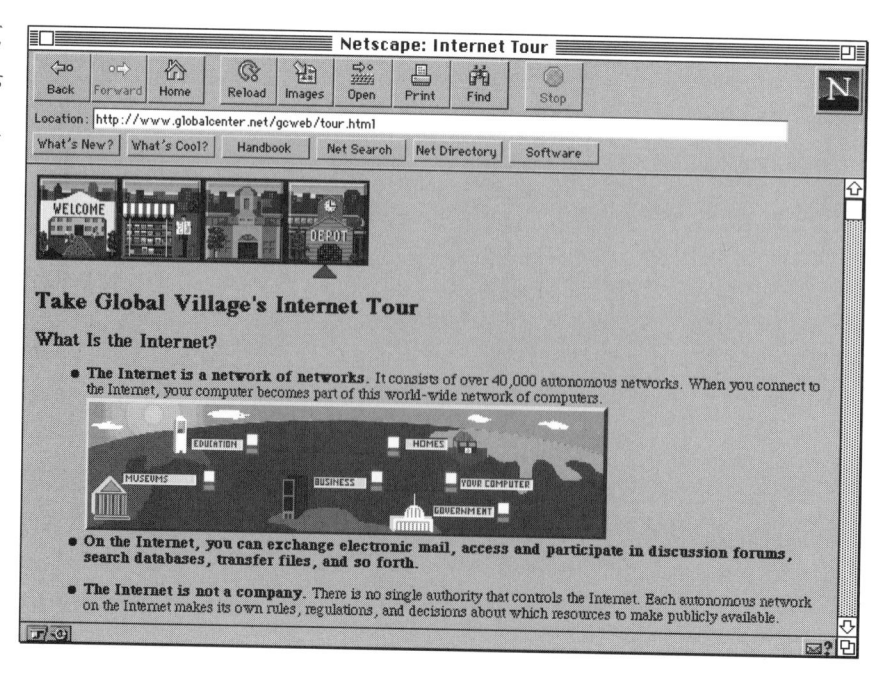

What could be more appropriate than starting your adventure with a tour guide? **Global Village** has a wonderful Web site that offers users the opportunity to become acquainted with the Net in a slow and gentle fashion (see

Figure 5.1). You get to stroll around, learn some of the tricks of the trade, and gradually get a real sense of the things you can see and do on the Net.

I recommend that you start here, and I guarantee that you will learn things that will serve you well on your future travels.

Great Overall Places

These are all good places to begin any Net journey. In fact, that is the first question you need to answer.

From where do you want to launch every time you log on to the Net?

If you are using an online service, then that service's main page will be your starting place. If you are using an ISP, you can set up your very own starting place. This starting place will be your home page, and as Dorothy says, there is no place like home.

If you are considering a site for a child, then look at the next section in particular. I have also listed a few quirky sites that you will want to explore when you are feeling adventurous.

Remember, your starting place is one you are going to return to every time you enter the Net or WWW. So pick a site that you really like. As a suggestion, you might try skimming though this chapter and then giving the pages that interest you a try.

> **Do You Know?**
>
> What the distance of the planet Mars from the sun is?
>
> For the Answer go to:
> http://bang.lanl.gov/solarsys/mars.htm

Yahoo

http://www.yahoo.com

Figure 5.2 Yahoo Home Page.

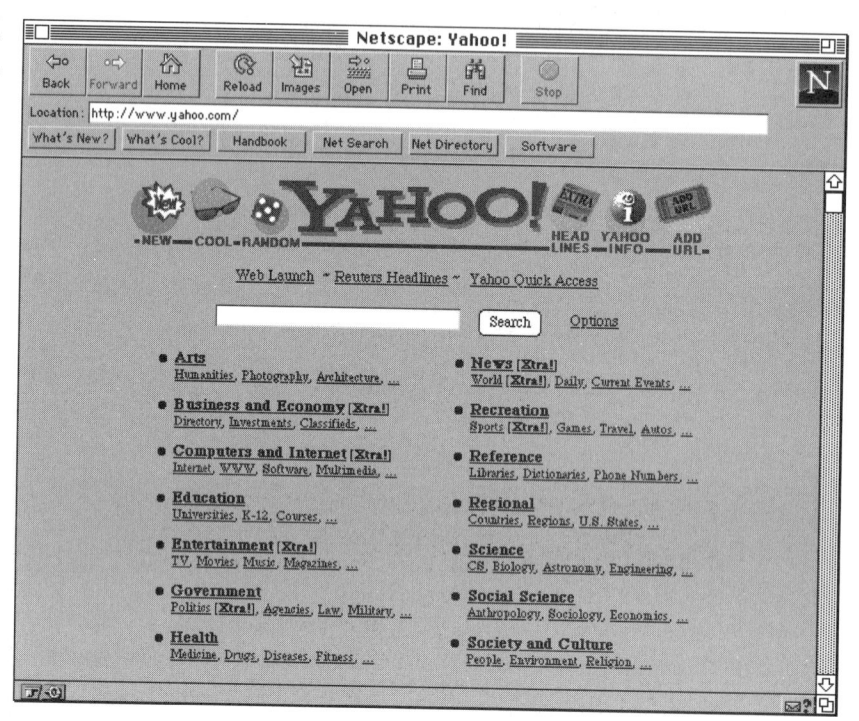

I use **Yahoo** as my home page, so obviously I think it's a great general page. Here are some of the reasons:

- It is organized to let you quickly go to topics of interest.

- It is a lot of fun to play around in and explore.

- It has good searching capabilities.

If you want to search for a specific subject all you have to do is enter your choice in the search area (see Figure 5.3).

Figure 5.3
Yahoo Searching Engine.

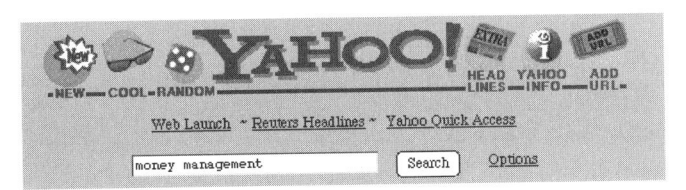

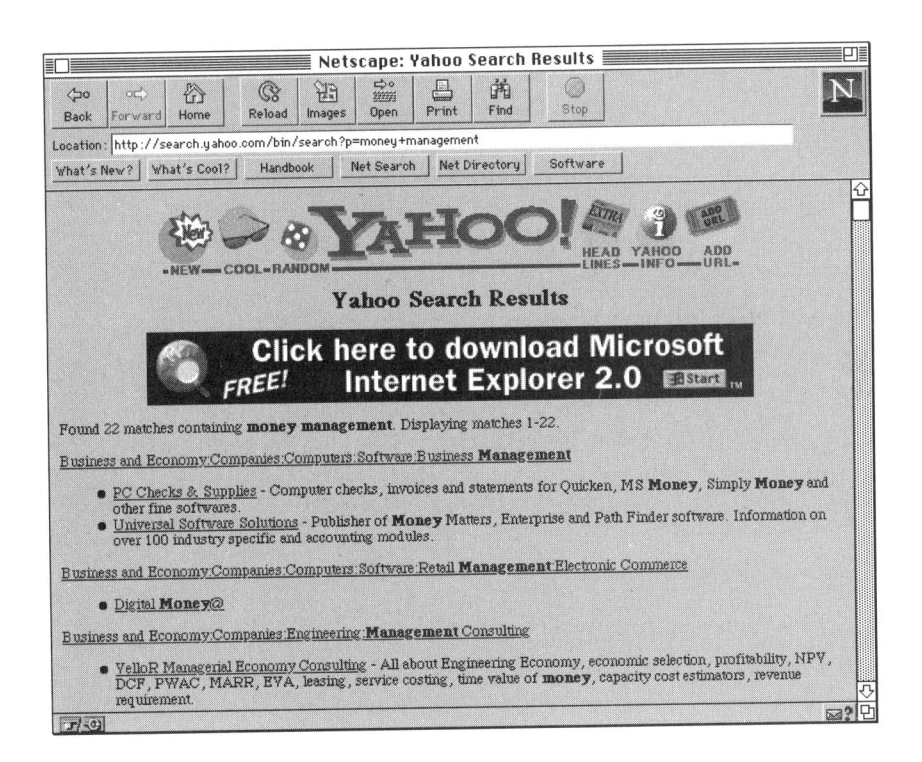

You can also look at Web sites in terms of someone's opinion of them. For example, you can look at **Yahoo's** opinion of cool sites (see Figure 5.4) simply by tapping the "Cool" image at the top of the page.

Figure 5.4
Yahoo Cool Links.

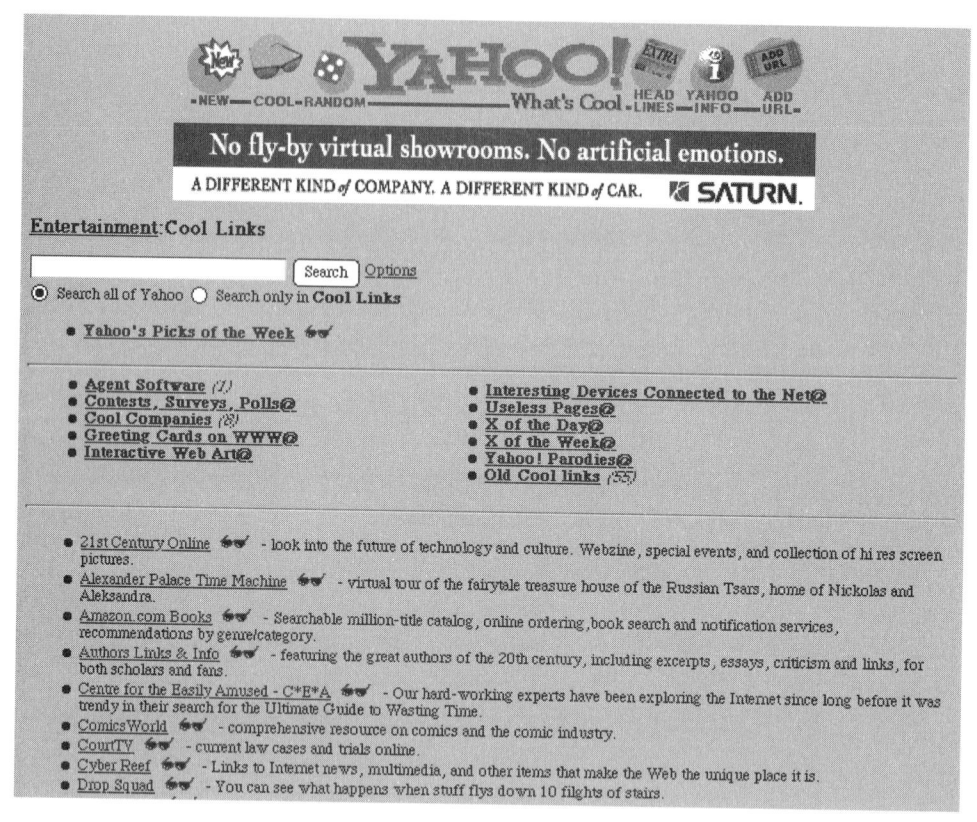

Who or What Is Yahoo?

Created in April 1994, **Yahoo's** mission is "To be the world's best guide for information and online discovery." Believe it or not, I think these folks do a good job living up to their goal. Until you find a site you like better, I would recommend you give Yahoo a try.

If you are a new user, you will also find **Yahoo's** "Info" button quite useful. It takes you to a link where almost any type of question can be answered (see Figure 5.5). In the "Info" area you will find help on:

- How to effectively search for a particular topic.

- Definitions of terminology (such as Internet, telnet, ftp, and so on).

- A FAQ (Frequently Asked Questions) sheet. As you might imagine, most people have the same sorts of general questions.

- How Yahoo goes about adding links into the information database.

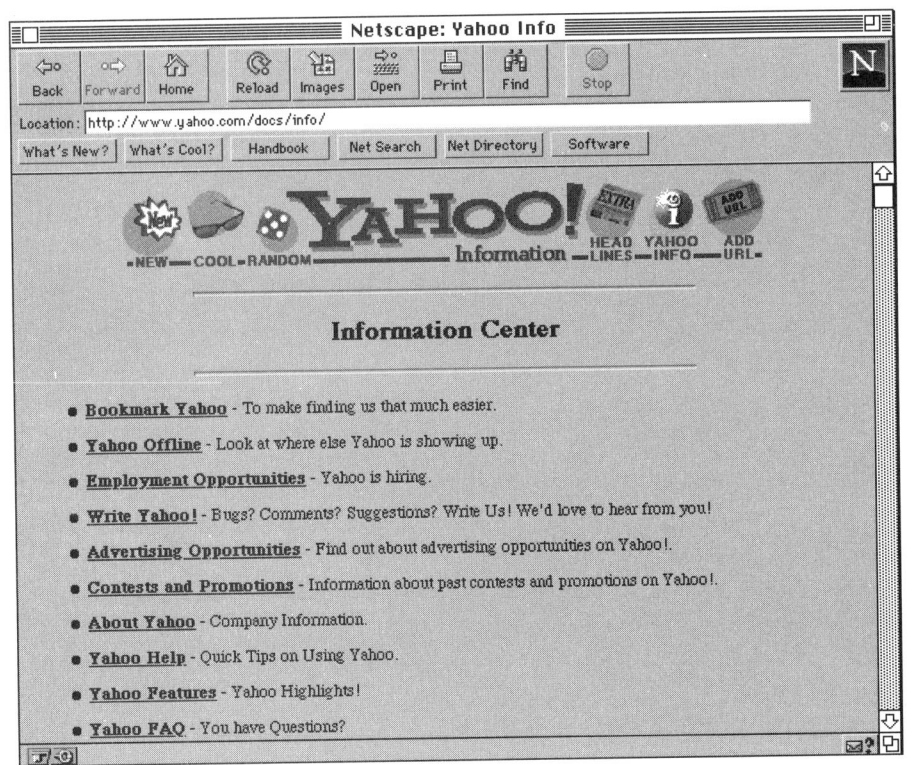

Figure 5.5
Yahoo Information Center.

Inter-Links

http://www.nova.edu/Inter-Links

Figure 5.6 Inter-Links Home Page.

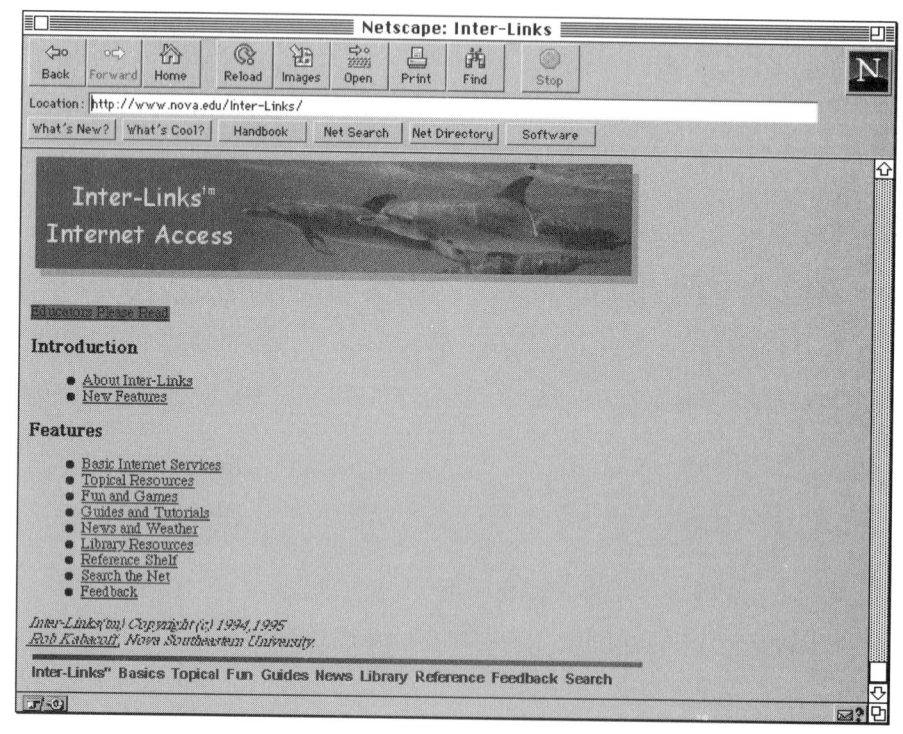

This is a great page for beginners for two very important reasons:

- It is easy to navigate.
- It is interesting.

Once you have visited a number of Net sites, you will realize how uncommon it is for a site to be both easy to use and interesting. With **Inter-Links,** you get a well-sifted selection of really good material (see Figure 5.6).

As Rob Kabacoff, the creator and maintainer of **Inter-Links** says: *"The goal ... is to provide a guide that is interesting, easy to use, and likely to yield useful information rapidly."* This page also offers access to other services besides the Web (such as Telnet), making it very comprehensive.

Under the topical resource section of **Inter-Links** you see subjects such as:

- Diversity
- Education
- Government
- Health and Medicine 
- Psychology 
- Commerce on the Net
- Consumer Information 
- Money Matters 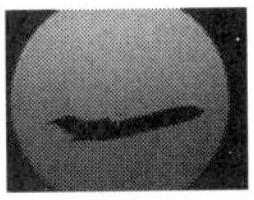
- Travel Information

Here, for example, is the material collected under Fun and Games. It is an interesting assemblage of amusing stuff (see Figure 5.7):

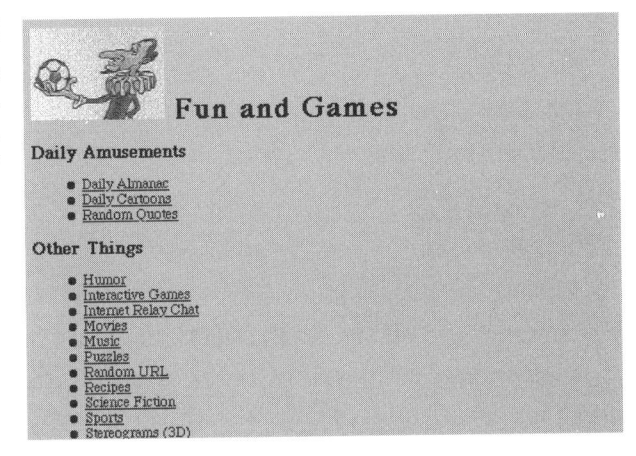

Figure 5.7 Fun and Games Section of Inter-Links.

Fun and Games

Daily Amusements
- Daily Almanac
- Daily Cartoons
- Random Quotes

Other Things
- Humor
- Interactive Games
- Internet Relay Chat
- Movies
- Music
- Puzzles
- Random URL
- Recipes
- Science Fiction
- Sports
- Stereograms (3D)

Tunneling down one more section into "Cartoons" you can see that **Inter-Links** has categorized cartoons into two sections (see Figure 5.8):

- Today's Cartoons

- Collections

If you are a real cartoon fan, you will want to delve deeply into the collection section.

Figure 5.8 Inter-Links Cartoon Page.

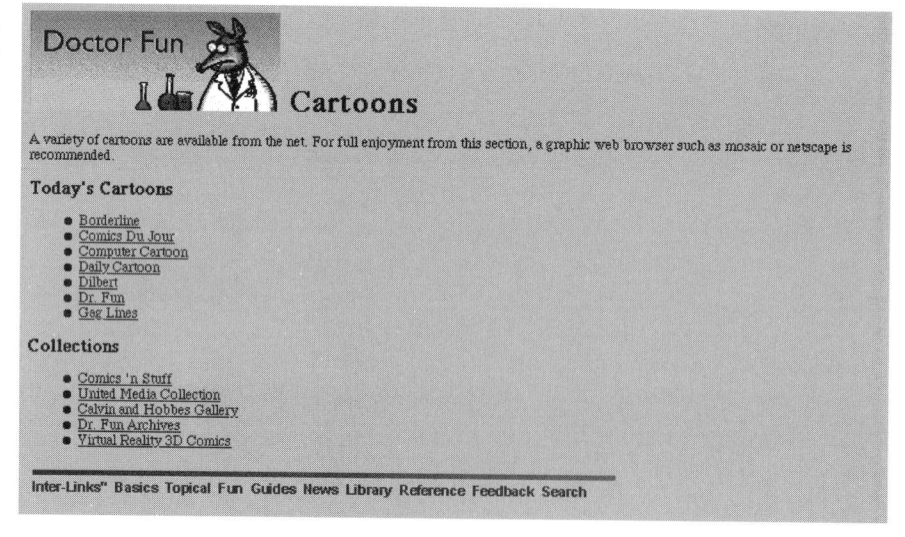

As I said before, **Inter-Links** pages will give you an idea of how straightforward it is to use. If any of the topics interest you, now is a great time to go take a look at them. In any case, I suggest you use either **Yahoo** or **Inter-Links** if you are just getting acquainted with the Net.

Next, we are going to turn to a couple of offerings that are worth looking at, even though they are maintained entirely differently. **Yahoo** and **Inter-Links** had a lot of preselection done to them. Now let's look at a page that has more girth.

Galaxy (Ei Net)

http://www.einet.net/galaxy.html

Figure 5.9 Galaxy Home Page.

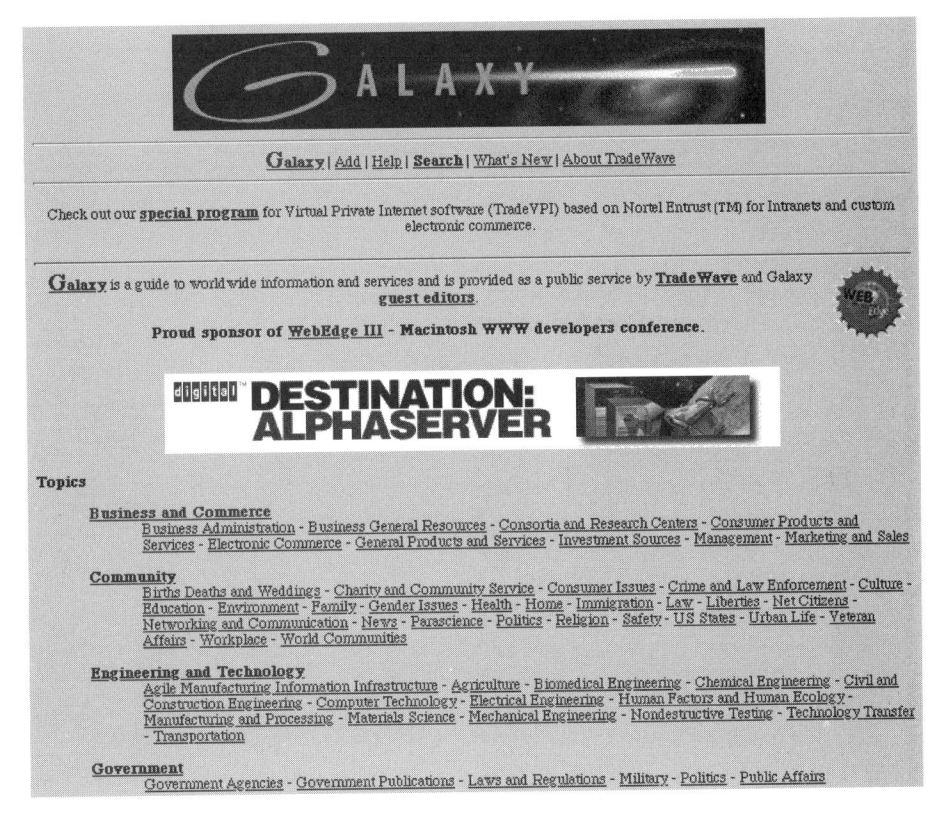

Galaxy offers a more traditional organizational approach to the subjects that it covers (see Figure 5.9). Organized similarly to a giant subject card catalog, subjects are categorized into various levels:

- Business and Commerce
- Community
- Engineering and Technology

- Government
- Humanities
- Law
- Leisure and Recreation
- Medicine
- Reference and Interdisciplinary Information
- Science
- Social Science

Under these sections, **Galaxy** also organizes subsections. For instance, Community has a subsection Family, which is itself categorized into sections:

- Family
- New Items
- Articles
- Guides
- Events
- Collections
- Periodicals
- And more...

There is a nice section in **Galaxy** called Just For Kids (see Figure 5.10) that contains a collection of material. Some of the pages it references are for pure childish amusement; others contain information about interesting educational materials that can be purchased and used by children.

Figure 5.10 Galaxy Just For Kids Page.

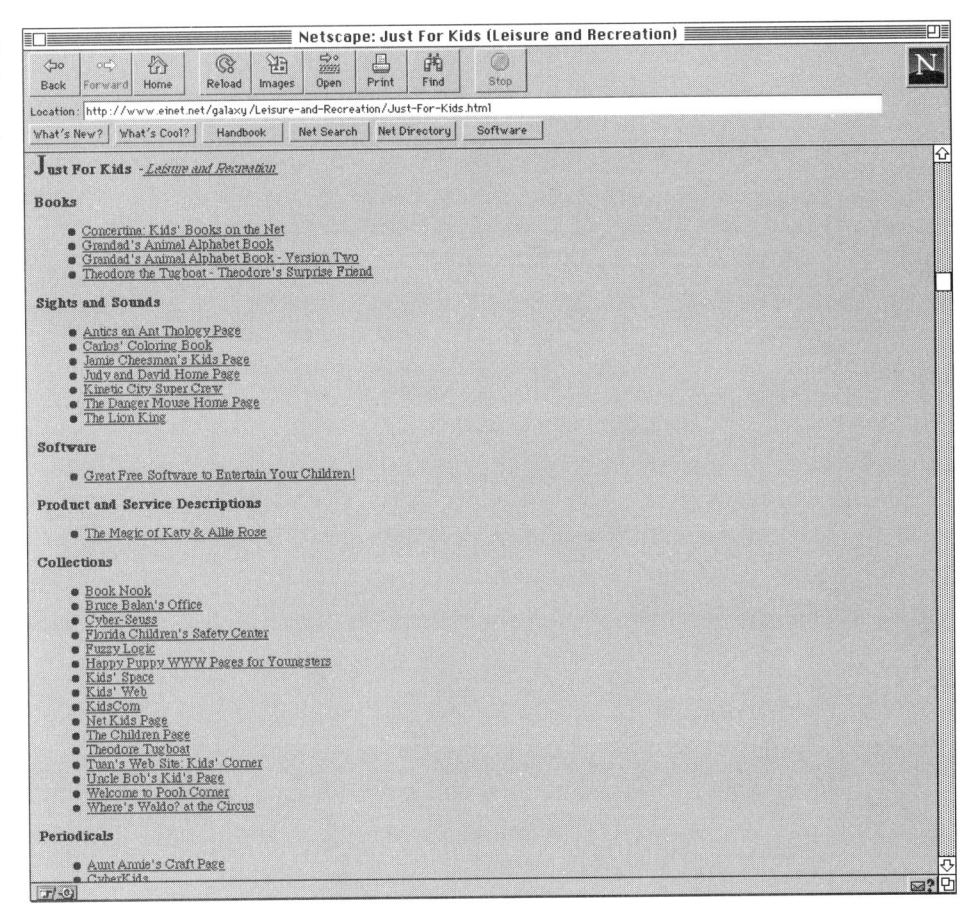

Galaxy's coverage differs from either **Inter-Links's** or **Yahoo's**. It has more traditional subjects, such as periodicals as well as more commercial information. Further, as it is maintained by a for-profit company, *TradeWinds*, you are likely to find more consumer information than you would in **Inter-Links** or **Yahoo**.

Chapter 5 Starting Places

The WWW Virtual Library

http://www.w3.org/hypertext/DataSources/bySubject/Overview.html

*Figure 5.11
WWW Virtual Library Home Page.*

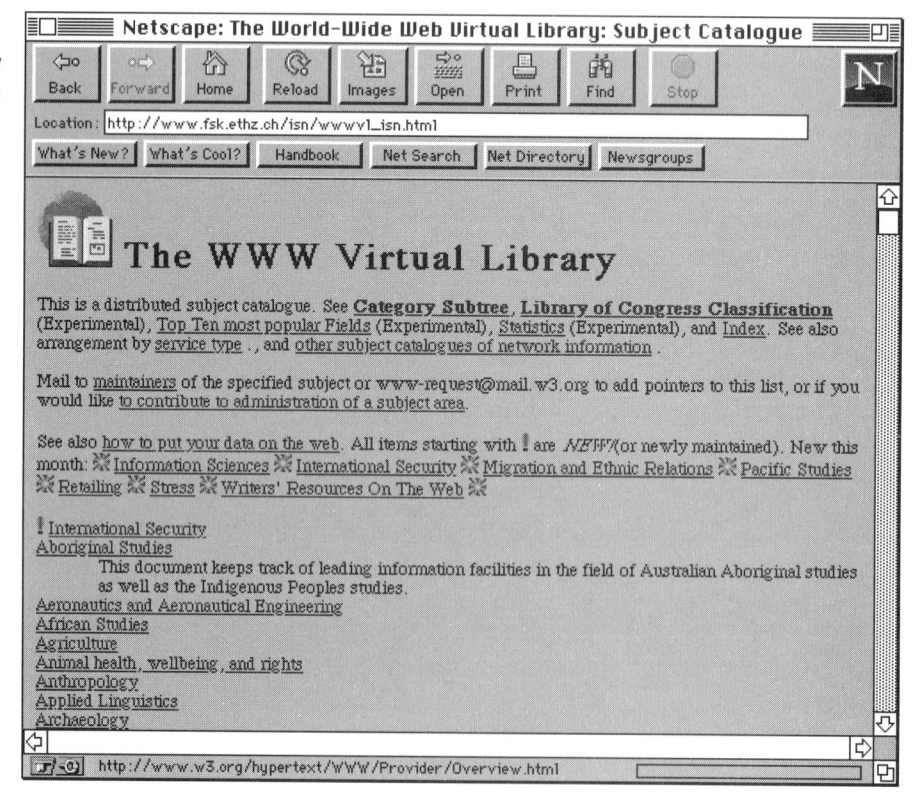

The great-granddaddy of all library sites is the **WWW Virtual Library.** It has been around longer than a lot of other sites and represents the most traditional organizational scheme. As you can see in Figure 5.11, this library offers a card catalog type approach to subjects.

When you are interested in learning about a particular topic (such as animal health) this is a page that you will visit repeatedly. As a general home page, it would probably suit librarians and other such organizationally minded people, but the rest of you are better served by one of the other pages.

Nevertheless, this is a great page. What it lacks in jazzy approach and fun sites it makes up in its breadth of topic coverage. For example, looking under the category of architecture we can see that the library offers a variety of choices on the subject (see Figure 5.12) and many different ways of looking at the information.

Figure 5.12 Architecture WWW Virtual Library Page.

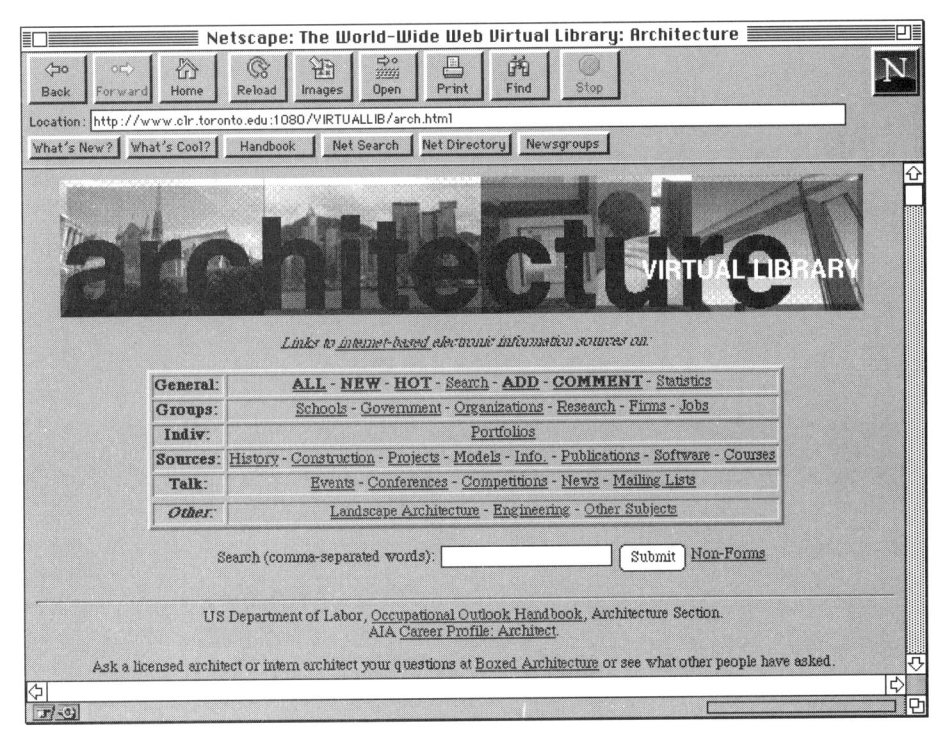

If we select what is "HOT," we get an even more specialized listing of sites based upon their popularity with Web folks (see Figure 5.13).

Now, finally, we are deep enough in the library that the next set of links will actually take us to a site with content. If we select the second item from the Hot page (I have always had a yen for the Sistine Chapel), we are sent off to look at that architectural site (see Figure 5.14).

The **WWW Virtual Library** is maintained by volunteers who are specialists in their subjects. What the **WWW Virtual Library** doesn't offer is much excitement as a day-to-day site. It isn't trying to pique your interest about material, but

138   Chapter 5 Starting Places

rather assumes you want information about a particular subject. It is certainly a site I would use for homework and other research.

Figure 5.13
WWW Virtual Library Architectural Hot Page.

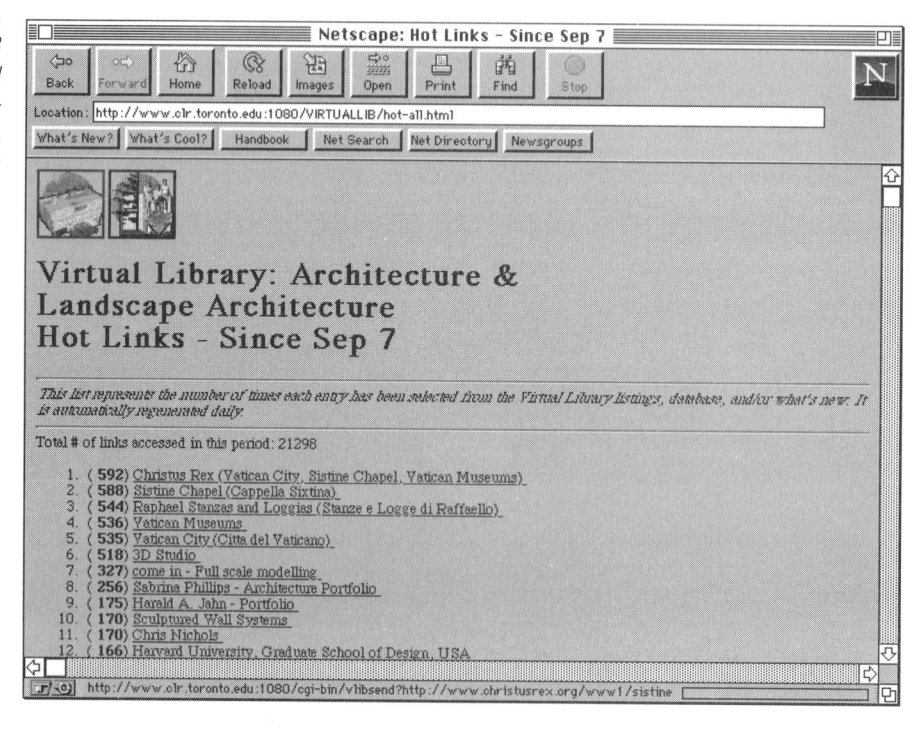

Figure 5.14
The Sistine Chapel in All Its Architectural Beauty.

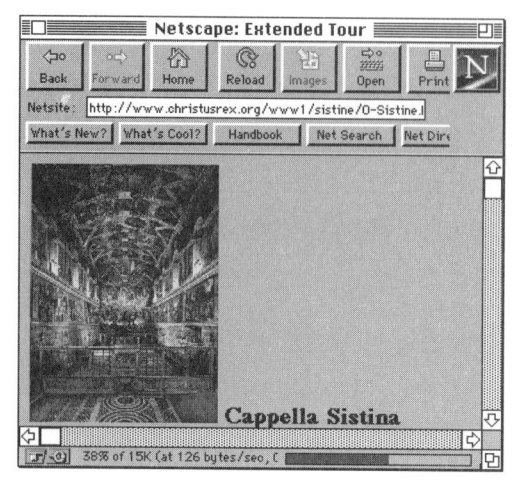

> **Hint:** Do you know how to change your home page in your Web browser software? With the Netscape Navigator browser it is as easy as using Preferences.

Great Kid Sites

Picking a site for your child to launch into the Net can be just as much fun as selecting one for yourself. Certainly, you will need to consider the age of the child. Many older kids (13 plus) might prefer to use **Yahoo** or **Inter-Links** as their home page. Younger children will probably prefer one of the other pages that more exclusively serves their interests.

The Ultimate Children's Internet Sites

http://www.vividus.com/ucis.html

The single greatest thing about this site is that:

- it organizes links according to the age ranges of children.

Any parent of a 4-year-old who has been forced to wade through dozens of sites aimed at teenagers will tell you that this feature alone makes this site worth its weight in gold. If you are new to the Net, then I heartily recommend that you use **The Ultimate Children's Internet Sites** as your starting point for explorations of the Web with your children (see Figure 5.15). This page also includes resource material for parents and teachers.

Figure 5.15
The Ultimate Children's Internet Sites Home Page.

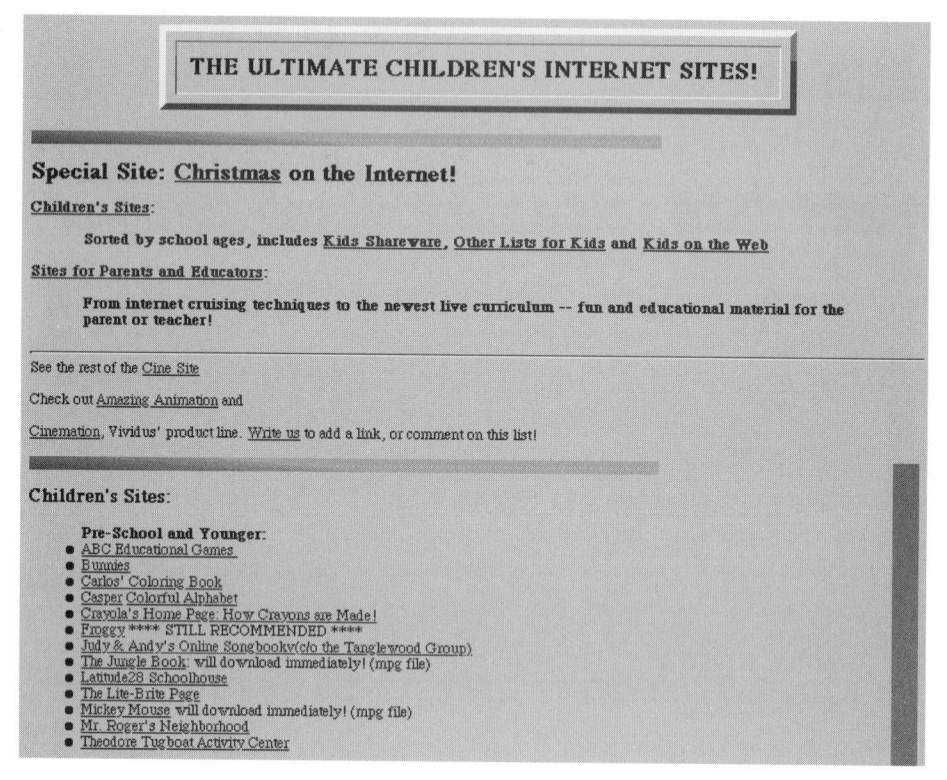

Uncle Bob's Kids' Page

http://gagme.wwa.com/~boba/kidsi.html

So who is Uncle Bob and what is this home page, anyway? Uncle Bob is Bob Allison, a guy responsible for a lot of pages on the Web (Bob says over 100).

*Figure 5.16
Uncle Bobs Kids
Page.*

WELCOME to Uncle Bob's Kids' Page. This page is a treasure chest of annotated links, with spotlights on special subjects.

Awards for this page:

- Picked as one of **CompuServe's Cool Sites of the Week** for August 28, 1995
- Placed in the **I-way 500** (best web sites in the world from I-way magazine)
- Included in the Premiere issue of **Virtual City**
- Placed in the **TOP 5% of All Web Sites** by the **Point Survey**
- Included in the June 1995 issue of **Online Access**
- Named **Cool Site of the Month!** on the Internet Advertising Solutions
- Awarded **"ThumbsUp!"** by the **Teenagers Circle**
- Featured in the September 1995 issue of **Internet & Comms Today**
- Included in the June 1995 issue of **NetGuide**
- Named **Cool Site of the Day** for February 2, 1995

Reviews for this page:

"A great resource of fun and content-rich sites for kids of all ages." - *CompuServe*

Reputed to have a large ego, Bob at least deserves some praise for having created a really good kids' page. It contains links that will appeal to a wide age range of kids and to their families.

Uncle Bob has divided his Kids' Page into seven sections that cover lots of topics. Here is a quick glance at the contents of two of them.

SECTION 1 of Uncle Bob's Kids' Page

You could spend months and months in any one of these sites (see Figure 5.17). Some of my favorite sites that Uncle Bob maintains links to are:

142   Chapter 5   Starting Places

Figure 5.17
Uncle Bob's Kids' Page, Section 1.

> **SECTION 1**
>
> ★★★★★★★★★★★★★★★★★★★★★
>
> - - The Michael Jordan Page - Talk about Michael's return to basketball, plus links to pages on the Bulls, NBA teams, schedules, fantasy basketball, and the FAQ.
> - - The Lite-Brite Page - Pictures created with different colored dots. Contains the current featured work, and a gallery of past pictures. You can edit a picture online.
> - - Sega - Sega News, Press Releases, Sega Genesis, CD, Game Gear, Genesis 32X, Sega Sports, Sega Club, Sega Toys, Sega Channel, Sega Visions, Sports Byline USA, plus Sega Mall and links to other places.
> - - Franklin Institute Virtual Science Museum - They 'bring the exhibits, resources, and fun of a museum visit right to your desktop' with virtual exhibits and hotlists.
> - - VidKids - California Museum of Photography's Web page for K-12 kids has an Interactive Gallery, Media Literacy Program, and Lesson Plans.
> - - Unicycling - Has links to the FAQ and mailing list archive, and info on games like unicycle hockey, plus a photo album and more.
> - - Helping Your Kids Learn Science - For parents. Do your kids ask Why is the sky blue, Why do things fall to the ground, How do seeds grow, What makes sound and music, Where do mountains come from, Well, look into this from the government.
> - - Global Show and Tell - Children show off their favorite projects, possessions, accomplishments and collections to kids (and adults) around the world.
> - - VolcanoWorld - Everything about volcanos. Includes a Hawaiian Tour Guide, volcano images, current and recent eruptions, and more.
> - - Fun Math - Math can be fun when you include math jokes, fractals, paradoxes, logic puzzles, crystals, hyberbolics and knots, plus the MATLAB Gallery of pictures.
> - - schoolsNET - A new organisation providing Internet access and educational resources to Australian schools. Has links to exibits, a hotlist, libraries and directories, and a demo pages.
> - - LEGO Information - Games, projects, pictures, plus the history and product lines.
> - - The Snow Page - Covers every aspect of the white fluffy stuff. Everything from snowboarding to travels, zines, trails, you name it.
> - - Museums - From the WWW Virtual Library. Has links to museums, exhibits, galleries, libraries, and further lists and links.
> - - Sea World - Main selections are Animal Information Data Base, Teacher's Guides, Shamu TV: Sea World and Busch Gardens Video Classroom
>
> ★★★★★★★★★★★★★★★★★★★★★
>
> SPOTLIGHT ON   OUTER SPACE
>
> "In the final phases of the descent after a number of program alarms, we looked at the landing area and found a very large crater. This is the area we decided we would not go into; we extended the range downrange. The exhaust dust was kicked up by the engine and this caused some concern in that it degraded our ability to determine not only our altitude in the final phases but also our translational velocities over the ground. It's quite important not to stub your toe during the final phases of touchdown."
> - *Neil Armstrong*

- The Lite-Brite Page

- Franklin Institute Science Museum

- Museums

- VidKids

- Helping Your Kids Learn Science

- VolcanoWorld

- Fun Math

- LEGO Information

SECTION 3 of Uncle Bob's Kids' Page

Figure 5.18 Uncle Bob's Kids' Page, Section 3.

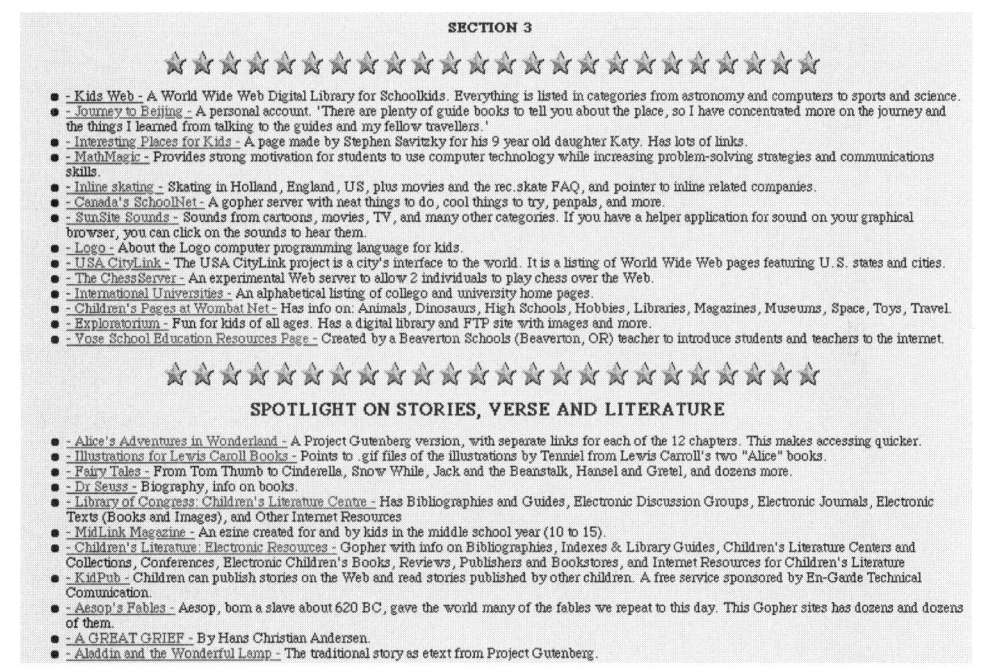

Section 3 contains lots of really great stuff as well (see Figure 5.18). My favorite sites are:

- Kids Web
- MathMagic
- Exploratorium

The Organization of Kids' Page

It is hard to tell what organizational scheme Uncle Bob uses in dividing material into the various sections. Sections can contain topics very different from each other. While this gives the site a sort of hodgepodge feel, I am sure you will find that it doesn't mar your enjoyment of the material.

CyberKids

http://www.mtlake.com/cyberkids/

Figure 5.19 CyberKids Home Page.

Art Gallery | Magazine | Multimedia | CyberKids Connection
Games | Young Composers | Launchpad

CyberKids is published by Mountain Lake Software (see Figure 5.19). This site offers nice links and sites for children. Some of my favorites are:

- Writing and art centers
- A bi-monthly magazine that features art and stories by teenagers

- Interactive areas where children can talk with each other

- Fun stuff, such as fonts for subscribers of CyberKids

CyberKids/CyberTeens Launchpad

http://www.cyberkids.com/cyberkids/Launchpad/Launchpad.html

*Figure 5.20
CyberKids Launchpad Home Page.*

Click on a category to see a list of Internet sites you can visit. If you have any comments or suggestions, please send email to webmaster@mtlake.com.

Click here for a text-only Launchpad

- Art
- Business
- Child Safety
- Children's Books Online
- Computers
- Educational Resources
- Entertainment
- For Kids By Kids
- Fun and Games

For exploring the Web, CyberKids offers the Launchpad (see Figure 5.20). It contains a wide variety of links to sites that will be interesting to children. The ones I like the most are:

146   Chapter 5 Starting Places

- Children's Books Online
- For Kids By Kids
- Fun and Games

Kids Web

http://www.npac.syr.edu/textbook/kidsweb/

Figure 5.21
Kids Web Home Page.

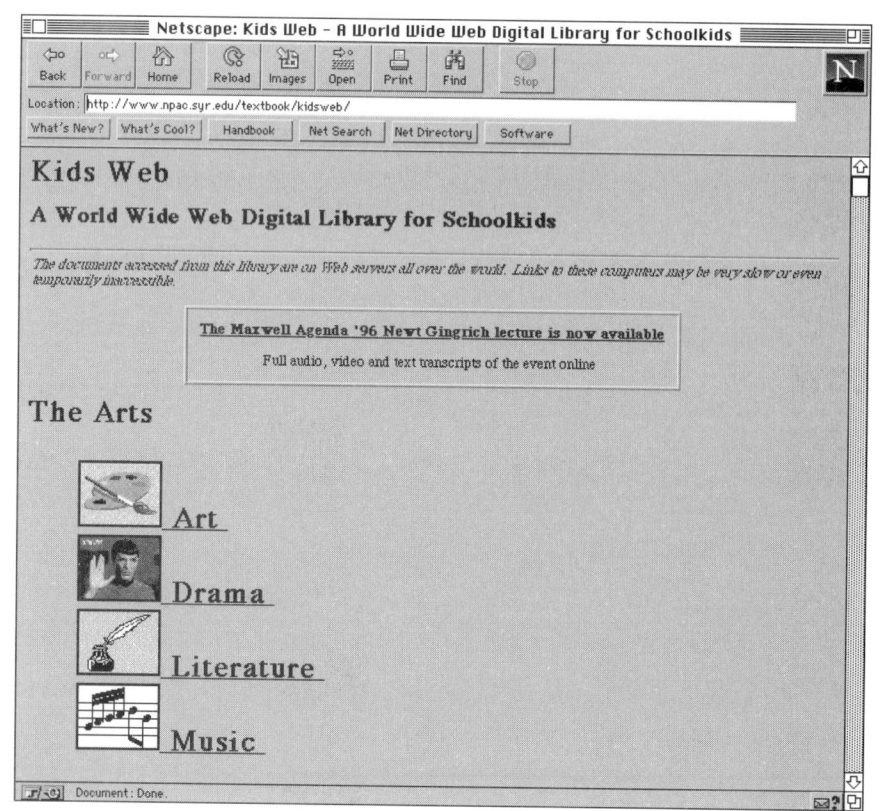

Great Kid Sites 147

Kids Web is a great page full of good links to sites all over the Web. Children will adore and use them over and over again. Material is in a two-tier organizational scheme of general subject and more specific topics:

The Arts

Art

Drama

Literature

Music

These are the great graphics and links available in Kids Web

The Sciences

Astronomy and Space

Biology and Life Sciences

Chemistry

Computers

Environmental Science

Geology and Earth Sciences

Mathematics

Physics

Science and Technology

Weather and Meteorology

Social Studies

Geography

Government

History

Miscellaneous

Fun and Games

Reference Material

Sports

Berit's Best Sites for Children

http://www.cochran.com/theosite/KSites.html

Figure 5.22
Berit's Best Sites for Children Home Page.

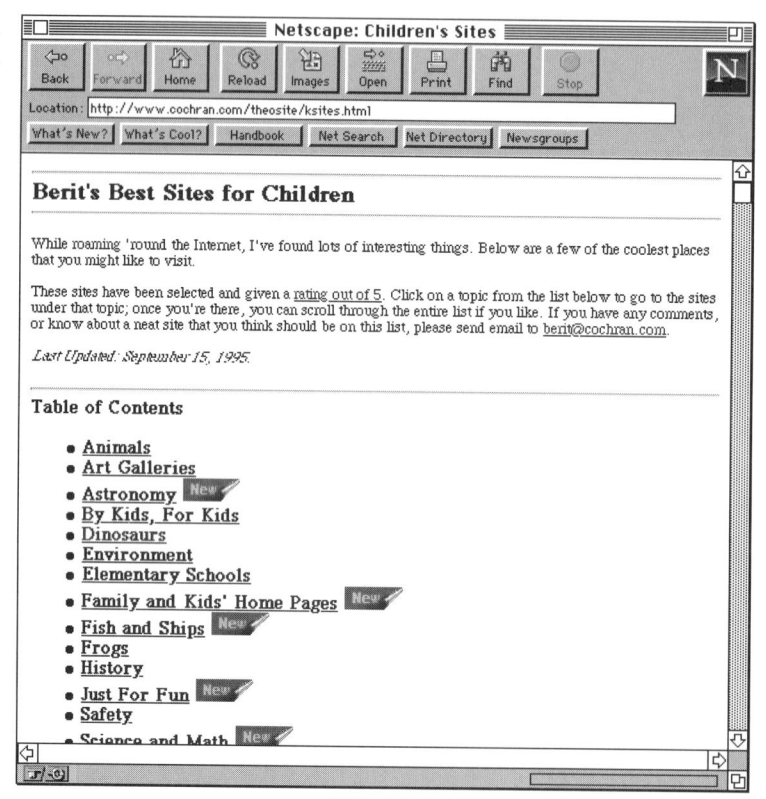

I really like this page (see Figure 5.22) because:

- Berit uses a rating system that gives you a good idea of the quality of the links.

- Each link has some annotation concerning its content.

Great Kid Sites 149

This sort of helpful categorization is very nice, as it makes the time you spend on the Net much more productive. Because of **Berit**, you won't need to go on as many dead-end or fruitless explorations. As many of the sites discussed here are targeted toward younger children, you also get to spend more time on material that is colorful and fun for the little people (not elves). These are a few of the topics that **Berit** covers:

- Arts and crafts
- Toys and games
- Science and math
- Safety, and more

Family World

http://family.com/indexGX.html

Figure 5.23
Family World Home Page.

This is an unusual page. It is put together by a large group of parenting publications and combines educational and parenting resources with calendars of regional features (see Figure 5.23). The features section of this page contains topics that will interest parents and teachers as well as children (see Figure 5.24).

Figure 5.24
The Family World Features Page.

Family World Features Page

activities | baby | book review | child development
dad | education | family file | fashion | health
home tech | parenting | travel

Activities | Baby | Book Reviews | Child Development | Education | Entertainment | Family Files | Fashion
For Dad's Eyes Only | Health | Home Tech | Parenting | Recreation and Travel

Quick Dip Spots

Sometimes you only have a few minutes to surf and you want to go right to something new and interesting. If that is the case, the following sites are really great places to go to find a treat.

The Fast-Food Approach to the Net

If your life is just too hectic to commit to more than a brief glance at the Net, you might want to select a page that focuses on a particular site instead of a whole bunch of them. If this is true, you are in luck because there are two really good site-of-the-day pages.

Cool Site of the Day

http://cool.infi.net/

Figure 5.25
The Cool Site Page.

As you can see in Figure 5.25, this site offers a daily cool place for you to visit. The only downside to this approach is that you will not know ahead of time if the site will be interesting or appropriate to you or your children. The upside is that this will expose you to a wide variety of "cool" stuff on the Net that would be hard to find on your own.

For more detailed exploration, you can also look at past winners of this prize by category.

Spider's Pick of the Day

http://gagme.wwa.com/~boba/pick.html

Figure 5.26 Spider's Pick of the Day.

THERE IS ALSO A SHORT VERSION OF THIS PAGE
CHECK OUT BOB'S KOOL LINK DAILY PICK

THE PICK

WELCOME to The Spider's Pick of the Day. The Spider may pick darn near anything. You know that crazy arachnid. There is a shorter version of this page for your convenience. It should load in 5 to 10 seconds on most systems. The Spider hopes you enjoy yourself ...

AND NOW, THE LINK D' JOUR ...

The Spider's Pick of the Day
Thursday, February 22nd, 1996

Bob is back. Bob Allison (alias Uncle Bob) also offers a pick-of-the-day page that is worth a look (see Figure 5.26). Once again, you won't know what you are getting, except that it seemed like a good site to Bob. It is certainly true that you could do far worse than to trust yourself to his discerning eye.

Yuppie Favorites

These sites are the staples of life in a modern world. What could be better than a cup of coffee and sitting down with any one of these web pages:

Yuppie Favorites   153

- PBS
- The New York Times
- CNN Interactive

PBS Online

http://www.pbs.org/

Figure 5.27 The PBS Home Page.

If Masterpiece Theatre is a date you won't break and your children are in love with Mister Rogers, this is the site for you (see Figure 5.27). **PBS** has put together a page that is both interesting and targeted to its loyal followers.

Several of the most popular shows have their own home pages. **PBS** also includes various activities that you can do with the whole family. Here is just a sprinkling of the offerings:

154   Chapter 5 Starting Places

- Bill Nye the Science Guy
- Evening at Pops
- Newton's Apple
- Reading Rainbow
- Masterpiece Theatre
- Nova
- Where in the World is Carmen Sandiego

PBS is still adding more material to this site, so if something that you love has not materialized yet, it might appear at any time. Take a look at the entries that **PBS** provides in the Contents page (see Figure 5.29) to see what it is currently covering.

The children's section of the **PBS** page contains material that will be familiar to any little watcher of "Mister Rogers' Neighborhood" (see Figure 5.28) and "Reading Rainbow." **PBS** also offers a variety of resources, including K-12 educational materials for children and teachers. There are various family activities, including a family newsletter, *PTV Families*, which contains everything from stories to articles on child safety.

Figure 5.28 Mister Rogers' Home Page.

Mister Rogers' Neighborhood

⇐ The Big Guy Himself

Mister Rogers and King Friday

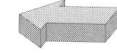

Figure 5.29
PBS Table of Programs.

For older children and adults there are more mature home pages. Two of these include the Merrow Report and an interactive page called The OnLine Newshour, which features interviews and news.

If all of that were not enough, you can also find out the times and channels of all of **PBS'** television programs. When you want to purchase the video of a show that you missed or any of the other PBS paraphernalia, you can zip over to the **PBS** store (see Figure 5.30).

PBS is a beautiful and fun place to visit. It also offers its visitors various useful pieces of information. Something that is both useful and pretty. What could be better than that?

156   Chapter 5 Starting Places

Figure 5.30
The PBS Store
Page.

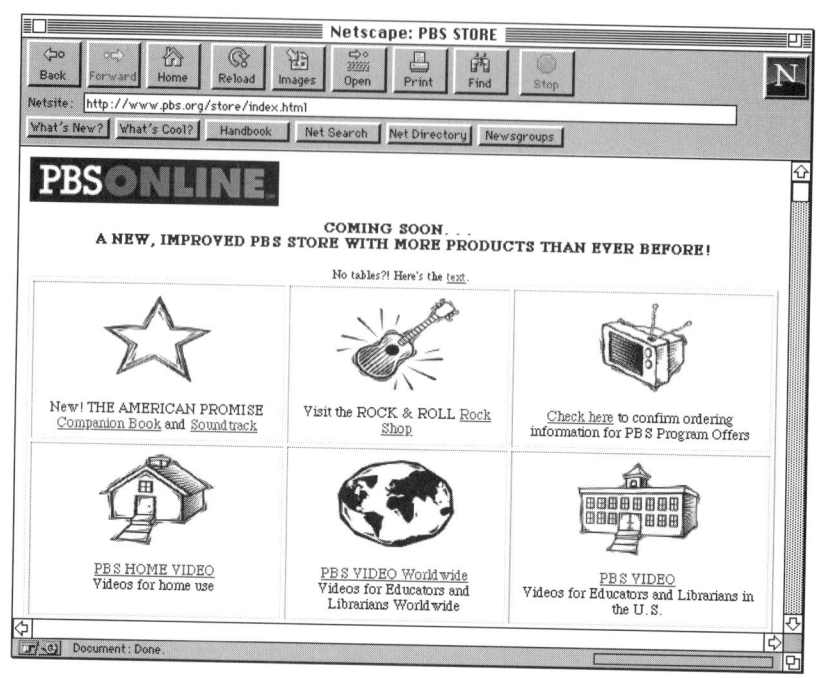

The New York Times Syndicate

http://nytsyn.com

What can one say about this page except the obvious. If you like the paper, you will like the page (see Figure 5.31). This site contains a wealth of information. Instead of settling down each night with your copy of the paper, you can log on and peruse this place. There are also live discussion groups that you can join if you are feeling opinionated about some subject.

Figure 5.31
The New York Times Syndicate Home Page.

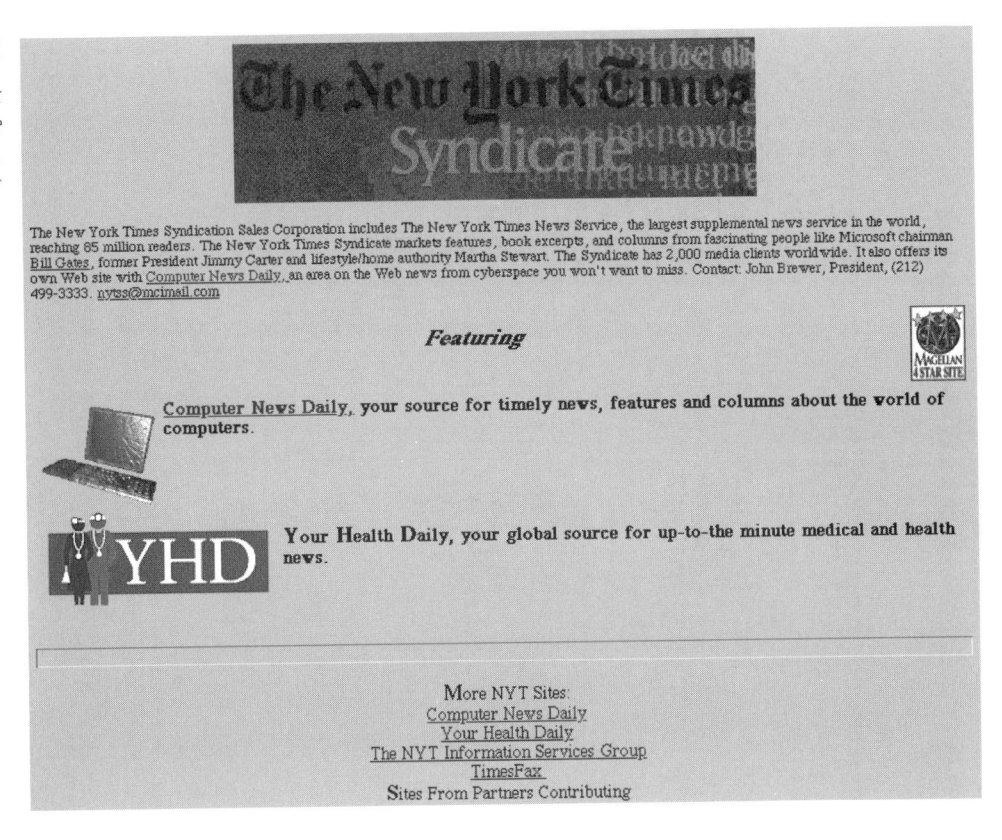

CNN Interactive

http://www.cnn.com/

For those of you who enjoy the cable channel, here is a Net version that includes a lot a snazzy articles complete with pictures, sound, and text (see Figure 5.32). Listen to a discussion and read about the United Nations peace plans for Bosnia or any of the other events that occur in our world (see Figure 5.33).

158 Chapter 5 Starting Places

Figure 5.32
CNN Interactive Home Page.

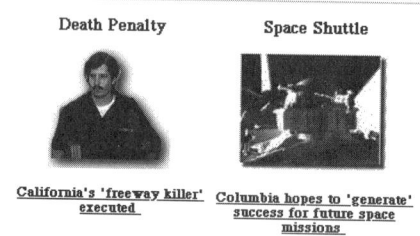

Kids will also find this a useful site for information on events to use in reports. They can do a search for particular events or topics and then read and use that material in their papers.

Figure 5.33
CNN World News Main Page.

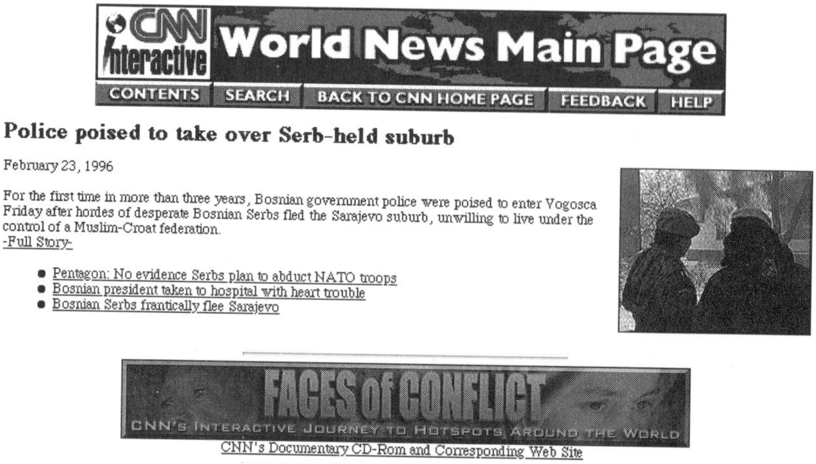

Chapter 6
News, Weather, and Sports

Covered in This Chapter
News
Weather
Sports

The Net is very useful for giving you information about day-to-day events. If it's news, weather, or who won the World Cup, then the Net is without peer. You can get specialized pages that offer news, weather, and sports (such as **ESPN** page), or you can rely on a Web library page like **Yahoo** to sort through this material for you. Either way, current information is attractively presented and easy to use.

News

Sources of news coverage on the Net come in all shapes and flavors. You can get local news, or look at what is happening all over the world. Sites range from charming small town news to top of the line commercial entries.

CNN News

http://www3.cnn.com

If you like your news with a multimedia flavor, then CNN's highly polished news page will be a pleasure to use (see Figure 6.1).

Figure 6.1
CNN World News Page.

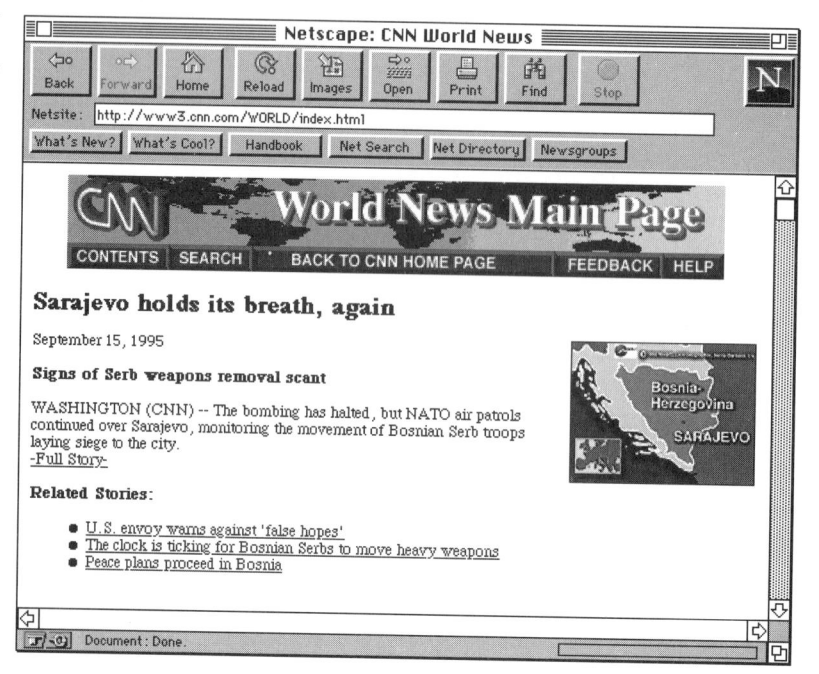

Newspapers

If your bent is the written page, the Net will hold many delights for you. Numerous newspapers and magazines offer excerpts or specialized versions of their publications on the Net.

The Electronic Newsstand–Newspapers

http://www.enews.com/papers.html

Figure 6.2 The Electronic Newsstand Home Page for Newspapers.

One place in which many newspapers have been gathered is the **Electronic Newsstand** home page (see Figure 6.2). From this page, you can cast off to almost any international publication, whether it be *India World* or the *Irish Times*. **Electronic Newsstand** also offers a variety of magazines and presents other types of news in a variety of formats.

The Financial Times of London

http://www.usa.ft.com/http://www.ft.com/

Figure 6.3
The Financial Times of London

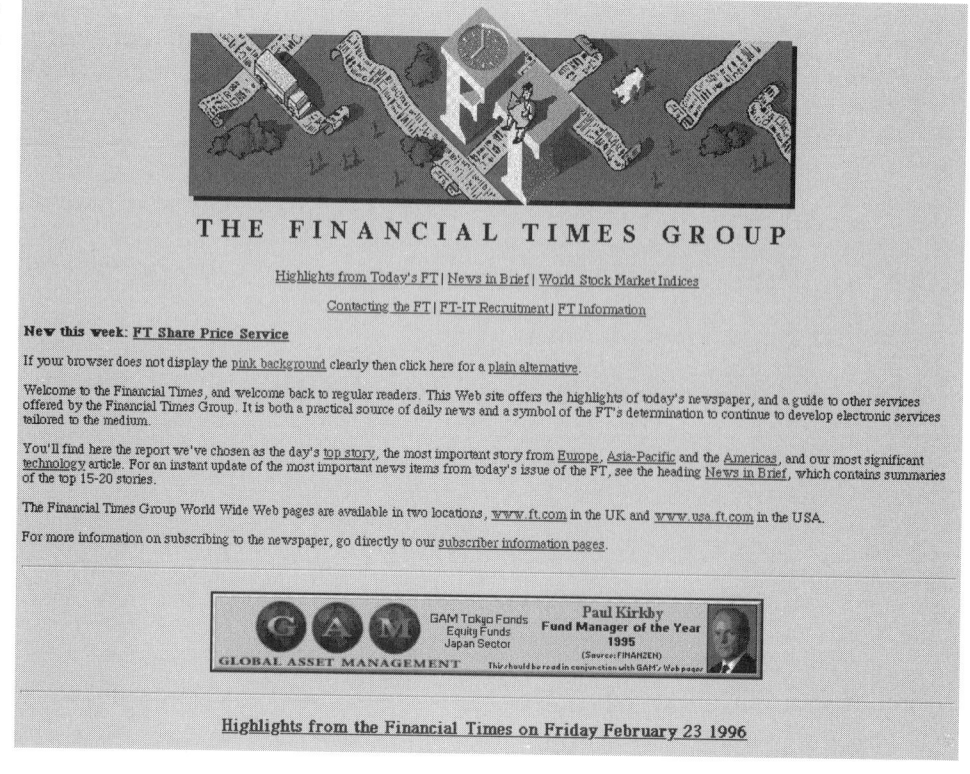

No longer does an expatriate need to wither away from lack of news of home. Even a British citizen can get a Net version of that old established paper *The*

Financial Times. Published since 1888, this newspaper now has a Net version that presents a very modern face (see Figure 6.3).

The New York Times

http://nytsyn.com

Figure 6.4
The New York Times Syndicate.

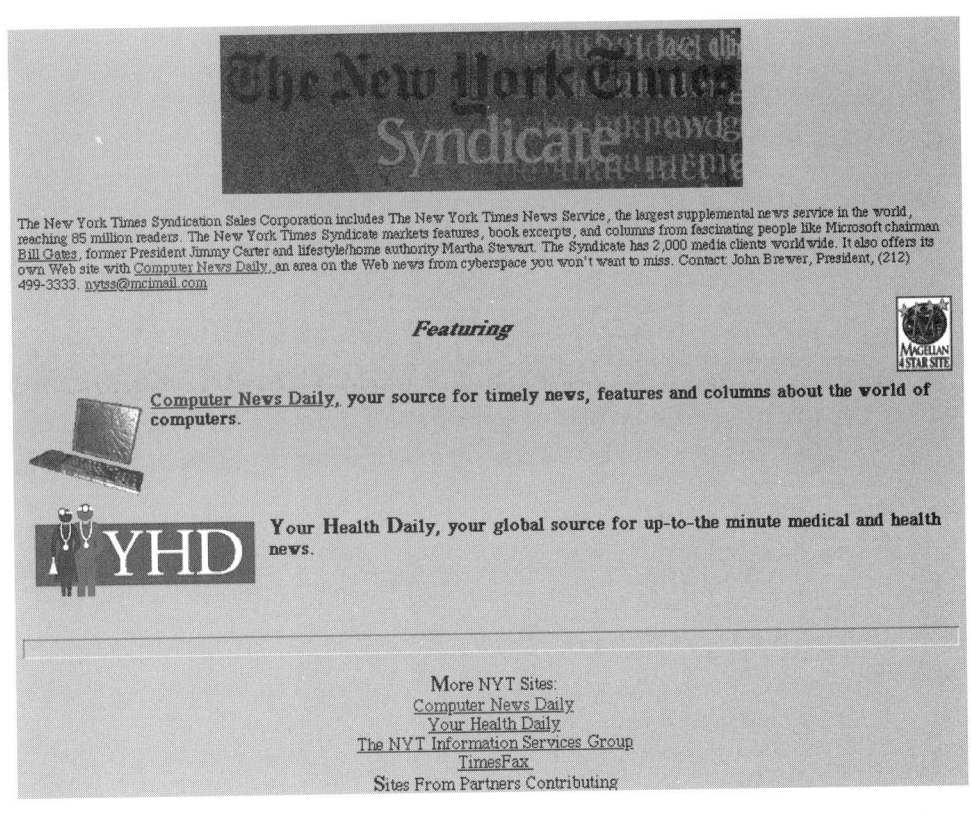

At last, you don't have to live in New York to get a copy of the *Times* (see Figure 6.4). The publishers of this fine newspaper have gotten together and created their very own Web page that contains standard articles on a variety of subjects as well as sections peculiar to the Net. You can also enter discussion areas to talk about important news events, critique articles, or discuss anything else that is on your mind.

164   Chapter 6   News, Weather, and Sports

Weather

People around the world love to talk about the weather. Now you can get information about forecasts, weather statistics, storm warnings, and satellite photos for virtually any place on the planet.

That is just because it's safer than talking about politics.

WeatherNet

http://cirrus.sprl.umich.edu/wxnet/

Figure 6.5 WeatherNet Home Page

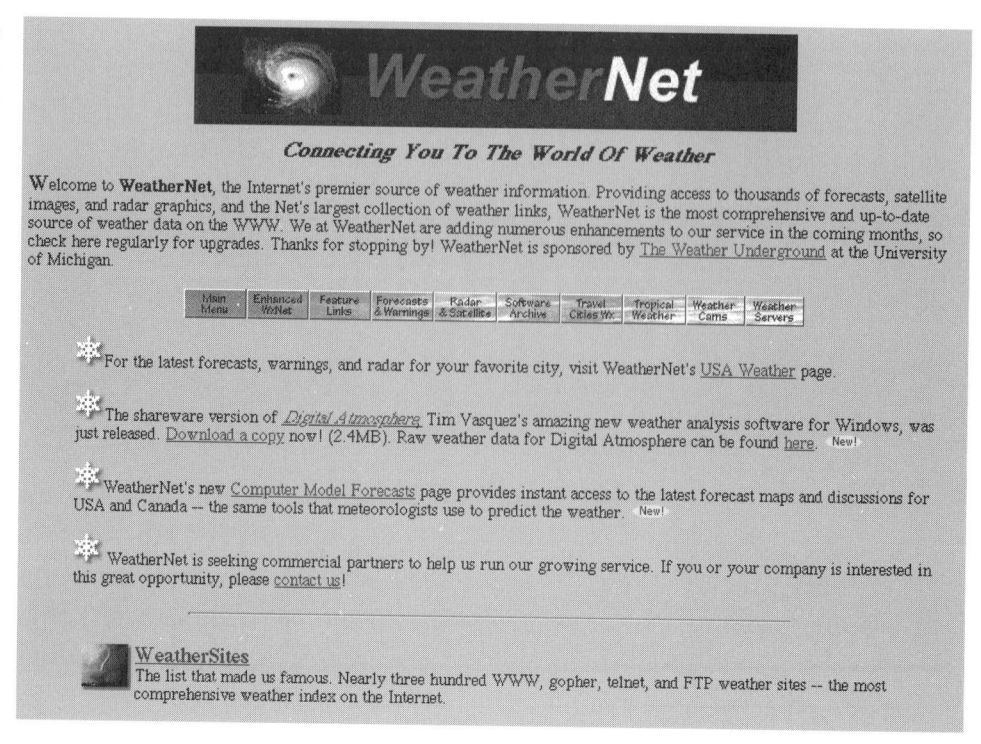

Welcome to WeatherNet, the Internet's premier source of weather information. Providing access to thousands of forecasts, satellite images, and radar graphics, and the Net's largest collection of weather links, WeatherNet is the most comprehensive and up-to-date source of weather data on the WWW. We at WeatherNet are adding numerous enhancements to our service in the coming months, so check here regularly for upgrades. Thanks for stopping by! WeatherNet is sponsored by The Weather Underground at the University of Michigan.

- For the latest forecasts, warnings, and radar for your favorite city, visit WeatherNet's USA Weather page.

- The shareware version of *Digital Atmosphere*, Tim Vasquez's amazing new weather analysis software for Windows, was just released. Download a copy now! (2.4MB). Raw weather data for Digital Atmosphere can be found here. **New!**

- WeatherNet's new Computer Model Forecasts page provides instant access to the latest forecast maps and discussions for USA and Canada -- the same tools that meteorologists use to predict the weather. **New!**

- WeatherNet is seeking commercial partners to help us run our growing service. If you or your company is interested in this great opportunity, please contact us!

WeatherSites
The list that made us famous. Nearly three hundred WWW, gopher, telnet, and FTP weather sites -- the most comprehensive weather index on the Internet.

Weather   165

This site offers a whole slew of topics related to the weather (see Figure 6.5). If you look at Figure 6.6 you can see some of these topics, including:

- Weather maps

- Ski weather

- Links to weather sites on the Net

- Tropical weather conditions

Another great feature of **WeatherNet's** site is its updates on important storm warnings. If you live in a hurricane area, then this is definitely a service that will come in handy.

Figure 6.6
More of the WeatherNet Home Page.

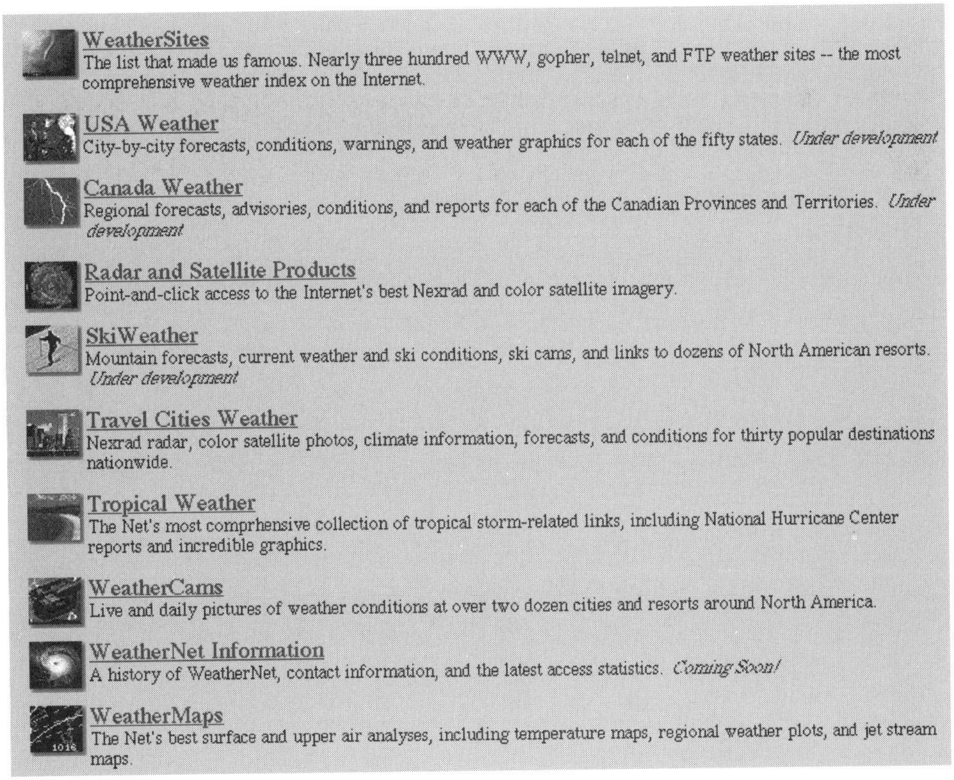

WeatherSites
The list that made us famous. Nearly three hundred WWW, gopher, telnet, and FTP weather sites -- the most comprehensive weather index on the Internet.

USA Weather
City-by-city forecasts, conditions, warnings, and weather graphics for each of the fifty states. *Under development*

Canada Weather
Regional forecasts, advisories, conditions, and reports for each of the Canadian Provinces and Territories. *Under development*

Radar and Satellite Products
Point-and-click access to the Internet's best Nexrad and color satellite imagery.

SkiWeather
Mountain forecasts, current weather and ski conditions, ski cams, and links to dozens of North American resorts. *Under development*

Travel Cities Weather
Nexrad radar, color satellite photos, climate information, forecasts, and conditions for thirty popular destinations nationwide.

Tropical Weather
The Net's most comprhensive collection of tropical storm-related links, including National Hurricane Center reports and incredible graphics.

WeatherCams
Live and daily pictures of weather conditions at over two dozen cities and resorts around North America.

WeatherNet Information
A history of WeatherNet, contact information, and the latest access statistics. *Coming Soon!*

WeatherMaps
The Net's best surface and upper air analyses, including temperature maps, regional weather plots, and jet stream maps.

NBC's Intellicast

http://www.intellicast.com/

Figure 6.7 NBC's Intellicast Home Page.

Intellicast's page offers updates of weather conditions, not only daily, but in many cases on the hour (see Figure 6.7). This is a beautiful page that is a pleasure to read. If you look in Figure 6.8, you can see the clickable **Intellicast** map where you can learn about the weather.

You can also download Intellicast's Satellite photos for the whole earth or by continent if you prefer. If you look at the Intellicast photos in Figure 6.9, you can see the weather for locations such as Australia or Africa.

Do You Know?

What the weather is like in Rome, Italy?

For the Answer go to:
http://www.intellicast.com/weather/cia/

Weather   167

Figure 6.8
Intellicast Earth Map for Weather Information.

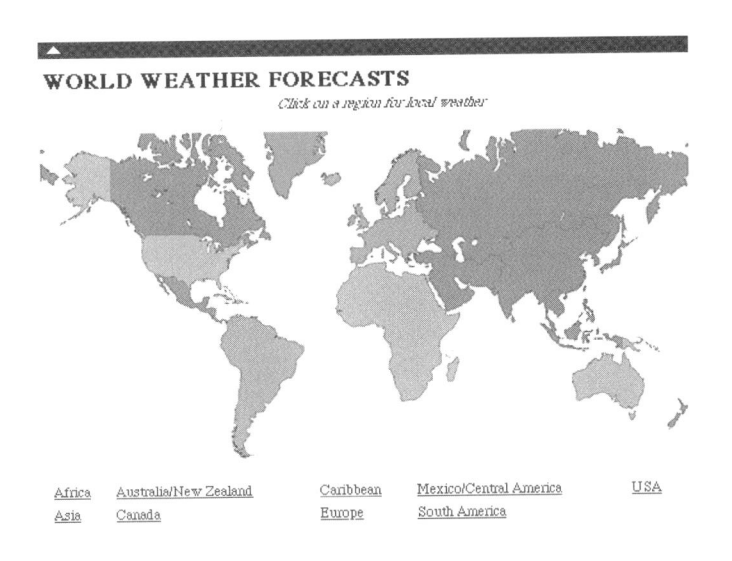

Figure 6.9
Intellicast Satellite Photo.

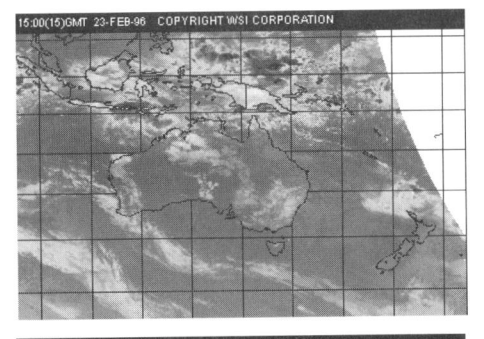

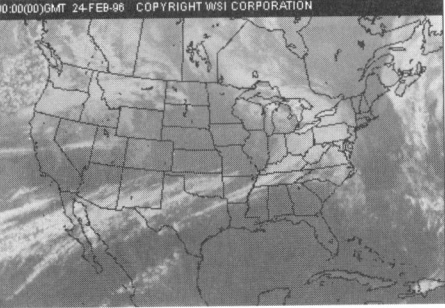

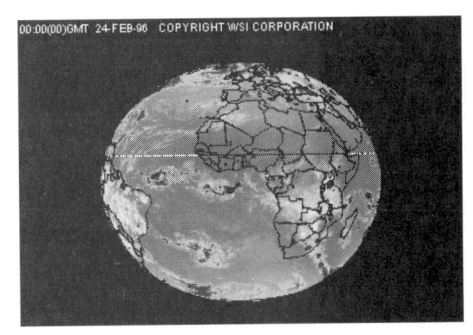

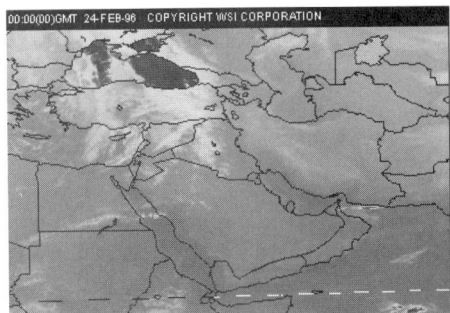

168   Chapter 6   News, Weather, and Sports

Sports

When people are not talking about the weather they are discussing the results of the latest sports match. The talk for some is soccer, for others it's football. If information about a sports event is important to you, then the Net is a great place to get it.

WWW Virtual Library's Sports Section

http://www.atm.ch.cam.ac.uk/sports/sports.html

Figure 6.10 WWW Virtual Library's Sports Page.

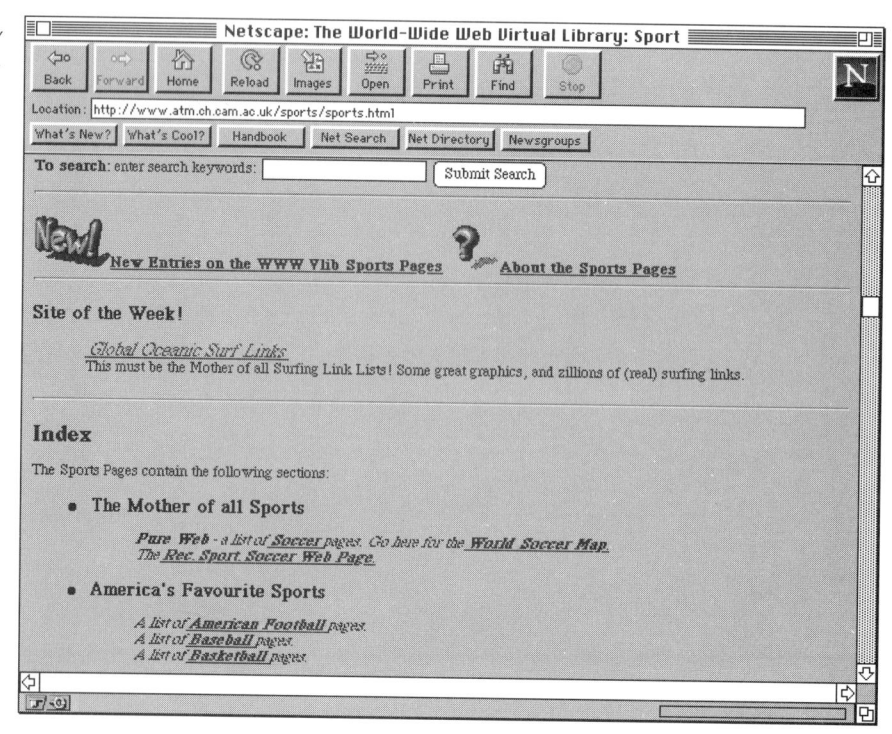

The **WWW Virtual Library** has a section on sports that is truly international in scope (see Figure 6.10). The volunteers who maintain this page do seem to have a particular passion for soccer—you will notice that they tend to view it as the most sacred of sports. Their reverence does not diminish their coverage, however. This is the best place to turn to for information about many other sports as well.

ESPN

http://espnet.sportszone.com/

Figure 6.11
ESPN Home Page.

170   Chapter 6   News, Weather, and Sports

ESPN maintains a sports page containing information about various sports happenings (see Figure 6.11). This is a slick, beautiful site well worth your time.

Sports World

http://sportsworld.line.com/

Figure 6.12
Sports World Home Page.

[Baseball] [Basketball] [Football] [Hockey]
[Golf] [Racing] [Tennis]

Main Topics
   News & Information
   Schedules
   Standings
   Statistics
   Discussion groups
   Live chat forum

Individual Game Information
Headline Sports News

Up to the Minute Scores
NBA Scores
NHL Scores
NFL Scores
College Football Scores

Other Sites
MensFitness
Tennis Country

Sports World also has a very good selection of material on virtually any aspect of American sports (see Figure 6.12). If you want to know the playing schedule of your favorite baseball or football team, this is the place for you. This page also covers college teams if you want to check out how your alma mater is faring.

Chapter 7
The Weird and Wonderful of the Net

Covered in This Chapter
A Walk on the Weird Side
The Wonderful Stuff

I threw this chapter into the book to give you an idea of both the wonderful and the silly things you can find on the Net. The weird pages got put in because I think you deserve to see them. Anyway, you wouldn't have believed me if I just described them to you. The wonderful pages are there to convey to you what an incredible thing the Net is becoming.

Let's start with the weird...

A Walk on the Weird Side

Obviously, one of your first questions is going to be what sort of criteria I used to pick a weird page. In a nutshell, for the page to make it here it had to be:

- Quintessentially strange
- Seriously tacky
- Too unbelievable for mere words
- Something so strange you would want to tell your friends about it

Anyway, that should give you some idea of what I mean by weird. Obviously these are my opinions and not necessarily those of the site creators (some probably think their sites are just dandy).

Weird for Parents

Caution: While I have only picked sites that are edging towards tasteless, as opposed to truly inappropriate, the parent sites are not really meant for small children. For the first two weird, but mild, sites, children will not even know why they are funny. The last weird parent site is the strangest of all and not really meant for children. Its content, however, is more along the lines of PG-13 material.

A Walk on the Weird Side 173

What Are Spooks Doing on the Net?

http://www.odci.gov/cia/

When a friend of mine told me that the CIA had a home page I glared at her and accused her of trying to fool me. "Really," I exclaimed, "you can't be serious. Those are people who specialize in keeping a low profile. They are spooks, after all." I went on to tell her, "Look, I've known some of those people and they won't even tell you their last names except on a need-to-know basis. What would ever possess the CIA to create a home page?" And then I figured it out (Yep, I read Tom Clancy)—the ultimate cover-up is to appear in the open. Anyway, here is the CIA on display (see Figure 7.1).

Figure 7.1
The Central Intelligence Agency Web Site.

One really useful research tool this phantom crew provides is the *CIA World Fact Book*. This site includes important statistical information on virtually every country and place on the planet. For example, if you look at Figure 7.2, you will see the maps they provide on Antarctica and Bosnia (the information fol-

174   Chapter 7 The Weird and Wonderful of the Net

lows the pictures). They also describe the country/place's population, economy, climate, history, geography, and government. This is another great resource for homework assignments.

Figure 7.2
CIA World Fact Book Pictures of Antarctica and Bosnia.

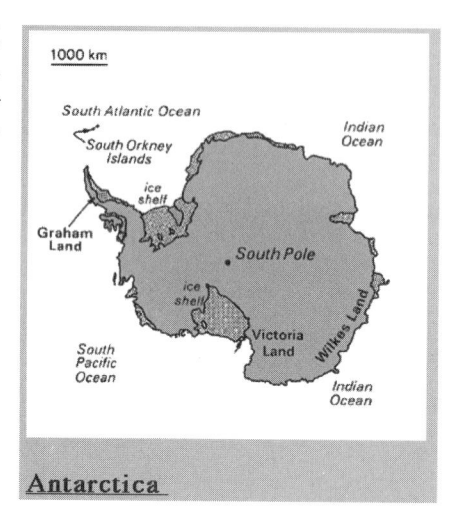

The Internal Revenue Service

http://www.irs.ustreas.gov

Okay, this is the last time I will pick on the United States government (I couldn't stop myself). If you look at the home page of this agency, you will see that it presents itself as an agency committed to:

- Customer Service

- Interplanetary Service (I'm not kidding)

Figure 7.3
Internal Revenue Service Site.

Look, some things I can swallow, other things forget it. Customer service was just too weird. Look at the home page for yourself. You can see in Figure 7.3 that these folks have a strange sense of humor.

The Conspiracy People (PG-13)

http://www.web.com/~conspire

In case you thought that Oliver Stone had a corner on the conspiracy market, you should take a look at this Web site (see Figure 7.4). The **50 Greatest Conspiracies of All Time** home page is very strange. These people talk about alien visitations like they were the relatives coming into town for the weekend.

176   Chapter 7 The Weird and Wonderful of the Net

Figure 7.5 contains just some of the links they have to sites that frankly discuss the ins and outs of alien visitations. If that is not enough fun, this place will also give you all the information you might ever want to have on:

- JFK's whereabouts until this very day

- How the Beatles were used as agents of Her Majesty's Secret Service in a plot to destroy the United States

- Elvis sightings

Figure 7.4
The Conspiracy People.

This is not what you would call quality educational material, but rather very strange stuff for a night when you are bored out of your mind. I do guarantee you that this will be more fun and less embarrassing than standing in line at the grocery store reading the *National Enquirer.*

Figure 7.5
The Conspiracy Theory of Alien Visitation and More.

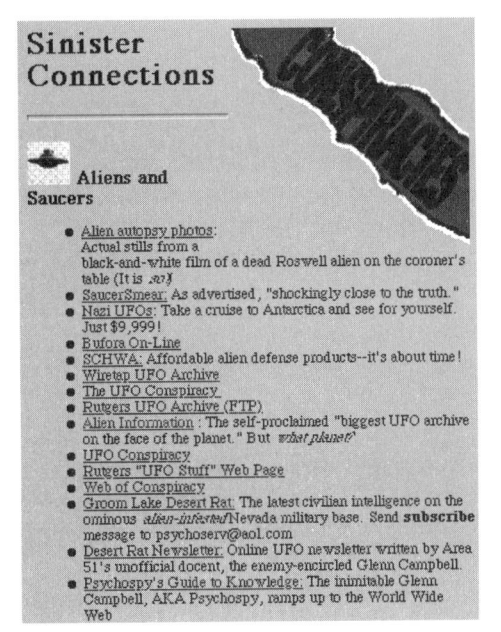

Weird for Kids

There are also a couple of strange offerings for children. What could be weirder than bugs, you might ask. I can tell you—it is the sound of the greatest starship captain in the history of American television singing the lyrics to Beatles songs. That's right— you get to listen to Captain Kirk (good old William Shatner) singing songs, and the results are very weird. That is not all; more of the crew of the *Enterprise* join in the fun.

Let's start with the bugs first.

178   Chapter 7   The Weird and Wonderful of the Net

The Yuckiest Site on the Internet

http://www.nj.com/yucky/index.html

Little kids will quite enjoy this strange place. It features slime and bugs. If you look at Figure 7.6, you will see that this site is the home of **Cockroach World**.

*Figure 7.6
The Yucky Page and Cockroach World.*

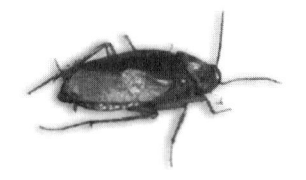

In **Cockroach World**, kids can learn about all sorts of cockroaches, including smelly and hissing ones. They can take an entertaining and fact-filled walk around the globe to visit the homes of these little creatures. This site, brought to the Net by entomologist Dr. Betty Faber and Liberty Science Center, also features her answers to questions about bugs and provides a plethora of entertaining material.

Captain Kirk Sings

http://www.ama.caltech.edu/users/mrm/kirk.html

I know that virtually every introductory book on the Web mentions this page (see Figure 7.7) and the next one, but that is because they are just too delicious

Figure 7.7
The Captain Kirk Sing-Along Page.

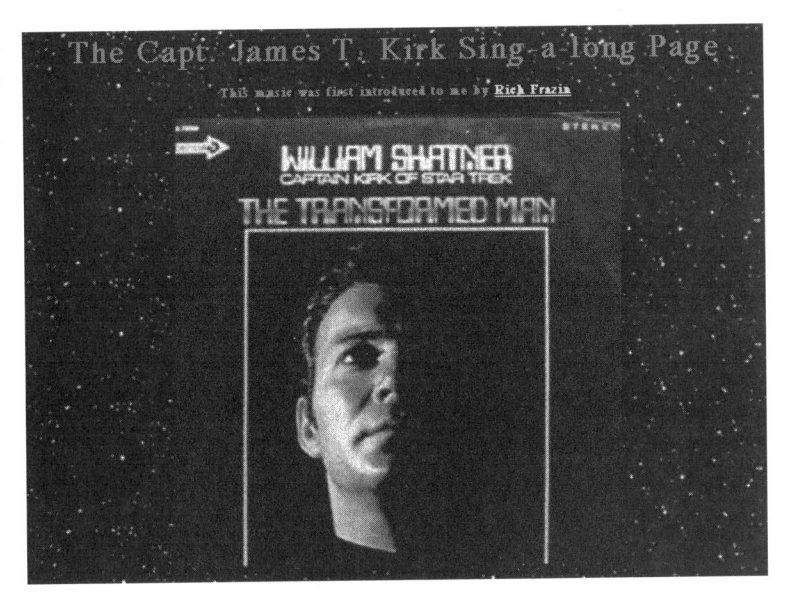

for mere words to describe. You have not truly experienced the Net until you have heard Captain Kirk (alias William Shatner) belt out a few rounds of…

- Lucy in the Sky with Diamonds
- Mr. Tambourine Man

William Shatner's musical talents rival my own (for embarrassing awfulness). It is still hard to believe that you can download his renditions of these and other musical favorites to the delight of your whole family.

Spock Sings Too

And just in case you thought Kirk was the only member of the Star Trek crew who made an attempt to break into the world of golden hits, here comes Spock (see Figure 7.8).

http://www.ama.caltech.edu/users/mrm/kirk/spock.html

Figure 7.8
Mr. Spock Gets into the Act.

William Shatner and Leonard Nimoy made some of the best TV I ever watched as a kid, but singers they are not. In fact, you would think that their unfortunate forays into the musical world would frighten off future crews of the *Enterprise*. Unfortunately, that is not the case. You can also get an earful of the singing of...

Data Does It Too

http://www.ama.caltech.edu/users/mrm/kirk/toot.au

Data sings too (see Figure 7.9). Maybe it is the side effect of having your bodies dissolved into tiny little bits of light and reassembled elsewhere countless number of times. I have no other explanation for it.

Figure 7.9 The Music of Data.

Someday, when you have the time to download the sound files of Kirk, Spock, and Data (approximately 2 to 5 minutes per sound file) you will find them interesting listening. I only hope the Herculean efforts of maintaining this splendid page never prove to much for its creator, Mark Meloon. If you haven't had enough of this sort of stuff yet, you can check out Mark's page on Godzilla (http://www.ama.caltech.edu/users/mrm/godzilla.html) for even more fun.

Chapter 7 The Weird and Wonderful of the Net

The Wonderful Stuff

As strange as the weird stuff is, the wonderful stuff can be enough to take your breath away. These pages are here for a variety of reasons. Some my children made me put in, some I included because they are just too darn neat for words, and one section is a tribute not to a site but a site creator, Bob. Come look and see some really great stuff.

Disney

http://www.disney.com

Where else would you expect to start a journey of delight and wonder? While Disney maintains several pages, this main one is used as a showcase for current Disney movies and a place of great fun and games for kids (see Figure 7.10).

Figure 7.10
The Disney Page.

If the great downloadable software and neat kid activities are not enough to enchant you, then you can take a virtual trip to Disney World…

Disney World

http://www2.disney.com/DisneyWorld/

Figure 7.11
The Disney World Home Page.

You can check out this or other theme parks, including a live video feed of folks walking around such places as Epcot and the Magic Kingdom (see Figure 7.11). You can visit the tour guide, who will make suggestions on where to stay and what to do.

Yahoo's Disney Information

Last, but not least, you can go back and check out **Yahoo's** Disney section for links to many other Disney fan pages.

http://www.yahoo.com/Business_and_Economy/Companies/Entertainment/Disney/

Movies and Times with MovieLink

http://www.777film.com/

I mentioned this site in my introduction to entice you onto the Net. I use it all the time and the idea is just so great and useful that I'm surprised it took so long for someone to come up with it (see Figure 7.12). You can look at what movies are currently playing, sort them by theater, and by title, and narrow them down to the zip code in which you live.

Figure 7.12 MovieLink Home Page.

See All the Places a Movie is Playing

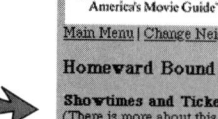

The Exploratorium

http://www.exploratorium.edu/

This is a really great site for kids and for finding projects to do with them. Modeled after the Exploratorium Museum in San Francisco, it offers children tons of interesting things to see and do (see Figure 7.13).

Figure 7.13 Exploratorium Home Page.

You know all those questions your kids ask you about things:

- "How does fog get made?"
- "What's inside a cow's eye?"
- "Who built the pyramids?

Well, the Exploratorium is the place to take your kids to explore the answers to such questions (see Figure 7.14 and Figure 7.15).

186 Chapter 7 The Weird and Wonderful of the Net

Figure 7.14
How to Make Fog.

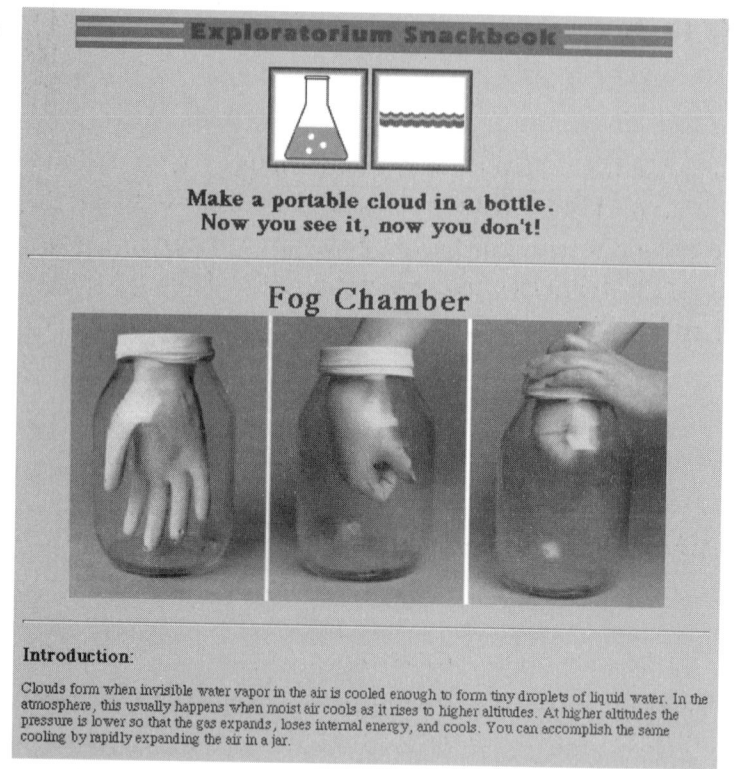

Figure 7.15
Exhibits Online.

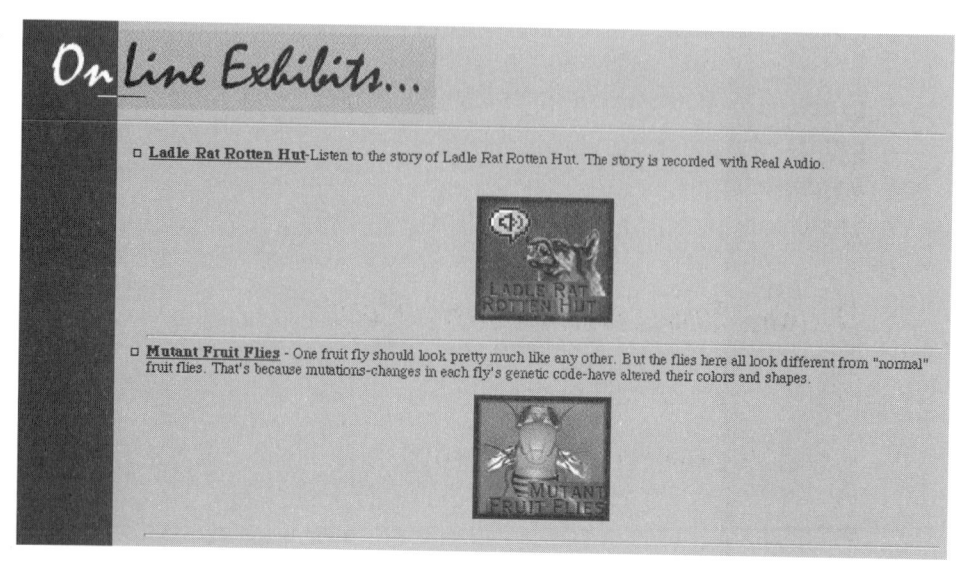

Star Wars

My son, Nicholas, has a serious love affair going on with the Star Wars saga. One day you can find him saving Han Solo from certain doom, the next day he is dodging meteors in the *Millennium Falcon* and escaping Darth Vader in the nick of time. With the help of the many Star Wars Web sites, this love affair is greatly enriched with pictures of his favorite characters, games, and much more.

Yahoo's Star Wars Collection

Yahoo has several categories dedicated entirely to those valiant heroes of the Rebellion (I admit, I love this story, too). You can either do a search on "Star Wars" or go directly to the following category.

> http://www.yahoo.com/Entertainment/Movies_and_Films/Genres/Science_Fiction/Star_Wars/

Official Star Wars Home Page

> http://www.tcfhe.com/starwars/

A must stop is the official home page of the movies (see Figure 7.16).

Chapter 7 The Weird and Wonderful of the Net

*Figure 7.16
Twentieth Century
Fox Star Wars
Page.*

You can find interviews, sound clips, story chapters, and all sorts of interesting stuff. When you have finished here, you can head on over to the Cantina (the bar at Mos Esiley Space Port) for a slew of interesting stuff.

Star Wars Archive

http://www.wpi.edu/ftp/starwars/

You can finish this adventure by looking at some of the great Star Wars things you can download from the Star Wars archive (see Figure 7.17).

Figure 7.17
Stars Wars Archive.

Planet Earth Home Page

http://www.nosc.mil/planet_earth/info.html

At some point, you might want to find out something about this planet we call home. If you do, this is the place for you. Dedicated to the planet we live on, and vivid in its description of its many wonders, this site talks about anything and everything having to do with it (see Figure 7.18).

190   Chapter 7 The Weird and Wonderful of the Net

Figure 7.18
The Planet Earth Home Page.

Plus, when you want to go exploring you can check out the WWW Virtual Library's floor plan, which will take you anywhere on the virtual planet Earth you want to go (see Figure 7.19).

Figure 7.19
Planet Earth WWW Virtual Library Floor Plan.

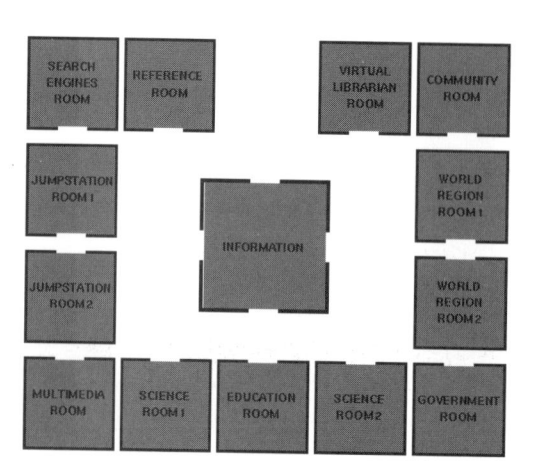

Museum of Paleontology

http://ucmp1.berkeley.edu/

What would the world be like without dinosaurs? How do children learn all of those extravagantly unpronounceable names that we have given to dinosaurs? This paleontology site is just dandy for finding out everything you need to know about those extinct critters (see Figure 7.20).

Figure 7.20
The Museum of Paleontology Home Page.

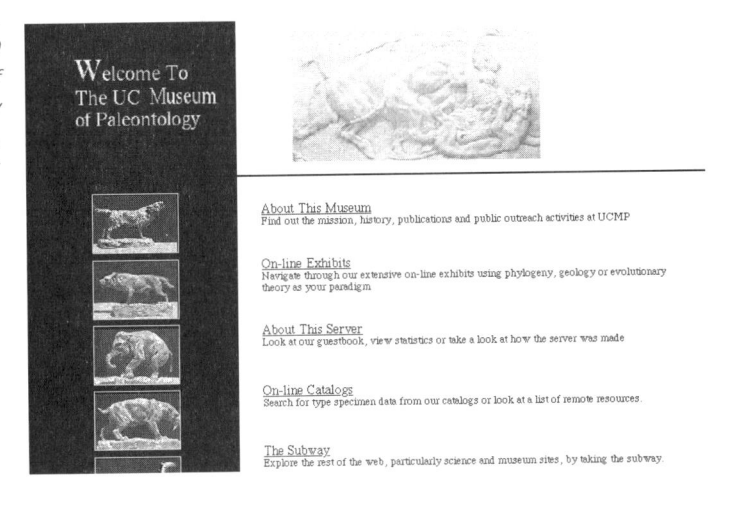

Plus, the **Museum of Paleontology** contains a virtual elevator to every kind of animal you can imagine. It points you to all the great collections of dinosaurs and other animals all over the world (see Figure 7.21).

Figure 7.21
The Web Lift at the Museum.

Late Show with Dave

How could we end a night without David Letterman's Top Ten List? Now you don't have to stay up or tape the show just to get those crucial items of information. You can just join Dave on the Net (see Figure 7.22).

http://www.cbs.com:80/lateshow/lateshow.html

Figure 7.22 The Late Night with David Letterman Page.

Welcome to the Official Late Show with David Letterman homepage where you'll find the daily Top Ten lists, today's guests, Dave's Lines and much more. You can order LATE SHOW and CBS stuff (t-shirts, caps, sweatshirts, etc.) from our catalog and don't miss the sites for THE LATE LATE SHOW with TOM SNYDER and Calvert DeForest.

The Top Ten List
"Signs Your Accountant Is Nuts"

As presented on the 04/10/96 broadcast of LATE SHOW with DAVID LETTERMAN

10. In several places on your tax forms, he's written, "Give or take a million dollars"
9. Tells you to put all your money into British cattle futures
8. You notice that his "calculator" is just a broken VCR remote
7. Insists that there's no such number as four
6. He laughed at the Bob Dole background check (I'm sorry -- that's a sign he's hypnotized)
5. Counts family of squirrels living in your yard as dependents
4. Advises you to save postage by filing your taxes telepathically

If Dave is not enough, you can also tune into the Web pages of all your favorite television shows. Late night, talk shows, soap operas, and even game shows have sites you can visit. In some, you can even win prizes in contests they sponsor. Just do a search in **Yahoo** on your favorite show's name and away you go into TV land.

What about Bob?

I've talked about Bob Allison before. He has created over 100 sites, many of which are downright great. Because of such dedication and creativity, I decided he deserved a slot in the "wonderful" section.

You will notice that he thinks he is good at this stuff, too; at least that is what littering his sites with testimonials indicates. A typical Bob page could have a long list of links in no particular order. In any case, for our last stop, I turn you over to the very capable hands of Bob. He will be your tour guide for this part of your Net journey.

BOBAWORLD

http://gagme.wwa.com/~boba/index.html

Figure 7.23 Bob's Home Page.

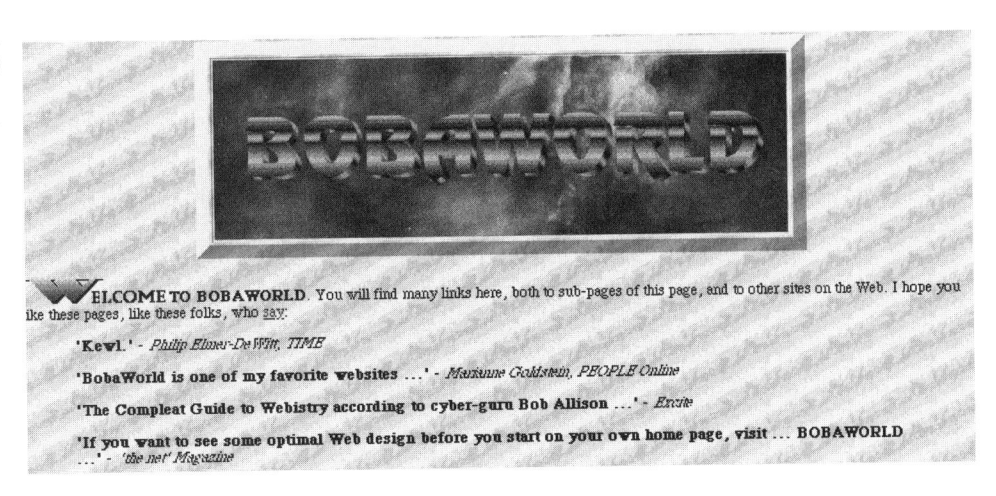

BOBAWORLD is one of Bob's pages and one that he calls his main page (see Figure 7.23). Like all the other Bob pages, it begins with glowing comments from Net users. Some of the links that this page offers include:

Chapter 7 The Weird and Wonderful of the Net

- Collections of home pages guaranteed by Bob to be interesting
- Help with browsing
- Links to other Bob pages
- Short and long lists of Newsgroups

The Spider's Web

http://gagme.wwa.com/~boba/spider.htm

Figure 7.24 The Spider's Web Home Page.

WELCOME to **The Spider's Web**. This is your gateway to some of the best things on the Web (and FTP and Gopher sites). Get ready to browse, because the Spider believes you will enjoy yourself, like these folks, who say:

"Do not walk. Do not wait. Run. Click. Whatever. Go see this place." - *VIBE Magazine on the Time-Warner Web*

"The Spider weaves the best links and many of them." - *Envie*

"Some of the coolest links on the Internet." - *CafeNet*

"... you'll find enough links to great sites here to keep you busy for a life time." - *iGUIDE inSITES*

The **Spider's Web** was placed at the top of **"The 12 Best Sites Out There"** list by **VIBE Magazine on the Time-Warner Web**, named **Geoff's Cool Site of the Day**, and included in the Spring 1995 **NetUser** magazine's list of **Jumping Off Points**.

The Spider's Web (see Figure 7.24) contains a nice set of links that are sorted into various combinations. It also contains some other very nice spider pages (see Figure 7.25). Bob also references FTP and Gopher sites as well as Web sites included in his links. This very eclectic list of links is well worth a look see.

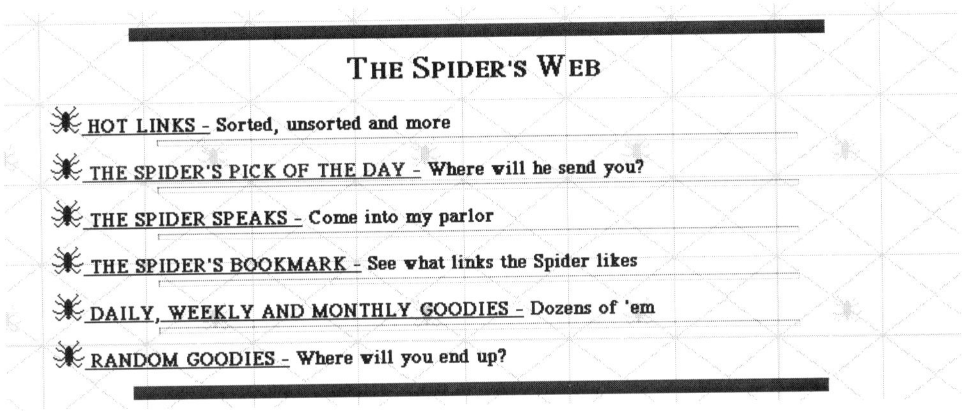

Figure 7.25
The Spider's Web Page Links.

THE SPIDER'S WEB

- HOT LINKS - Sorted, unsorted and more
- THE SPIDER'S PICK OF THE DAY - Where will he send you?
- THE SPIDER SPEAKS - Come into my parlor
- THE SPIDER'S BOOKMARK - See what links the Spider likes
- DAILY, WEEKLY AND MONTHLY GOODIES - Dozens of 'em
- RANDOM GOODIES - Where will you end up?

The Spider's Pick of the Day

http://gagme.wwa.com/~boba/pick.html

If you do not have a lot of time to spend on the Net, then you should go right to **The Spider's Pick of the Day** (see Figure 7.26). This site contains a newly selected "great" site (using Bob's criteria of greatness). It also contains links for:

- A Few of The Spider's past picks
- The current month's picks
- Last month's selections
- An index of selections

As you can see, virtually anything your heart could desire can be found in **The Spider's Pick of the Day.**

Chapter 7 The Weird and Wonderful of the Net

Figure 7.26
Spider's Pick of the Day Page.

THERE IS ALSO A SHORT VERSION OF THIS PAGE
AND SEE BOB'S KOOL LINK DAILY PICK

THE PICK

WELCOME to The Spider's Pick of the Day. The Spider may pick darn near anything. You know that crazy arachnid. There is a shorter version of this page for your convenience. It should load in 5 to 10 seconds on most systems. The Spider hopes you enjoy yourself...

AND NOW, THE LINK D' JOUR ...

The Spider's Pick of the Day
Saturday, March 9th, 1996

Fun and Games

http://gagme.wwa.com/~boba/fun.html

Figure 7.27
Fun and Games Page.

FUN & GAMES

Each selection will take you to a server containing games, gimmicks, jokes, and other goodies. If you know of any links that are not included here, email me the URLs. Feel free to add a link to this page to your home page or hotlist, and to add a bookmark. This page is served through the courtesy of WorldWide Access.

- - Last Month's Sites From SPotD and BKL -
- - TV Land -
- - Star Trek -
- - Peanuts -
- - Casey's Top 40 -
- - The Biz -
- - Interactive Movie Reviews -
- - Before They Were Stars -
- - Gamers Ledge -
- - Argon Zark! - Comic book
- - Dialing Dr Durango -
- - Movie Studios -
- - World Wide Trivia -
- - Desk Potato -
- - Electric Origami Shop -
- - Uncle Bob's Kids' Page - Lot of links just for kids
- - Out Of My Mind - Cartoon
- - Trivia -
- - Science Adventures For Kids -
- - The Marilyn Pages -
- - Interactive Story -

- - Broadway -
- - Mad About You -
- - Space Telescope -
- - HiFi on WWW -
- - TV Net -
- - Sega -
- - Supermodels FTP Server -
- - The Lite-Brite Page -
- - Multi-User Dungeons (MUDs) -
- - Barbie -
- - Seattle Mariners - Baseball team
- - Humor on the Net -
- - FalconStar Comics -
- - Anonymous Messages - Write and read anonymous notes
- - Mr Potatohead - No kidding
- - Enternet Skateboarding -
- - Star Trek Archives -
- - Guitar World on the Internet -
- - Silly Zone -
- - How to Keep an Idiot Busy for Hours -
- - Daily, Weekly, Monthly and Random Goodies -

As you might imagine, *Fun and Games* is one of Bob's most popular sites (see Figure 7.27). If you want links for jokes (good and bad), games, "Star Trek," cartoons, entertainment tidbits, and bunches of other strange and fun sites, this is definitely the place for you.

More of Bob's Pages

Bob has lots of other sites that you can explore on your own and I will leave it up to your own ingenuity to find them. As a last stop, however, you should join in a few *fa-la-la-la-las* on his Christmas page (see Figure 7.28).

http://gagme.wwa.com/~boba/christmas.html

Figure 7.28
Bob's Christmas Page.

At this lovely seasonal site you can:

- Find links to great Christmas sites the world round

- Email a customized letter to St. Nick

- Talk to Santa or the Elves

- Learn about Christmas traditions around the world

Chapter 8
All Sorts of Stuff for Parents

Covered in This Chapter
Advice
Resources
Family Home Pages

There is stuff all over the Net for parents. Each day more families from all over the world join the Net community, and with them they bring their collective experience and wisdom concerning children. They also bring all of their mistakes. Taken together, they create the weird and wonderful adventures of parenting on the Net. Some of the stuff you will find here will be absolutely useless, some will sound okay, and some will be worth its weight in gold.

Advice

If you want advice on parenting, there are plenty of places to get it on the Net. Just like in your day-to-day life, there is no shortage of people willing to tell you how to raise your kids. Nicely enough, sometimes the advice from the Net actually helps.

Ask the Parents

What better resource can you imagine than the accumulated thoughts and wisdom of millions of parents who every day wonder and worry over some part of parenting. If you are trying to figure out what to do in a situation, many of these parents may have already faced that situation and may have some helpful advice. Of course, you might think some of the advice is just short of crazy. You could be right.

Ask the Newsgroup Parents

One of the most interesting parts of the Net is undoubtedly the newsgroups. The ones devoted to parenting and children are certainly no exception. To get the newsgroups relevant to parenting, you can do a **Find** on any of these words: "kids," "parent," and "education." You can also do a search in **Yahoo** and that will yield much the same results.

Here is an annotated list of newsgroups that have to do with parenting. It is by no means exhaustive; they are just the ones I am familiar with:

> *Free Advice:* If this is your first exposure to a newsgroup, then you would do well to re-read the material in Chapter 1 dealing with the rules of Net behavior. Plus, I recommend that you lurk in newsgroups for at least one month before posting a question or giving advice. That will allow you plenty of time to gain a true understanding of the variety and behavior of newsgroup posters (which, I must admit can be, at its worst, pure ranting).
>
> Lurking refers to the honorable activity of hanging around a newsgroup reading what other people write without entering the discussion yourself. You stay as quiet as a little fly on the wall.

misc . kids

This newsgroup can get questions on virtually anything to do with children or parenting (see Figure 8.1). This is also the largest collection of information on children and certainly a fun stop. People here will discuss anything from toilet training to papier mâché.

Figure 8.1 Exert from misc.kids Newsgroup.

```
▷  6    Blowing Bubbles    What Is "Magic Cards"? - Enlighten Me Please
   -    kate@anatomy.uc…   Re: Help! 20 month old likes time out!
▷  3    Cissy . Thorpe     Re: HOW LONG FOR STRIDE-RITE?
▷  2    Greh3595           Re: Fluoridation vs. Breast feeding
   -    Terri A. Rivkin    Re: Re: "Pulling up" too early?
▷  2    Frances I Fourn…   Re: english first?
▷ 48    Patrick Draper     Re: Pro-circ delusions
   -    Terri A. Rivkin    Re: Night diapers not working at all!!!
▷  3    Terri A. Rivkin    Re: baby swings:  too soon?
▷  8    Maryann Mcnamara   Re: best toy ever, in your opinion
   -    Donna Kinney       Re: Crying over Music from Childhood
   -    Susan R. Martin    Camping w/ nursing children
   -    Dana               Re: Help! How to make Paper Mache?
   -    zorn               Re: Explaining "bad" people (was 10 Keys To Successful Parenting)
   -    Jan Penovich       Re: Worthless Gift - Tell The Giver?
```

misc . kids . health

Questions regarding children's health are directed to this newsgroup. If you want to know how to get rid of head lice, what to do about changing pediatricians, or what type of milk kids should drink, then this is a place to look for opinions (see Figure 8.2). Another topic that occupies a lot of space in this

202 Chapter 8 All Sorts of Stuff for Parents

newsgroup is the raging debate concerning infant circumcision. I must tell you that both sides on this matter have very firm opinions and are relentless in their attack upon the other side. Much like a modern-day political campaign, this is fun to watch but rough if you get in the middle. Consider yourself warned.

Figure 8.2 Exert from misc.kids.health Newsgroup.

```
-       choward@abacus....  Headlice!
-       Sarah               Asthma Survey (please help!)
▷ 5     Jim Burris          Re: Fat content of 2% milk
-       Zeying Zhu          HELP!!! Infant not eating
▷ 2     J. Rachael Haml...  Re: Human milk (was Re: BROCCOLIZE THE WATER!!)
-       Andrea Wilson       New Web Site
▷ 6     Makem punt          Re: Why do humans drink milk? (was BROCCOLIZE the water)
-       Della Noche         Re: How common is child death by Cerebral Hemmorage?
▷ 3     Melanie Typaldos    Changing doctors
-       Alex Gostevskikh    PLEASE, PLEASE ADVISE!
```

misc . kids . computers

This is where people go to ask questions about children's software and to participate in the never-ending debate on what is the best computer to buy (Figure 8.3). You can also find software for sale in this group.

Figure 8.3 Exert from misc.kids.computers Newsgroup.

```
-       DDunker303          Games as education, vice-versa
▷ 3     Stephen R. Savi...  Re: One computer, four kids!
▷ 2     Gary E. Bloom       Re: Teaching Logo and programming to young children
-       Gary E. Bloom       Re: Construction Game
-       CWind63350          Request: recomm. Windows chess for 7year old
▷ 2     Perry Denton        Re: ReaderRabbit IJ on sale for $35.00
▷ 2     Russell Anderson    Re: Typing tutorial software wanted
▷ 2     Barbara             WANTED BOOK WITH REVIEWS OF EDUCATIONAL SOFTWARE
-       LIPMAN JOSEPH K...  Re: Dinosaur Safari- need some help
-       CoNnEcTiOnS         Re: Parent Control Your PC
-       Dave Timoney        Re: BEGINNERS! EVERYTHING to see PICS on 1 disk -wifeproof
-       Teresa              Fun keypal needed
-       Jerry Rakar         FS: New Edmark CDs: $ 10 Each Shipped or 3 for $ 25 Shipped
-       Susan Watkins       Re: Letters & Numbers software for 3-year-old?
```

alt . parenting . solutions

If you have questions about a parenting issue, this is a place to look for opinions (see Figure 8.4). You will see all sorts of questions, from "Should children be spanked?" to "How do I handle a terrible two-year-old?"

Figure 8.4
Exert from alt.parenting.solutions Newsgroup.

▷	46	serendp@azstarn...	Re: Ritalin/ADD
▷	4	Spiros Triantaf...	Re: Views of high cost of parenting.
▷	2	Spiros Triantaf...	Re: FRANTIC MOTHERS
▷	4	Kimberly Sylva ...	Baby Faces video?
▷	8	Marilyn Berry	Re: Former Teen Runaway--Glad they didn't label me "ADD/ADHD"
-		Gnosis	3 views
-		Hypothetical	Hypo 7: Twins?
▷	2	Hypothetical	Hypo 6: Who do I look like?
▷	3	Katie's Mommy	Re: public/private schools (was Re:School dress codes/uniforms)
▷	3	Tafarrar3	Re: The law steps in - finally
-		Lynn	Re: Please read...My baby's dependancy is slowly driving me NUTS!me
▷	11	S Urwick	Re: Do you like your mini-van?
▷	3	MmeFerauge	Re: Bilingual Households
-		MarilynStn	Re: How To Boss Your Kids Around
-		Maryann Mcnamara	Re: Hold son back from kindergarten?
▷	2	KKarastury	Re: Family Bed?
▷	4	groemer@wingsbb...	Re: Super Terrible Two's any help please!
-		Dean Shipley	Bedwetting Solutions

misc.education

This is a great stop if you want to see the ongoing debates about schools, both public and private (see Figure 8.5). There are also lively discussions on school vouchers and on the use of Ritalin as a behavior-shaping tool.

Figure 8.5
The misc.education Newsgroup.

▷	11	Michael Zarlenga	Re: Public Education vs. Private Potentials
▷	6	fritzw@UWYO.EDU	Re: The Drop in SAT Scores?
▷	9	Don Detweiler	Re: Internet policy
▷	20	Alberto C Morei...	Re: mathematics TA with angst
-		Nancy K	OBE: "Longing" for the Old Model T
▷	14	Nancy K	Re: UN Treaty Undermines Parents
▷	7	Frolicking Gilb...	Re: Public School Teachers Who Send *their* Children to Private Schools
▷	3	I Adams	Re: Grouping children other than by age--Kentucky
-		Jan Cooper	Re: public/private schools (was Re:School dress codes/uniforms)
▷	3	Bite	Re: DOPPLER EFFECT
-		Nancy K	Nevada Rejects Goals 2000...
▷	6	Brian M. Scott	Re: It's means it is or it has
▷	11	Curt Howland	Re: Individual vs. society (was Re: Public Education vs.)
▷	2	Mario Taboada	Re: School of Hard Knocks.
▷	8	Charles L. Hunt...	Re: Stock Holders (Prev: Fool the people...)
▷	2	N. Hagerstown H...	How Can A School Improve Attendance?
-		Hank Mai	Vocational Education Newsgroup
▷	5	John E. and Joa...	Re: aRe: Establishment "Educators" Push Drugs On Disruptive, Fussy , Children!/...
-		Karl M. Bunday	Possessive Plural Forms of English Words (was It's means it is or it has)
-		Karl M. Bunday	Question of teaching
-		Karl M. Bunday	teacher tenure
-		Karl M. Bunday	VOUCHERS ARE ANSWER
▷	5	Karl M. Bunday	20/20 Report on Tenure

misc.education.home-school.misc

This newsgroup is where to turn if you want information on home-schooling your children (see Figure 8.6). Resources, friendly advice, and stories about why people home-school abound at this site. You can also participate in the ongoing debate between those who believe children benefit from home-schooling and those who believe that children need an in-school setting to grow up normally.

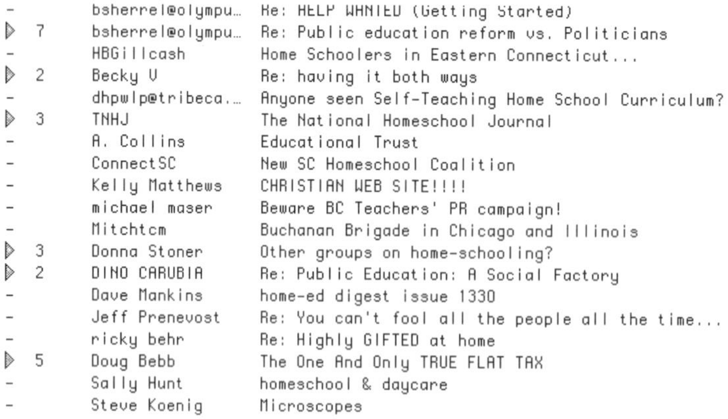

Figure 8.6 The misc.education.home-school.misc Newsgroup.

```
-        bsherrel@olympu…   Re: HELP WHNIEU (Getting Started)
▷  7     bsherrel@olympu…   Re: Public education reform vs. Politicians
-        HBGillcash         Home Schoolers in Eastern Connecticut...
▷  2     Becky V            Re: having it both ways
-        dhpwlp@tribeca.…   Anyone seen Self-Teaching Home School Curriculum?
▷  3     TNHJ               The National Homeschool Journal
-        A. Collins         Educational Trust
-        ConnectSC          New SC Homeschool Coalition
-        Kelly Matthews     CHRISTIAN WEB SITE!!!!
-        michael maser      Beware BC Teachers' PR campaign!
-        Mitchtcm           Buchanan Brigade in Chicago and Illinois
▷  3     Donna Stoner       Other groups on home-schooling?
▷  2     DINO CARUBIA       Re: Public Education: A Social Factory
-        Dave Mankins       home-ed digest issue 1330
-        Jeff Prenevost     Re: You can't fool all the people all the time...
-        ricky behr         Re: Highly GIFTED at home
▷  5     Doug Bebb          The One And Only TRUE FLAT TAX
-        Sally Hunt         homeschool & daycare
-        Steve Koenig       Microscopes
```

Ask a Doctor

Believe it or not, on the Net you can ask a pediatrician questions about your children's health. At this tremendously useful site, which is part of **ParentsPlace** (Figure 8.7), you can look through questions other parents have asked, and if you don't find yours answered, you can ask the doctor yourself. In this case, the doctor is Robert W. Steele, M.D., a pediatrician at Children's Hospital Medical Center in Cincinnati, Ohio. He is also a parent of two children and thus knows, on a firsthand basis, the kinds of concerns parents have about their children's health.

Advice 205

http://www.parentsplace.com/readroom/health.html

Figure 8.7
Dr. Robert W. Steele, Questions and Answers.

ParentsPlace.com
Health Issues and Your Children

Ask the Pediatrician

A **ParentsPlace.com exclusive**: the Web Doctor answers your pediatric questions. PLEASE read the posted answers before posing a question to the Web Doctor.

Preventive Healthcare: Articles by a Family Nurse Practitioner

1. Stocking a Medicine Chest for Your Child
2. Stocking a Medicine Chest for Your Infant
3. Understanding Cold and Cough Medications NEW
4. Fevers: Taking Temperatures and Treating Fevers NEW
5. Children's Acetaminophen: Information and Dosing NEW
6. Children's Motrin®: Information and Dosing
7. Prevention, Classification and Care for Burns
8. Poisonous Plants
9. Fluoride Issues and your children
10. Dental Hygiene for Kids
11. Pregnancy and Vitamin A

Get a Second Opinion

Since everybody should be able to get a second opinion on a medical problem, there is yet another doctor available to parents and caretakers on the Net. As you can see in Figure 8.8, this is a nice page brought to you by Lewis Wasserman, M.D. It contains lots of general medical advice on everything from infant care to discussions of the new chicken pox vaccine.

http://members.aol.com/AllianceMD/parents.html

Figure 8.8
Dr. Lewis Wasserman's Page.

-=+=-
Parents' Page
-=+=-

Brought to you by
Lewis Wasserman, M.D.
Orlando, Florida
Originated December, 1994
Last update 1/25/96

NOTICE:

This is a source of friendly advice and helpful hints. It is NOT a substitute for medical care or your doctor's attention. If your child is sick, please seek the advice of your pediatrician or family doctor.

Any correspondence received becomes the property of Lewis Wasserman, M.D., and may be published online or in other media. Privacy of Email can not be guaranteed.

Keep watching for future additions to this page -- I am constantly looking for useful things to add. If you have any information or links to include, please Email me.

You are visitor number 2 0 7 0 since 1/1/96, according to the Web Counter.

Guided Tour

To sample some of the highlights of the Parents' Page, I have included a brief guided tour. To follow the tour, just click on the Tour icons, and they will take you to the next part of the tour. Read down to the next Tour icon, and then click on the Tour icon to continue your tour. Feel free to get side-tracked if you wish. If you want to take the tour, you can begin right now:

Resources

There are also some good parent resource sites on the WWW. These sites combine advice with resource material and links to other valuable places.

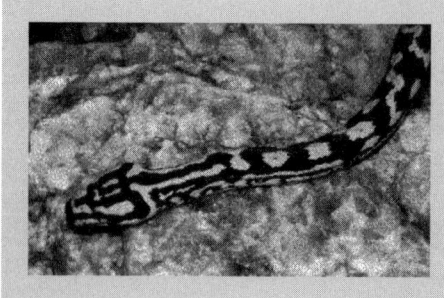

Do You Know?

How the Carpet Python got its name?

For the Answer go to:
http://www.bev.net/education/SeaWorld/
/carpet_pythonab.html

ParentsPlace

http://www.parentsplace.com/

Figure 8.9
ParentsPlace Home Page.

ParentsPlace.com
The Parenting Resource Center on the Web (TM)

February 24-25, 1996

Today's Features:

1. **SLEEP:** The conversation on Family Bed continues. Essay by Sora Feldman.
   Dialog Room: Come meet other parents who are trying to figure out how to get a good night's rest.
2. **INFANT NUTRITION:** Sue Gilbert answers: My baby just switched to formula; how do I know if he is getting enough? and Feeding a 9-month old.
3. **THE LAW:** Peter Fritz, Esq. follows up on the question: Can an employee be forced to request FMLA when using paid temporary disability leave for childbirth?

Main Selections:

The ParentsPlace.com Mall. Catalogs, stores and services designed exclusively for the parenting market.

ParentsPlace.com Reading Rooms. Selected topics include: book reviews, twins, fathering, single parenting, step-parenting. Lots of great material for new and experienced parents.

When I found this page (see Figure 8.9), I immediately told two friends of mine that they had to see it. **ParentsPlace** is a beautifully crafted site that is packed with extraordinarily valuable information. You can get thorough, helpful advice and resources on such important topics as childcare, health issues, family leave, divorce and custody rights, and much more. The creators of this site have thought through the needs of modern parents and collected resources that would be difficult to get on your own without great time and expense. I

208   Chapter 8 All Sorts of Stuff for Parents

have looked at a lot of sites on the Net about parenting, and I can tell you that this place is head and shoulders above most other sites.

ParentsPlace is one of my favorite parent sites on all of the Net.

I assume that I have so enticed you now that you are immediately running to your computer to check it out. That is an excellent idea. If you need just a little bit more incentive, look at a handful of the things **ParentsPlace** has to offer:

- Legal consultants who give custody and parenting advice

- Products for Children — everything from diapers to strollers

- Children and parenting books and book reviews

- Childcare and nanny referrals

- Newsletters for single parents, stay-at-home dads, and more…

- Reading Rooms that give information and advice from doctors and midwives, stepparents, and so on

ParentSoup

http://www.parentsoup.com/

Figure 8.10 Parent Soup Home Page.

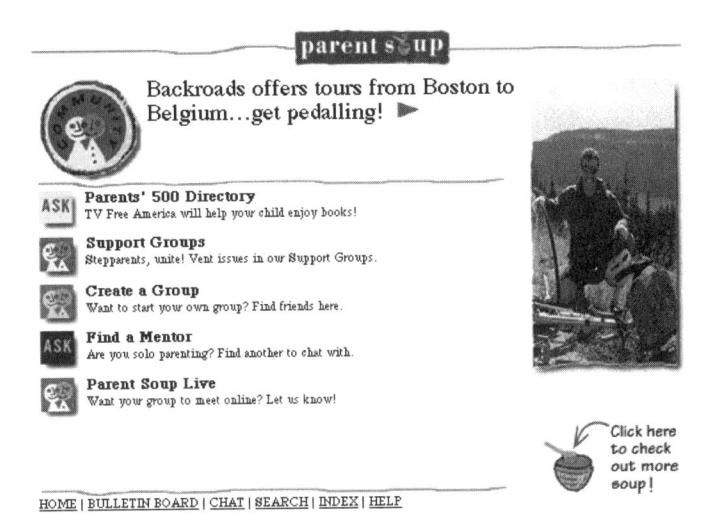

Parent Soup is another eclectic site full of wonderful resources, including everything from magazines to support groups for parents (see Figure 8.10).

Family Planet

http://family.starwave.com/

This Web site (see Figure 8.11) is beautifully presented, though somewhat graphics-intensive and therefore slow. You can get advice on child-rearing from various experts or explore very nice material with your children.

Chapter 8 All Sorts of Stuff for Parents

Figure 8.11
Family Planet Home Page.

Family Planet has a number of really good resources for parents:

- The Parents Resource Almanac (an index to books on virtually any parenting topic)

- Movie and book reviews

- Fun activities to do with kids

- Parents Choice Awards (choices for toys, videos, comics, and so on)

Note: If you have a slow modem you might want to view this site in text-only mode as it is graphically intensive. If you don't, you will find yourself waiting a long time for a page to load.

Parenting Newsletters

You can find virtually any kind of parenting newsletter on the Net. Are you a single working mother, a stay-at-home dad, a grandparent raising a grandchild? If you are one of these or anyone faced with raising children, you can probably find a support group or newsletter on the Net. Here are just a few of the choices available.

The At-Home Dad Newsletter

http://www.parentsplace.com/readroom/athomedad/index.html

This newsletter contains all sorts of commentary about life as a stay-at-home father (see Figure 8.12).

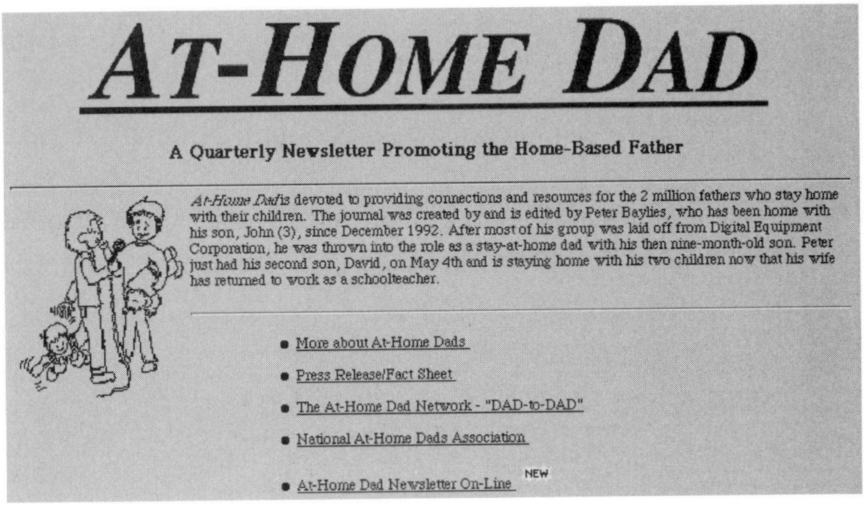

Figure 8.12
The At-Home Dad Newsletter.

Chapter 8 All Sorts of Stuff for Parents

For Divorced Parents

http://www.primenet.com/~dean/

Like many parents in our modern world, you might be someone who has to cope with parenting after a divorce. If so, this site is a worthwhile stop (see Figure 8.13).

Figure 8.13
The Divorce Page.

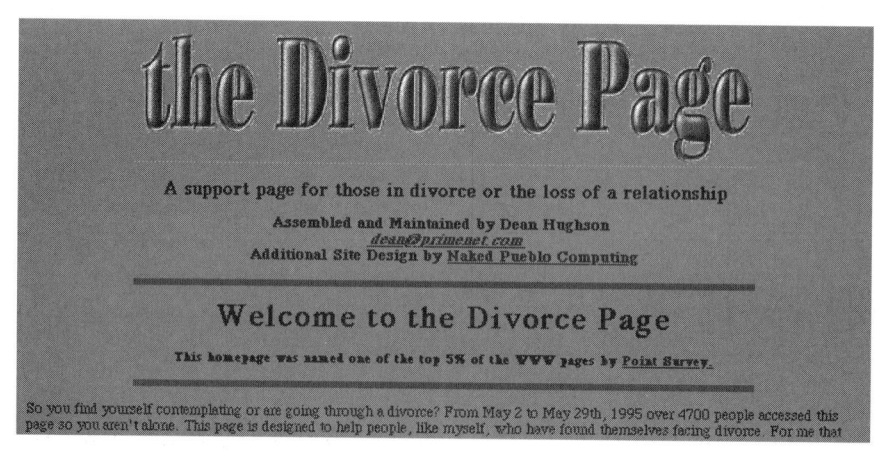

Parents of Twins

http://www.twinsmagazine.com/

While I can't imagine the amount of trouble that comes with having two children at once, there are some people who know all about it. If you want a newsletter for double installment children, Twins Magazine would be a good stop (see Figure 8.14).

Figure 8.14
Twins Magazine.

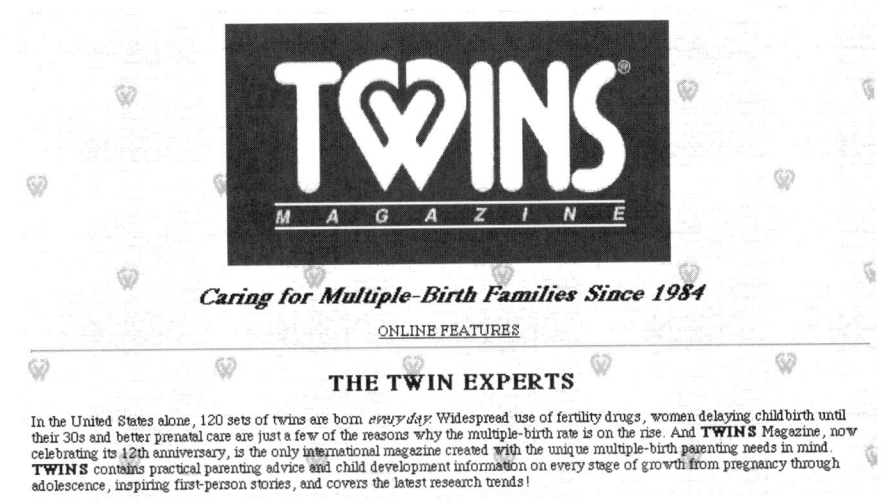

Family Home Pages

At some point in your Net adventures you will contemplate creating a Web page for your family. Why not check out some of the pioneer families who have gone before you. Here are just a few samples…

A British Family Home Page

http://ds.dial.pipex.com/ian.grey/

We can start our international tour with a stop in Great Britain. Here is a British family to get to know (see Figure 8.15).

214   Chapter 8   All Sorts of Stuff for Parents

Figure 8.15 The Grey's Home Page.

Ian and Karen Grey's Home Page

- Welcome to our home page. As we are limited to 0.5 Meg, don't expect to find too much here! Some of our hobbies and Interests:

  - Eighteen Plus
  - Walt Disney World
  - Joe Jackson
  - John Shuttleworth

  - Theatre & Cinema architecture
  - Stage Lighting (mainly historical)
  - Dinosaurs (TV show)

Ian is a freelance Project Engineer working in Telecommunications and Entertainment Technology. Karen is a Manager for British Telecom Operator Services. We live in Morley, a small town in Leeds, West Yorkshire, England, UK. As people have asked us to elaborate, Leeds is the Capital of Yorkshire, about 200 miles north of London, higher than the Midlands (capital Birmingham), lower than the North East (Capital Newcastle upon Tyne).
We can be contacted by e-mail at: ian.grey@dial.pipex.com

An American Family Home Page

http://www.redshift.com/~deutsch/

Our American family is opposed to Net censorship (see Figure 8.16).

Figure 8.16 The home page of Rick, Amy, Matt & Zach.

Welcome to "A-Nother Site"

Home of Rick, Amy, Matt & Zach

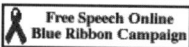

THE ONLY WAY THEY'LL TAKE MY INTERNET AWAY IS WHEN THEY PRY MY COLD, DEAD FINGERS FROM MY KEYBOARD!

Free Speech Online Blue Ribbon Campaign
Join the Blue Ribbon Anti-Censorship Campaign!

An Australian Family Home Page

http://ourworld.compuserve.com/homepages/David_Martin/

We go in an opposite direction to visit our next family. This time our stop is down under in Australia (see Figure 8.17).

Figure 8.17 The Martin home page.

The Martin Family HomePage

Hi! We're a family of four living in Canberra, Australia. In many ways we're typical of many other families in Australia and the rest of the western world - both parents working, two kids, a mortgage and all the rest of it ...

A Kathmandu, Nepal Family Home Page

http://home.supernova.net/~rjpsingh/Singh/

Figure 8.18 The Singh Family home page.

Singh Family Home Page

Life: Indulgence vs Seeking Truth, which is your forte? - Sinfay_Khalifa

Welcome to Singh Family Home Page! This home page is evolving.

This family page is dedicated to decendents of Ram Krishna Singh of former Tulsipur Rajya, now present day Dang Deukhuri Tulsipur, Nepal. Immediate anchestors of Ram Krishna Singh migrated from former State of Tulsipur, India during the Moghul invasion of North-West Indian frontier. Decendents of Ram Krishna Singh moved to Kathmandu in 1850 A.D. A short VANSHAVALI is available.

Here are some of the interesting sites via the World Wide Web:

- Global Nepali Orgaization Home Page TND Foundations
- Home Page Provider SuperNova Technologies and SuperNova-NEPAL Technologies
- Search the Web - Your Roadmap to Internet via Infoseek or Yahoo

If you want to visit with some people from Katmandu, then this is a good place to start (see Figure 8.18).

A Japanese Family Home Page

http://www.st.rim.or.jp/~tate/index.html

To add to your international experience, here is a Japanese page to admire (see Figure 8.19).

Figure 8.19
The Tatebayashi Family home page.

Another thing that makes this page nice is that you can view it in either Japanese or English. Further, each member of the Tatebayashi family has her or his own home page, which you can reach by clicking on the corresponding buttons at the bottom of the page.

Yahoo's Complete List of Families

http://www.yahoo.com/Entertainment/People/Families/

Yahoo lists a ton of home pages of families from all over the world. A fun thing to do is search for a family with interests similar to yours and correspond with them. You can also look for a family who lives in a place you have always wanted to learn about and write to them.

Chapter 9
How to Find Things on the Net

Covered in This Chapter

Finding People
Finding a Certain Topic
Going to the Library

Finding what you want on the Net can be a daunting task. There is so much stuff that sometimes it can be hard to figure out where to start. For example, how do you:

- Find some long-lost relative or friend on the Net?

- Research homework on the Net?

- Find out if a place is a good vacation spot?

- And, last but not least, find the really interesting sites without wading through all the boring ones?

Finding People

Yes, it's true. The Net is the ultimate finder of lost loves. Do you wonder what happened to that best friend of yours from college? Chances are getting better every day that she or he is somewhere on the Net. If so, you can email a hello from the past.

What if you don't want to find someone who is lost but someone who is new? Maybe your child or classroom wants a pen pal from Japan or Peru. If so, what better way to correspond than over the Net?

Finding an Old Friend

I think the Alta Vista search engine is the best way to find an old friend.

> http://altavista.digital.com/

Provided to you by the good folks at Digital Equipment Corporation, this is one of the best and fastest search engines on the Net (see Figure 9.1). Introduced in the Fall of 1995, this searching engine efficiently handles over 2 million requests per day. Because it searches not only the titles of documents but the contents of them as well, it does a great job of finding things. It also searches in a variety of places, including newsgroups and Web sites.

Figure 9.1 The Alta Vista Home Page.

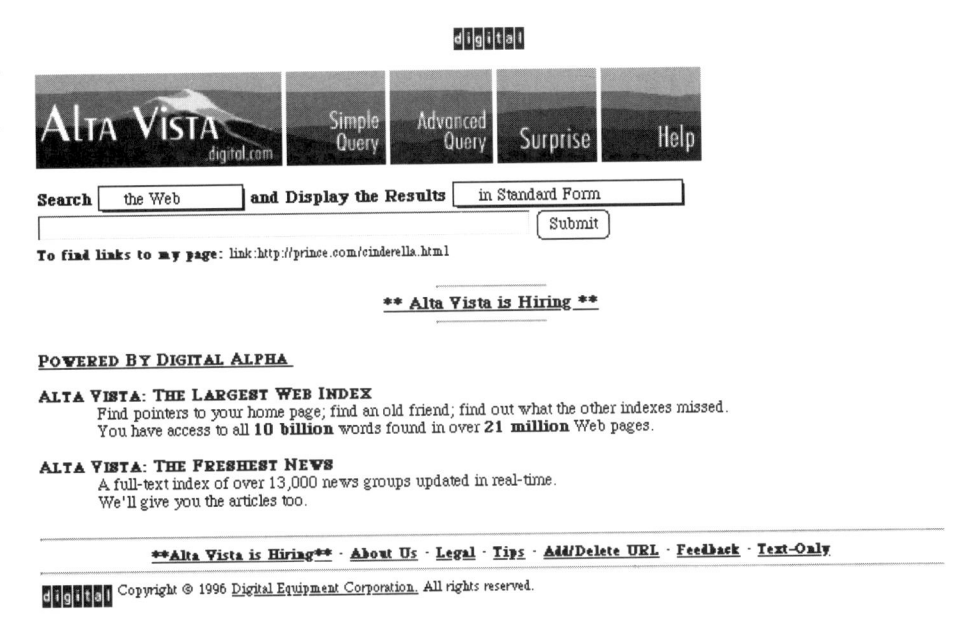

Using a Search Engine

You use this search engine by entering the name of the person you are looking for in the Search box. You surround the person's name (such as Jane Doe) with double quote marks, like this:

"jane doe"

This tells the search engine to look for that exact name and ignore things like "Jane has a doe as a pet."

Finding Someone with a Common Name

Let's go find someone to show you how it works. Mark Anderson is a friend of mine who I haven't talked to for a couple of years. Let's see if I can find him (see Figure 9.2). Figure 9.3 shows the result of that search:

Figure 9.2 First Attempt to Find Someone.

Search [the Web] and Display the Results [in Standard Form]
["Mark Anderson"]   [Submit]

Figure 9.3 First search for Mark Anderson.

Word count: Mark Anderson: about 1000
Documents 1-10 of about 1000 matching some of the query terms, best matches first.

Alta Vista found me about 1000 sites with the name Mark Anderson somewhere in them. Clearly, I do not want to wade through all of these to find my friend, so I need to narrow the search. Before doing that, however, I need to make two important points about looking for someone.

- People with common names are hard to pinpoint.

- People with unusual names are easy to locate, if they are on the Net at all.

If you are looking for someone named "Loring Fiske-Phillips," you will find him on the first attempt. If you are looking for a guy named John Smith, you get a whopping number of returns (Figure 9.4).

Figure 9.4 Two Name Searches, One Common, One Not.

Word count: Loring Fiske Phillips: 7
Documents 1-7 of 7 matching some of the query terms, best matches first.

Word count: John Smith: about 7000
Documents 1-10 of about 5000 matching some of the query terms, best matches first.

Narrowing the Search

Anyway, let's get back to finding my friend, Mark Anderson. Now I am going to add another criterion to help narrow the search. I know he teaches somewhere in Baltimore. Figure 9.5 shows what my search yields with this addition.

Figure 9.5 Second Search for Mark Anderson.

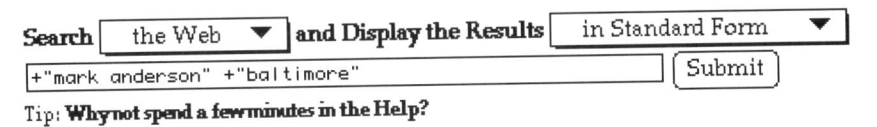

Search [the Web ▼] and Display the Results [in Standard Form ▼]
[+"mark anderson" +"baltimore"   ] [Submit]
Tip: **Why not spend a few minutes in the Help?**

Word count: mark anderson: about 1000, baltimore:203353

Documents 1-10 of 36 matching some of the query terms, best matches first.

That helped quite a bit. However, I'd still rather not wade through 36 matches. I also know that he got his bachelor's degree from Harvey Mudd college. Let's try the name of the college as a further narrowing criterion. To do that, we enter all three items (see Figure 9.6) like this:

+"mark anderson" +"maryland" +"harvey mudd"

Rule of Thumb: I didn't use uppercase letters in my search because of how the search engine works. It assumes nothing about case if you use lowercase letters. If you use uppercase letters, the engine only returns exact matches of words exactly like you typed them.

This may not be a problem with a name like anderson but definitely is with "mckeehan." If you search for "Mckeehan" it will not return "mckeehan" or "McKeehan," for example. As a rule of thumb, use lowercase letters.

Note that a "+" character before a phrase specifies to Alta Vista that the phrase is required; without a "+," the phrase is optional and won't help in narrowing down the search. With all three of these required phrases, we have a fairly

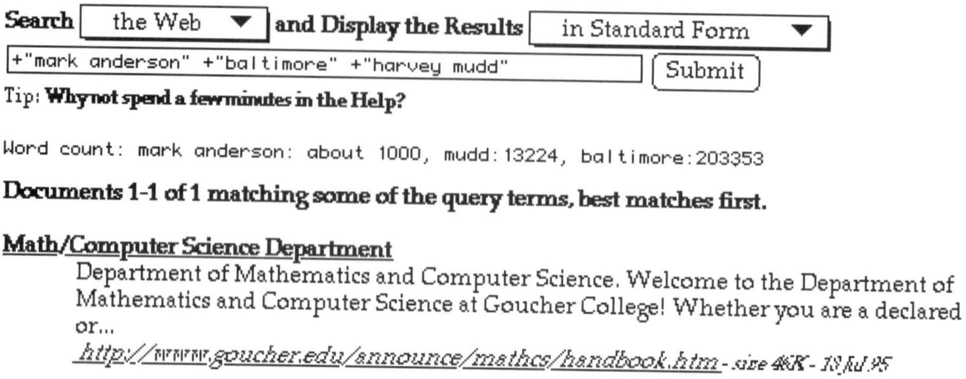

Chapter 9 How to Find Things on the Net

Figure 9.6
Third Search for Mark Anderson.

Search [the Web ▼] and Display the Results [in Standard Form ▼]
[+"mark anderson" +"baltimore" +"harvey mudd"] [Submit]
Tip: **Why not spend a few minutes in the Help?**

Word count: mark anderson: about 1000, mudd: 13224, baltimore: 203353

Documents 1-1 of 1 matching some of the query terms, best matches first.

Math/Computer Science Department
 Department of Mathematics and Computer Science. Welcome to the Department of Mathematics and Computer Science at Goucher College! Whether you are a declared or...
 http://wwww.goucher.edu/announce/mathcs/handbook.htm - size 46K - 19 Jul 95

narrow search. Indeed, Alta Vista returns exactly one site that fits the bill. Let's take a look and see if that is my friend. When I get to the site Alta Vista found, I do a **Find** on "Mark Anderson" to see where his name is in that document (see Figure 9.7).

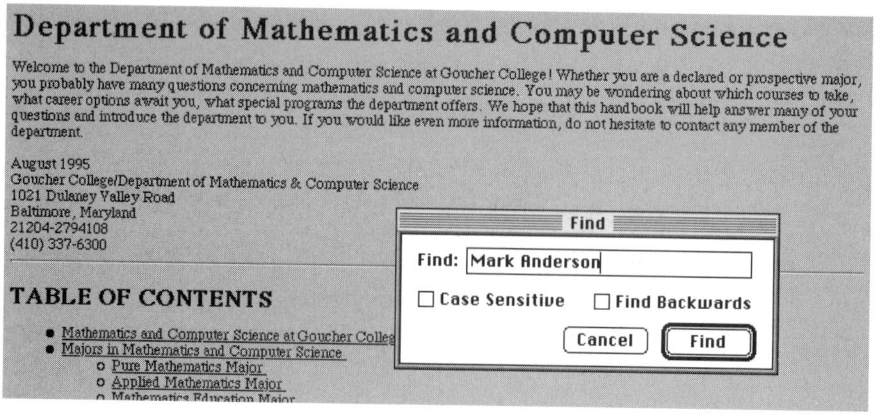

Figure 9.7
Looking for Mark in a Site.

Department of Mathematics and Computer Science

Welcome to the Department of Mathematics and Computer Science at Goucher College! Whether you are a declared or prospective major, you probably have many questions concerning mathematics and computer science. You may be wondering about which courses to take, what career options await you, what special programs the department offers. We hope that this handbook will help answer many of your questions and introduce the department to you. If you would like even more information, do not hesitate to contact any member of the department.

August 1995
Goucher College/Department of Mathematics & Computer Science
1021 Dulaney Valley Road
Baltimore, Maryland
21204-2794108
(410) 337-6300

--- Find ---
Find: [Mark Anderson]
☐ Case Sensitive   ☐ Find Backwards
[Cancel] [Find]

TABLE OF CONTENTS
- Mathematics and Computer Science at Goucher Colle
- Majors in Mathematics and Computer Science
  - Pure Mathematics Major
  - Applied Mathematics Major
  - Mathematics Education Major

Having done that find, I get the faculty member shown in Figure 9.8. This is indeed my friend, who I can now call or email to find out how he has been for the last couple of years.

*Figure 9.8
The Found Mark Anderson.*

THE FACULTY

MARK ANDERSON

- B.S. (Mathematics) Harvey Mudd College
- M.S. (Computer Science) University of California, San Diego
- Ph.D. (Computer Science) University of California, San Diego

As an undergraduate, I majored in mathematics. During my junior year a class in the theory of computation captured my attention. My senior research project was to implement a matrix computation algorithm on a prototype parallel architecture related to systolic arrays. So when it came time to apply to graduate school I decided to pursue computer science. Although not my original intention upon entering graduate school, my dissertation ended up dealing with systolic arrays. I've held a variety of jobs in the computer field from programmer, to system administrator, to user support consultant working on machines as diverse as the Macintosh and the Cray. My theoretical background was an asset on every one of these jobs. An employer once said, "There is nothing more practical than theory." I emphasize this to students and stress the necessity of a strong theoretical background.

Remember, when running a search to find someone, the important thing is to add keywords that will distinguish who you are looking for from any one else. You should also read the help sections on search engines to determine the correct way to notate a search for that particular engine.

Finding a New Pen Pal

Finding a pen pal, or whole class or school, to correspond with is a much different sort of problem. First, I recommend that you search in **Yahoo** on the word "pen pal" (see Figure 9.9).

*Figure 9.9
Yahoo Search Request.*

Such a search will yield more than enough material (see Figure 9.10). Now all you have to do is look through these 20 sites to see which contains the most appropriate pen pal information.

Figure 9.10
Yahoo Search Results.

Yahoo Search Results

Found 20 matches containing **pen pal**. Displaying matches 1-20.

Here are Some of the Results:

Society and Culture:Friendship:**Pen Pals**

- Cafe Vanda's Mail-**Pal** Page
- Canadian International **Penfriends** - a postal **penpal** service published on a quarterly basis. Free listings by email!
- E-Mail Key **Pal** Connection
- Grandparent **Pen Pals** - a **pen pal** list for grandparents. includes grandparents that are participating in our 'surrogate grandparent/mentor' program.
- Intercultural E-Mail Classroom Connections - free service to help teachers and classes link with partners in other countries and cultures for e-mail classroom **pen-pal** and project exchanges
- L.B. Alberti **Pen-Pal** Connection
- **Pen Pal** Connection [HLC]
- **Pen Pal** Page [bestmall.com]
- **Pen Pal** Page [dds.nl] - A Page for People who searching for **Pen**/Key **pals**.
- **Penpal** Chat - Webchat Broadcasting System
- **Penpal** Connection - browse ads or place free online **penpal** ads. Primarily serving the gay community.
- **Penpal** Lists (Email and Snail)
- Soccer **Pen Pal** Connection - Soccer loving kids from around the world share thoughts, stories, ideas, and more.
- TCM - **Pen Pal** - A place for students to be matched with other students for Internet **Pen Pals**. More to be added later.

Finding a Certain Topic

As any good librarian will tell you, searching is a refined and sophisticated art. Happily, there are a number of places on the Net that make this task much easier. First, let's take a look at how a child could use the Net to research a topic for a homework assignment. Next, we will talk about how you can find something for yourself. Last, we will visit the library.

Homework Research

A good first stop for children looking up a topic is an encyclopedia. The Net offers kids a couple of wonderful resources for this. I would, however, always start off such a project with a search in **Yahoo's** Reference section in case new encyclopedias have been added (see Figure 9.11):

http://www.yahoo.com/Reference/

Figure 9.11 Yahoo's Reference Section.

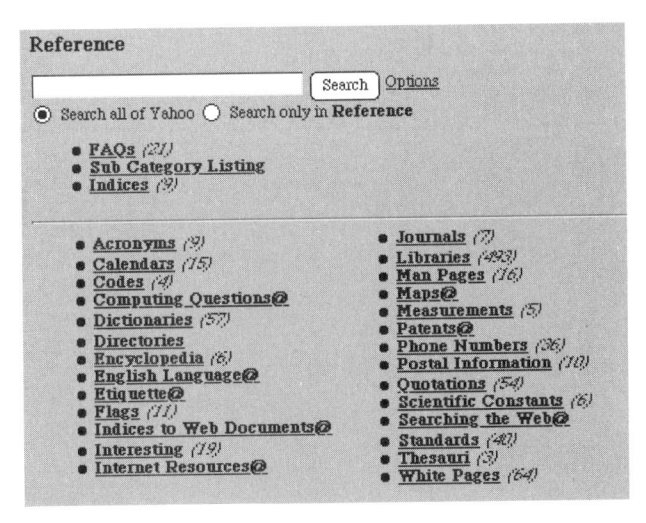

Here you can find all sorts of lovely things, like dictionaries, quotations, thesauri, and, as the next stop, encyclopedias.

Encyclopaedia Britannica

The *Encyclopaedia Britannica* has entered the information age, and so can you. At Britannica's Web site, you can go through the risk-free sign up process (that means no credit card information) to get a 7-day free trial (see Figure 9.12).

226   Chapter 9   How to Find Things on the Net

---

http://www.eb.com/

Figure 9.12 Home Page of Encyclopaedia Britannica.

BRITANNICA

An Information Service from the Editors of *Encyclopaedia Britannica*

Welcome to *Britannica Online*, the first encyclopedia on the Internet!

From the editors of the *Encyclopaedia Britannica*, *Britannica Online* combines the authority and breadth of the highly respected print version of *Britannica* with the vast resources of the Internet to put reliable and comprehensive information at your fingertips. Sign up for a free trial or an annual subscription, or try some of the free features on this page.

Besides all the normal subjects you would expect to find in an encyclopedia, Britannica also has a couple of new features that include:

- Information on all the nations of the world
- Important events of the Year (1993 and 1994)
- And much, much more (see Figure 9.13)

Figure 9.13 Britannica's Features.

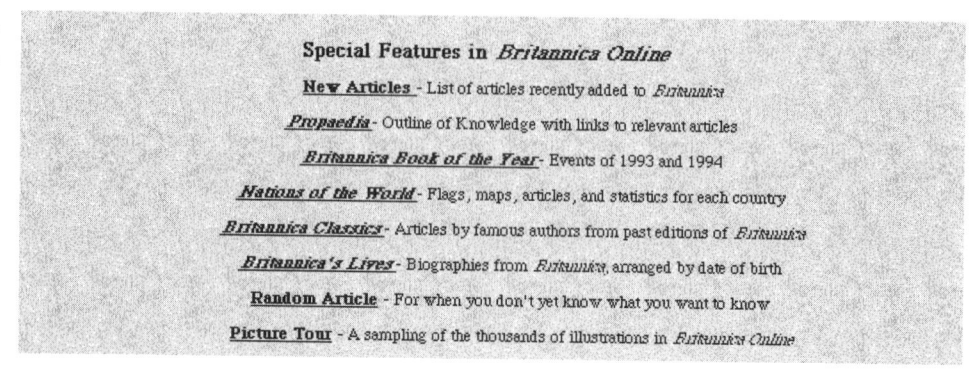

Special Features in *Britannica Online*

New Articles - List of articles recently added to *Britannica*
Propaedia - Outline of Knowledge with links to relevant articles
Britannica Book of the Year - Events of 1993 and 1994
Nations of the World - Flags, maps, articles, and statistics for each country
Britannica Classics - Articles by famous authors from past editions of *Britannica*
Britannica's Lives - Biographies from *Britannica*, arranged by date of birth
Random Article - For when you don't yet know what you want to know
Picture Tour - A sampling of the thousands of illustrations in *Britannica Online*

What Does Britannica Cost?

You subscribe to this encyclopedia service on a yearly basis. The fees vary some depending upon who you are:

Personal/Family $150 per year ($25 one time charge)
College Student $120 per year
Business $300 per year ($50 one time charge)

Subject Searching in Britannica

One of the really nice things about this encyclopedia is that you can use natural language to look for things. That means I can type sentences like this when searching:

- "Why is Mars red?"
- "How long do flies live?"
- "What is the difference between fission and fusion?"

Figure 9.14 shows an example of a search in Britannica.

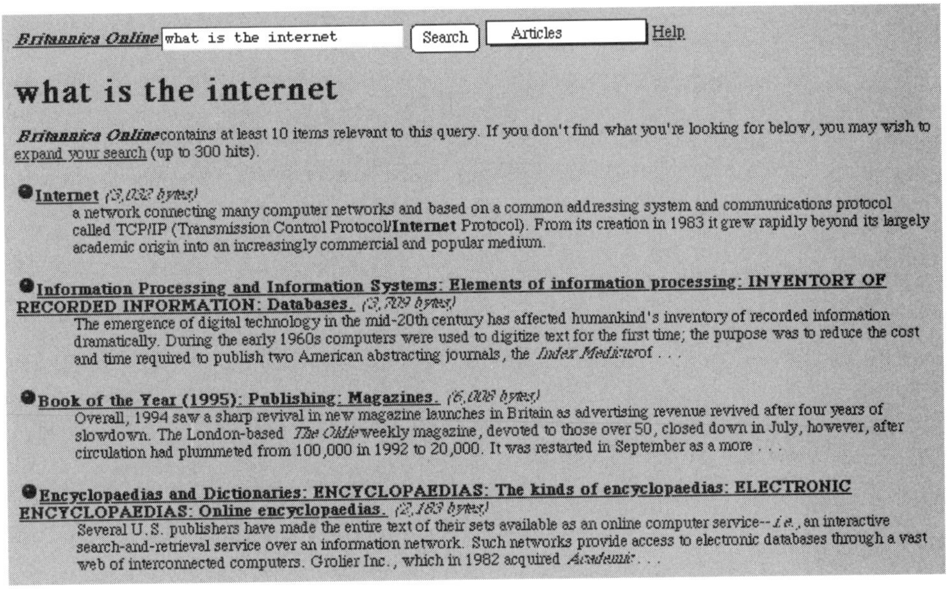

Figure 9.14 Subject Search in Britannica.

Chapter 9 How to Find Things on the Net

Having found all these lovely articles on the Internet, all you have to do is open one to find the answer. In this case, I opened the first one (see Figure 9.15).

Figure 9.15 What is the Internet.

Internet,

a (INDEX) network connecting many computer networks and based on a common addressing system and communications protocol called TCP/IP (Transmission Control Protocol/**Internet** Protocol). From its creation in 1983 it grew rapidly beyond its largely academic origin into an increasingly commercial and popular medium.

By mid-1994 the **Internet** connected an estimated two million computers in more than 100 countries, serving some 23 million users. Many commercial computer network and data services also provided at least indirect connection to the **Internet**.

The primary uses of the **Internet** are (INDEX) electronic mail (commonly called "e-mail"), file transfer (using ftp, or file transfer protocol), bulletin boards and newsgroups, and remote computer access (telnet). More recent developments have made possible book and magazine publishing, video conferencing, and audio broadcasts.

The **Internet** had its origin in a U.S. (INDEX) Department of Defense program called ARPANET (Advanced Research Projects Agency Network), established in 1969 to provide a secure and survivable communications network for organizations engaged in defense-related research. Researchers and academics in other fields began to make use of the network, and at length the (INDEX) National Science Foundation (NSF), which had created a similar and parallel network called NSFNet, took over much of the TCP/IP technology from ARPANET and established a distributed network of networks capable of handling far greater traffic. NSF continues to maintain the backbone of the network (which carries data at a rate of 45 million bits per second), but **Internet** protocol development is governed by the **Internet** Architecture Board, and the InterNIC (**Internet** Network Information Center) administers the naming of computers and networks.

Amateur radio, cable television wires, spread spectrum radio, satellite, and fibre optics all have been used to deliver **Internet** services. Networked games, networked monetary transactions, and virtual museums are among applications being developed that both extend the network's utility and test the limits of its technology. (B.Ka.)

Another sort of question you can ask is "Why do camels spit?" (see Figure 9.16).

Figure 9.16 Why Do Camels spit?

camel

(INDEX) (genus *Camelus*), either of two large ruminating mammals (family Camelidae, order Artiodactyla) used as draft and saddle animals in desert regions, especially of Africa and Asia. The (INDEX) Arabian **camel**, or dromedary (*C. dromedarius*), has only one hump, but the (INDEX) Bactrian **camel** (*C. bactrianus*) has two. The limbs are long, and the feet have no traces of the second and fifth toes; the wide-spreading soft feet are adapted for walking upon sand or snow. Horny pads on the chest and knees support the weight when kneeling. The animals run with a characteristic pacing gait, the legs on each side moving in unison. In adaptation to wind-blown deserts and other unfavourable environments, **camels** have double rows of protective eyelashes, haired ear openings, the ability to close the nostrils, and keen senses of sight and smell. **Camels** are docile when properly trained and handled but, especially in the rutting season, are liable to fits of rage. They **spit** when annoyed and can bite and kick dangerously.

Britannica is very good at answering general subject questions like:

- "What caused World War I?"
- "What is pottery & what is its history?"
- "Where does metal come from?"

It is also pretty good at answering current event questions such as:

- "What caused the war in Bosnia?"
- "What problems does Israel face in the modern world?"

All in all, if you have several children in school who are writing reports on a regular basis, this service can be a very good deal. The only thing that tends to scare people off is having to pay the service fee up front ($150). If you average that out over 12 months, however, it will look more attractive ($12.50 per month).

Electric Library

http://www.elibrary.com/

Another encyclopedia service that you can subscribe to is the Electric Library. It uses a different approach to collecting information. It accesses a wide variety of newspapers, magazines, television, and radio interviews, all of which are part of its database of information.

What Does Electric Library Cost?

This is also a fee-based encyclopedia service.

Monthly Cost $9.95 (available 20 hours per day)

Subject Searching in Electric Library

Electric Library has a searching engine that allows you to ask questions in English. If you look in Figure 9.17, you will see the type of question that a student could ask.

Chapter 9 How to Find Things on the Net

Figure 9.17
Using the Electric Library.

The Electric Library then returns the search results in order of how many of the words were matched in the citation (see Figure 9.18). It also provides other information about the item, including:

- How good a match it was

- The name of the article/report

- The type of source (magazine, radio)

- The date and size of file

- The reading level required for comprehension

Saving the best for last, when you open one of the citations you can use the thoughtfully provided "GO TO" button to go directly to the most relevant portion of the article. The matched words are also bolded (Figure 9.19).

Electric Library offers a free evaluation visit, and I suggest that you use it to decide if this is a good service for you. What I found was that it was a fairly good resource for researching a current event (such as global warming or the

*Figure 9.18
Results from Electric Library Search.*

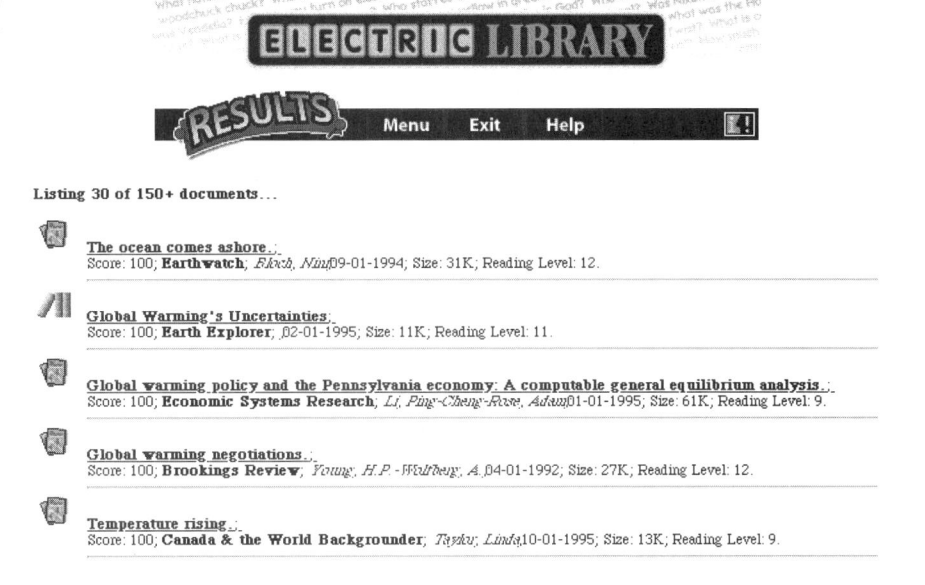

Bosnian war). It was not very helpful for researching a more general topic (such as: "What caused World War I?" or "Why do camels spit?").

*Figure 9.19
An Article on Global Warming.*

232   Chapter 9 How to Find Things on the Net

Other Encyclopedias and Dictionaries

It is also worth checking out the other offerings. Currently, there are several encyclopedias, dictionaries, and reference items worth looking into.

The Free Internet Encyclopedia

---
http://www.cs.uh.edu/~clifton/ encyclopedia.html

The Free Internet Encyclopedia is both very good and free (see Figure 9.20). It is the brainchild of Cliff Davis and Margaret Adamson Fincannon. While they do not write the articles (those were written by folks all over the Net) they do a great indexing job to help you find a subject. The encyclopedia is divided into two sections:

- a MacroReference Section
- a MicroReference Section

Figure 9.20
The Free Internet Encyclopedia.

Supporting Access to Information
The FREE Internet Encyclopedia

Free Speech Online
Blue Ribbon Campaign

Free Internet Encyclopedia

Beta test Version 1.0 - Created and Maintained by Clif Davis and Margaret Adamson Fincannon, MLS

This Page Under Construction and only partially spellchecked!!

The MacroReference... ...The MicroReference... ...Credits... ...Editorial...
...What's New and Coming ...Your Comments ...The FAQ

What is this anyway?

This is an encyclopedia composed of information available on the Internet. There are two main divisions. The MacroReference contains references to large areas of knowledge, FAQs where available, and pointers to relevant areas of the MicroReference. The MicroReference contains short bits of information and references to specific subjects, sometimes with instructions on finding the specific subject inside a general reference. Each specific subject will reference its general subject in the MacroReference if one is present.

The MacroReference Section

This area contains references to wide areas of knowledge. In fact, it is better to think of this section as one large alphabetic index to material. By using this index you can get to a particular site. You will find that the sites it references vary in quality and format (I found most to be quite good). An example of some of the material you can find in a section is shown in Figure 9.21. To give you some idea about the kind of site you might find, here is a sample article about learning a foreign language (see Figure 9.22).

Figure 9.21 The MacroReference Section.

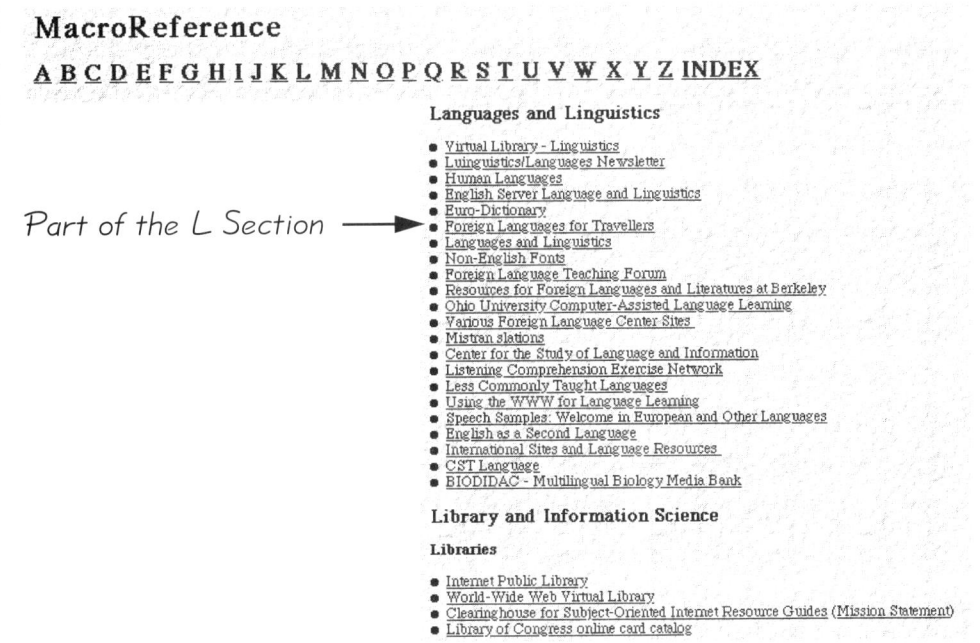

MacroReference
A B C D E F G H I J K L M N O P Q R S T U V W X Y Z INDEX

Languages and Linguistics

- Virtual Library - Linguistics
- Luinguistics/Languages Newsletter
- Human Languages
- English Server Language and Linguistics
- Euro-Dictionary
- Foreign Languages for Travellers
- Languages and Linguistics
- Non-English Fonts
- Foreign Language Teaching Forum
- Resources for Foreign Languages and Literatures at Berkeley
- Ohio University Computer-Assisted Language Learning
- Various Foreign Language Center Sites
- Mistran slations
- Center for the Study of Language and Information
- Listening Comprehension Exercise Network
- Less Commonly Taught Languages
- Using the WWW for Language Learning
- Speech Samples: Welcome in European and Other Languages
- English as a Second Language
- International Sites and Language Resources
- CST Language
- BIODIDAC - Multilingual Biology Media Bank

Library and Information Science

Libraries

- Internet Public Library
- World-Wide Web Virtual Library
- Clearinghouse for Subject-Oriented Internet Resource Guides (Mission Statement)
- Library of Congress online card catalog

Part of the L Section →

The MicroReference Section

This area contains short bits of information and references to particular subjects that can also be found in the general reference area (see Figure 9.23). The Free Internet Encyclopedia is certainly a nice place to wander around in and it contains some very nice links to material. While it does not offer the powerful natural language searching capabilities found in the Encyclopedia Britannica or Electric Encyclopedia, it is free.

234 Chapter 9 How to Find Things on the Net

*Figure 9.22
The VCU Trail Guide Site.*

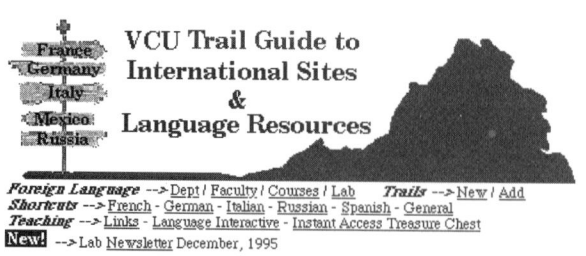

VCU Trail Guide to International Sites & Language Resources

Foreign Language --> Dept / Faculty / Courses / Lab   Trails --> New / Add
Shortcuts --> French - German - Italian - Russian - Spanish - General
Teaching --> Links - Language Interactive - Instant Access Treasure Chest
New! --> Lab Newsletter December, 1995

Scenic Side Trails

WebMuseum (English) Ever-expanding gallery of art & music, plus tour of Paris
Wrapped Reichstag (German) Christo's lastest project in word and deed
Cuban Music (English/Spanish) Listen to sound samples from the forbidden Isle

Explore by Map

- Worldwide WWW sites (Virtual Tourist -- country by country list of servers)
- Country and City Guides (CityNet -- pointers to many other resources)

*Figure 9.23
The MicroReference Section.*

MicroReference

Select the first letter

A B C D E F G H I J K L M N O P Q R S T U V W X Y Z

A

Abbey, Edward

Academy Awards®

ACM
   Professional Computer Science dedicated to advancing information technology

Adams, Ansel

Adams, Douglas

Adobe Systems Incorporated

Yahoo's Dictionary Collection

http://www.yahoo.com/Reference/Dictionaries/

The next time you have Swedish relatives coming into town who do not speak a word of English you will have nothing to worry about. **Yahoo's** dictionary collection comes to the rescue. You can find translations of virtually any language into any other language (see Figure 9.24). There are also plenty of types of technical and subject specific dictionaries as well.

Figure 9.24 Yahoo's Dictionaries.

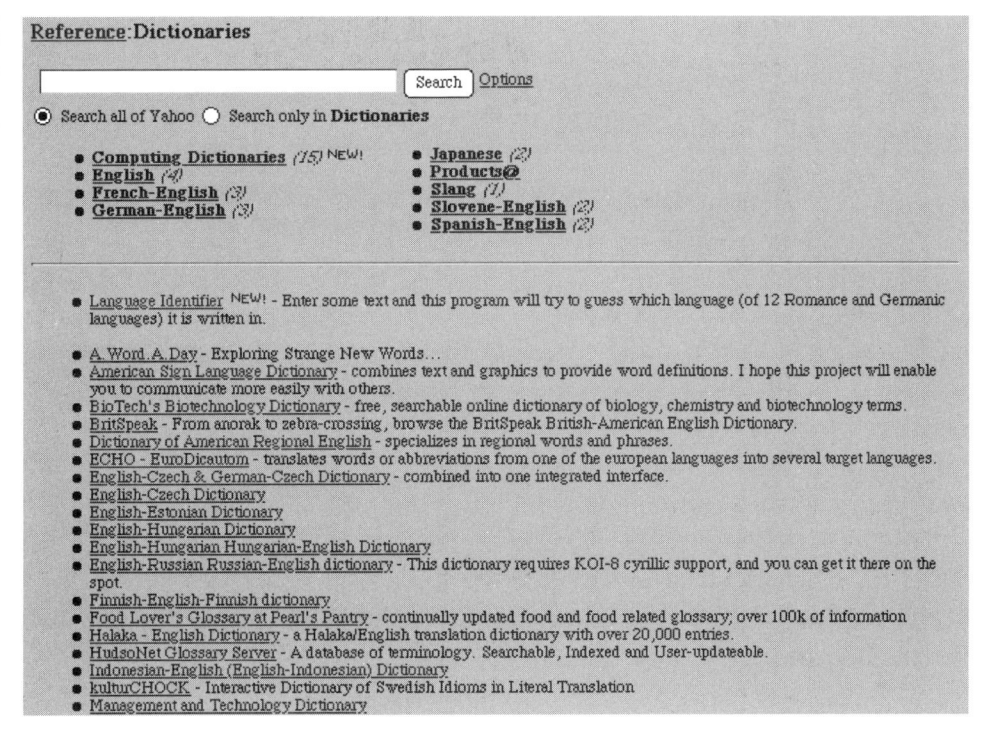

Using Net Search Engines

Okay, now it is time to talk about how you find a subject of interest. I recommend using Yahoo's search engine as a first attempt to find something. If that doesn't return any useful results, then it is time to turn to the heavy hitters. In this case, I recommend either of these two choices:

- Savvy Search
- MetaCrawler

Savvy Search – An International Search Engine

This is a great all-in-one search engine. This means that this engine will:

- submit your search to various search engines
- organize the results
- return the results in a standardized format

If that is not enough for you, it also allows you to search in any one of 15 different languages. If you look at Figure 9.25, you can see Savvy's Search's home page and some of the criteria it allows you to specify in a search.

http://www.cs.colostate.edu/ ~dreiling/smartform.html

Figure 9.25
The Savvy Search Page.

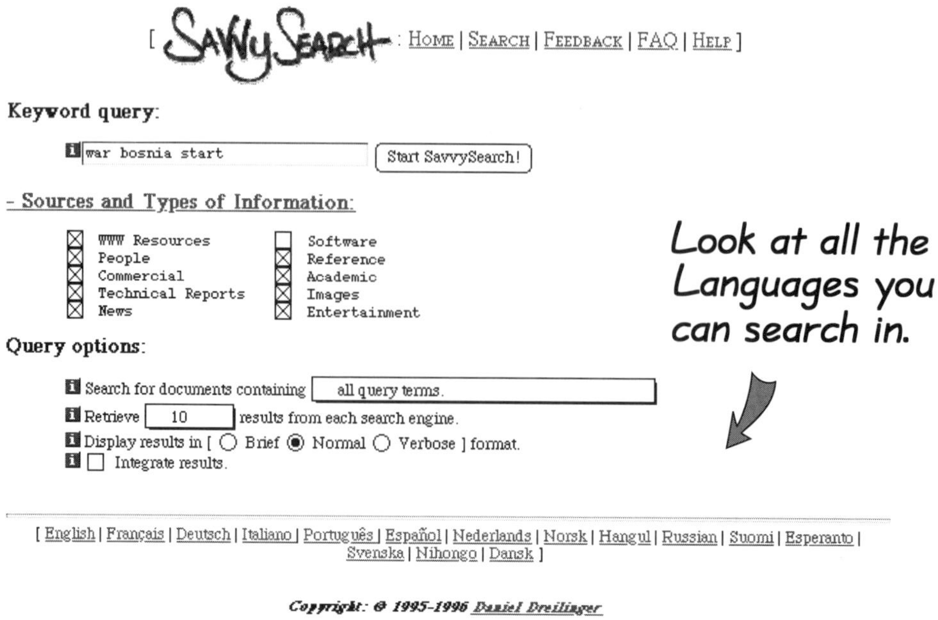

[SAVVY SEARCH : HOME | SEARCH | FEEDBACK | FAQ | HELP]

Keyword query:

[war bosnia start]   [Start SavvySearch!]

- Sources and Types of Information:

- ☒ WWW Resources
- ☒ People
- ☒ Commercial
- ☒ Technical Reports
- ☒ News
- ☐ Software
- ☒ Reference
- ☒ Academic
- ☒ Images
- ☒ Entertainment

Query options:

- Search for documents containing [all query terms].
- Retrieve [10] results from each search engine.
- Display results in [○ Brief ● Normal ○ Verbose] format.
- ☐ Integrate results.

Look at all the Languages you can search in.

[English | Français | Deutsch | Italiano | Português | Español | Nederlands | Norsk | Hangul | Russian | Suomi | Esperanto | Svenska | Nihongo | Dansk]

Copyright: © 1995-1996 Daniel Dreilinger

I did my standard query about what started the war in Bosnia. In this searching format, I entered keywords and chose between looking for any of the words, all of them, or an exact phrase. Here are the results that Savvy Search returned (see Figure 9.26).

Figure 9.26
Savvy Page Search Results.

AltaVista Results:

Bosnia War Hits Close to Home (AltaVista)
   Size: 8K, **Date**: 24 Jan 96
   Description: Bosnia War Hits Close to Home. by Melony Swasey Not long ago, Maja Markovic was like most high school students. She lived at home with her parents and younger brother in...
War in Bosnia (AltaVista)
   Size: 16K, **Date**: 30 Jul 95
   Description: My mission is to get the world to be a better place, specifically creating a set of new communities, not a single global community.' -- Esther Dyson. Mercury News photo...
War in Bosnia: Timeline (AltaVista)
   Size: 5K, **Date**: 9 Mar 95
   Description: War in Bosnia: Timeline. 1990-91. Croatia and Slovenia declare their independence from the Yugoslav Federated Republic. In Croatia ethnic Serbs and Croats begin a long,...
No Title (AltaVista)
   Size: 4K, **Date**: 15 Dec 95
   Description: Solutions. The war in Bosnia has raged on for more than four years now. Many attempts to halt the fighting have proven to be unsuccessful. For three years the United...
The war in Bosnia index (AltaVista)
   Size: 6K, **Date**: 14 Feb 96
   Description: 02/14/96 - 06:37 PM ET - Click reload often for latest version. The war in Bosnia index. Stories from December 1995. Additional stories are archived by month. Click on...

This searching engine did a great job locating material that answered my question. The only issue you would need to consider in using this type of research is the source of the information. When using something like *Encyclopaedia Britannica*, you have some notion of the quality of the scholarship. With a site found by SavvySearch, any bozo's opinion can show up in the material. This means you will have to evaluate each article returned on a case-by-case basis. It could be from a professor of history at Harvard or from a lunatic who lives on Mars.

MetaCrawler–A Slow But Thorough Searcher

MetaCrawler is another searcher that submits your query to a bunch of other search engines. The nice touch that this page adds is that you can optionally specify that it retrieve the reference as well, search it, and ensure that the docu-

238   Chapter 9   How to Find Things on the Net

ment really does contain the subject in question. This makes for slow but thorough searches. (Most searches do not actually open documents and look to see if they contain the relevant subject matter.)

With MetaCrawler, you can specify that all the words, any of the words, or a phrase is used in a search (see Figure 9.27):

http://metacrawler.cs.washington.edu:8080/index.html

Figure 9.27
The MetaCrawler Search Page.

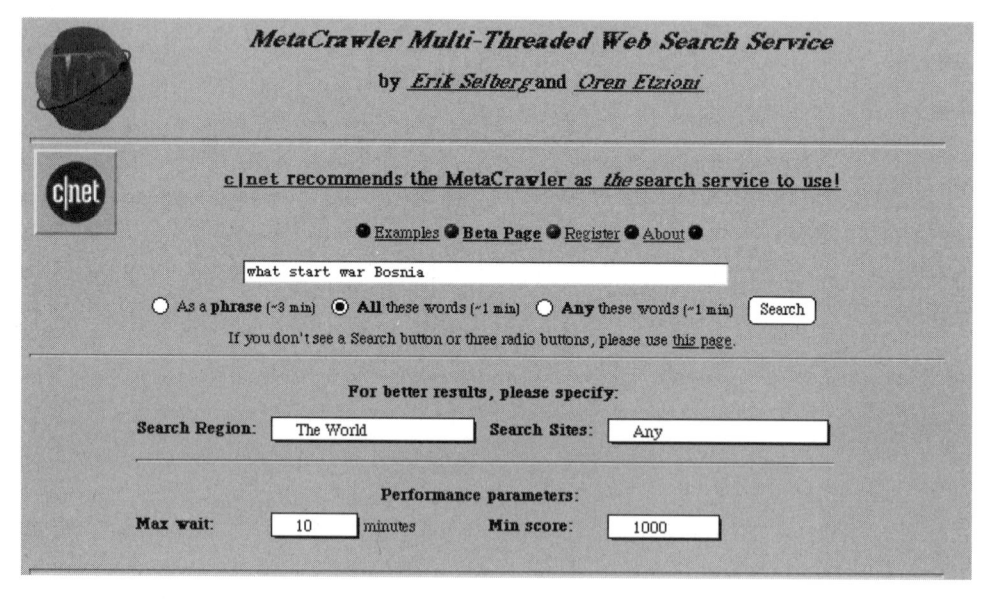

You can also limit the areas that you search to:

- particular continents
- your country
- the type of reference you want returned (that is, educational, commercial, military, and so on)

MetaCrawler is a very good choice as a search engine if you don't want to wade through a lot of material and you have the time to wait for an extended search. Conducting the search on "what start war bosnia" yielded these results after about a 5 minute wait (see Figure 9.28).

Figure 9.28 MetaCrawler Search Results.

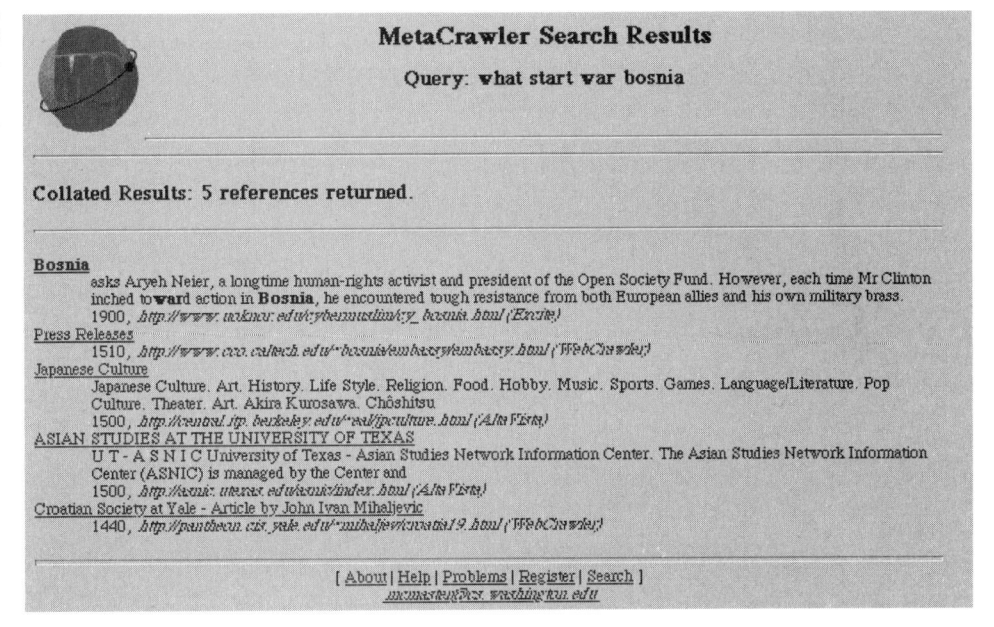

As was true of the other multi-engine searchers, the quality of the response is somewhat variable. You can limit the type of responses you get to a certain extent by specifying the field type (such as only educational references), but that doesn't guarantee that some clown won't be the one writing the article. Each article will need to be evaluated on a case-by-case basis as to whether it is written by someone with a respectable opinion.

Going to the Library

Where else would you go to find something interesting but to the library? Librarians are in the forefront of innovative content providers on the Net. They like this new medium, and many have done an amazing job of organizing material in new and useful ways. After checking out what is available on **Yahoo's** library page you can go see two of my favorite libraries.

The Smithsonian Library

http://www.sil.si.edu/

Figure 9.29
The Smithsonian Library Page.

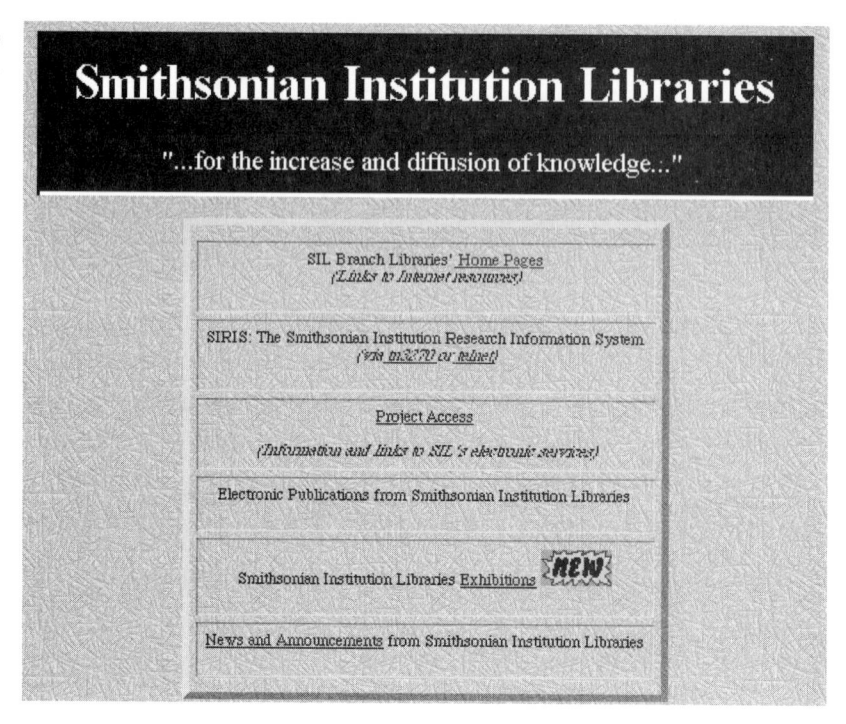

One of my favorite places on the Net, The Smithsonian, also has one of the best libraries (see Figure 9.29). This library offers abundant subjects and some very nice rooms to explore. One of my favorite sites here is **The National Museum of American History,** which is jam-packed with links to subjects like:

- Inventions
- History of computers
- Foundation information
- Museums, like the American Museum of Papermaking
- Libraries, such as the National Library of Medicine

The Internet Public Library

http://ipl.sils.umich.edu/

Another great library to explore is the Internet Public Library (see Figure 9.30). You can go into any one of a number of rooms and browse to your heart's content. For example, the Reading Room has publications from all over the world. You can read the *Pravda Press* from Czechoslovakia, *The St. Petersburg Press* from Russia, or *The Irish Times* from Ireland.

The children's section has delightful resources for even the littlest of children. These include:

- Chatting with authors about their books
- Doctor Internet, who explains the workings of math and science
- Writing Contests, and much, much more…

Figure 9.30
The Internet Public Library.

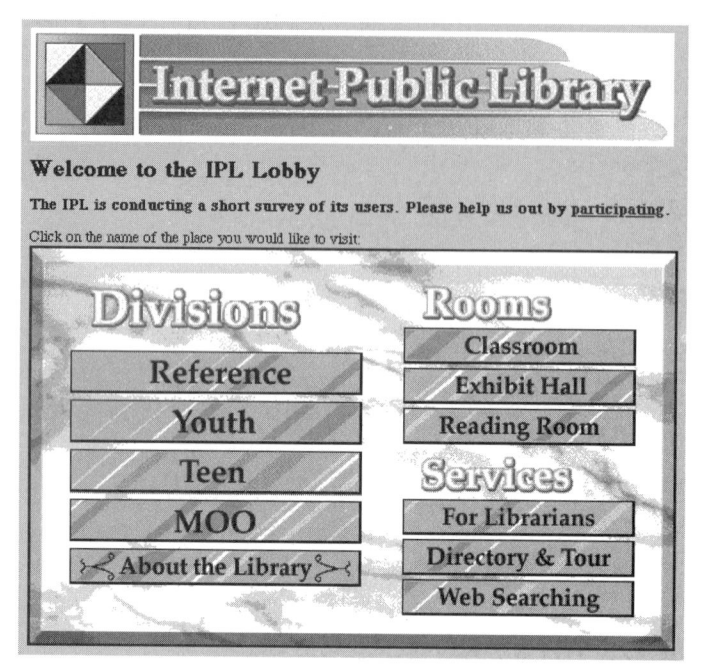

The Youth section contains lovely material for young children (see Figure 9.31).

Figure 9.31
The Internet Public Library, Youth Section.

Going to the Library   243

Children can go to Story Hour to read books aloud (see Figure 9.32).

Figure 9.32
The Internet Public Library, Story Hour.

And the books are full of delightful pictures and words (see Figure 9.33).

Figure 9.33
Do Spiders Live on the World Wide Web?

244 Chapter 9 How to Find Things on the Net

The Teen section is filled with music and movies, books, and college information (see Figure 9.34).

Figure 9.34 Teen Division of Internet Public Library.

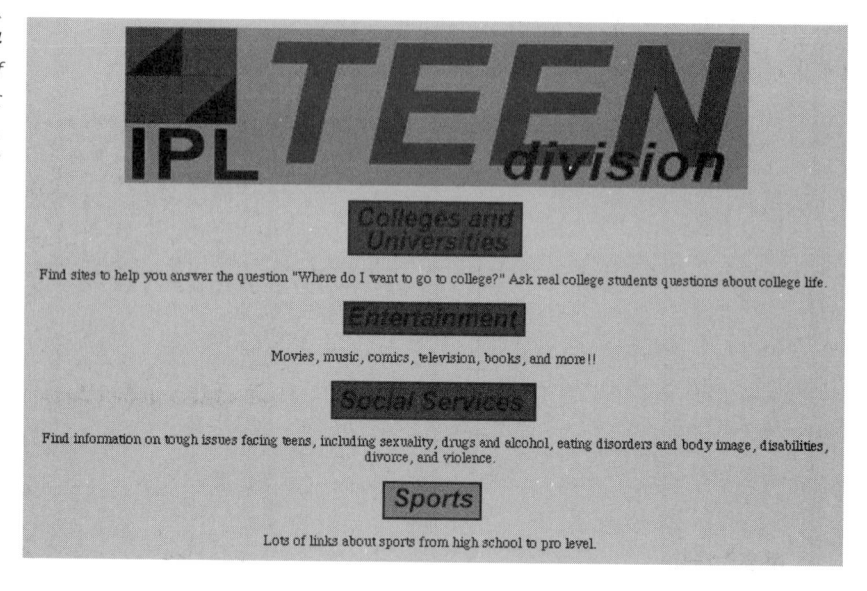

Plus, there is a Reference Center, where you can look through any number of wonderful things… (see Figure 9.35)

Figure 9.35 The Reference Room of the Internet Public Library.

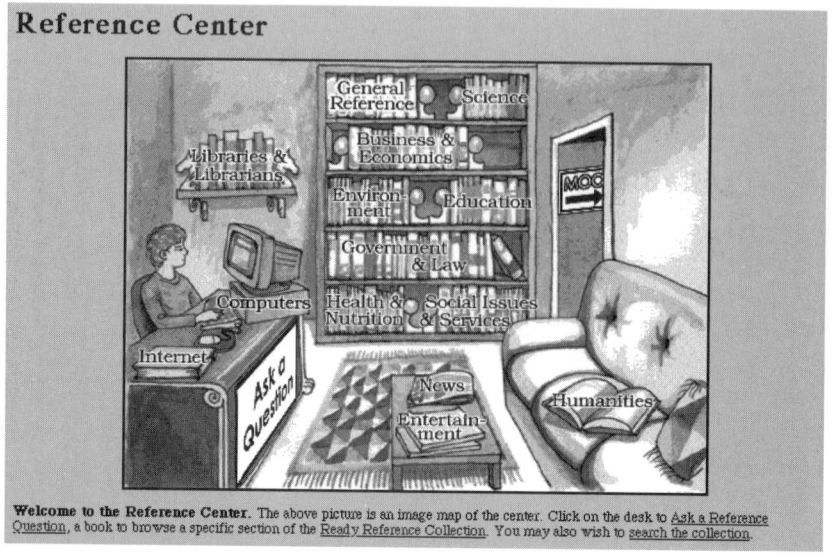

Best of all, there are no fines for overdue books!

Part Three

Being Safe on the Net

United Nations

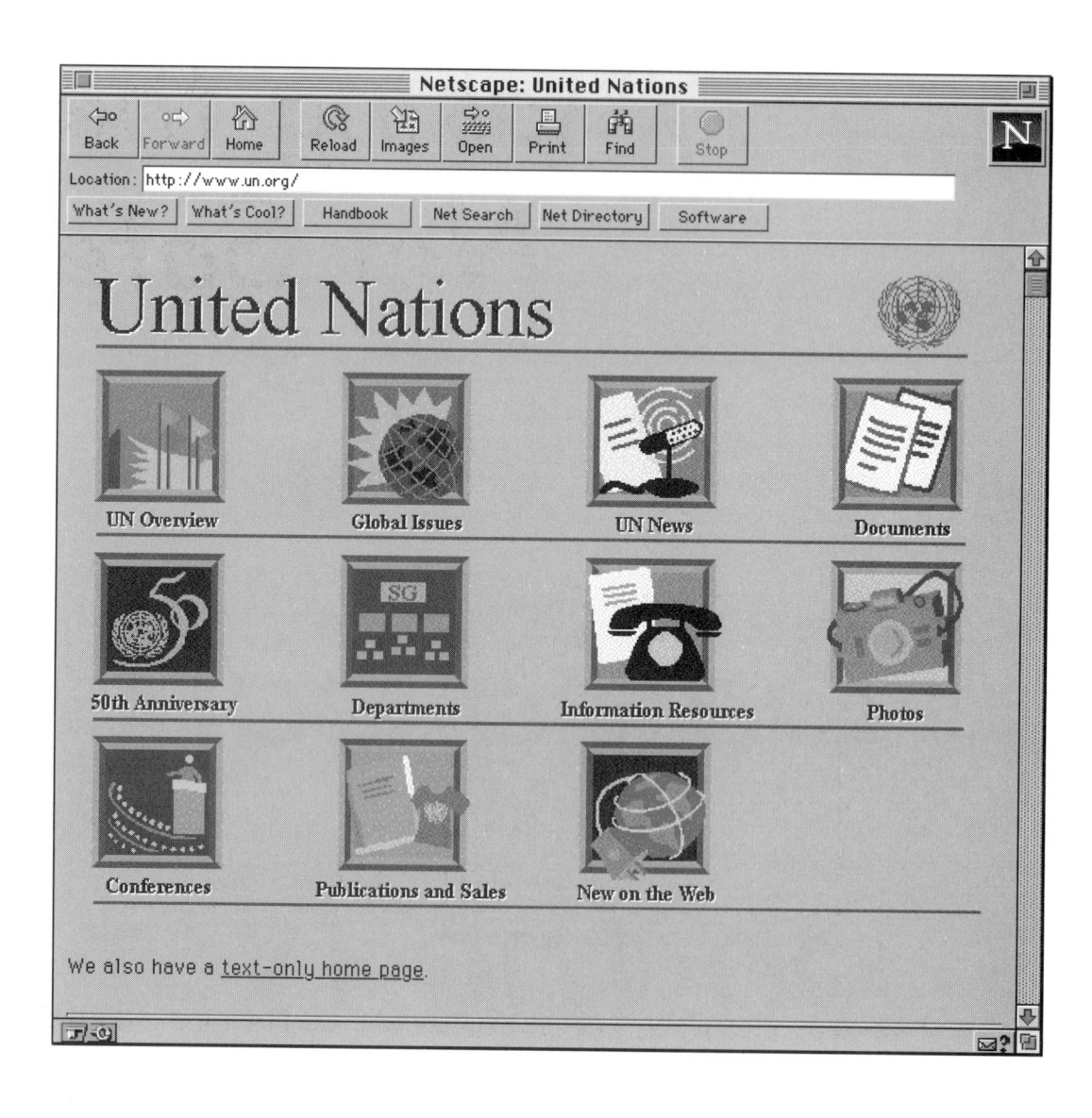

- UN Overview
- Global Issues
- UN News
- Documents
- 50th Anniversary
- Departments
- Information Resources
- Photos
- Conferences
- Publications and Sales
- New on the Web

We also have a text-only home page.

Chapter 10
Making the Net Safe

Covered in This Chapter
Why the Net Is Not Safe
Net Safety Rules
Online Rules of Behavior
Safe Web Sites for Kids

Perhaps the best analogy I can give you for what the Net is like is the Old West. (At least Hollywood's view of the Old West.) You know…

There were lawless criminals all over the place, but they usually didn't last long. Justice was swift, because Matt Dillon, Wyatt Earp, and Judge Roy Bean always rode the rascals out of town. Likewise, Butch Cassidy and the Sundance Kid were rakish but lovable bad guys pulling countless jobs and almost never getting caught. Basically, people lived and died without a lot of laws to tell them how to do it. Because of that two things were true. One, people who lived the longest were the ones who knew how to take care of themselves, and two, everybody knew how to shoot a gun.

So, if you are going to let children on the Net, you need to become Net savvy. That means you need to learn the ways of the frontier with all its adventures and challenges. There is nobody out there to shield your kids from the bad stuff but you, which means that you better learn to shoot straight.

If you follow the few simple rules I give you in this chapter, your kids will be safe and have a wonderful experience as well. These are the rules that I use with my own children or would use with anyone else's kids. Before talking about how to make the Net safe, however, I want to explain why it's a place that children should not wander around without your guiding hand.

Why the Net Is Not Safe

When I explain to people the kind of things that are on the Net that children should not see, I am mostly met with disbelief.

"Surely," they say "it can't be as bad as all that."

Upon reflection, I have decided that I get this response for a couple of reasons. Part of it is that many people don't have these types of books or magazines lying about in full view on their coffee tables, so they find it difficult to believe that they could just be lying about in full view on the Net. Another part of it is that people naively assume that laws that pertain to minors and adult material are somehow also enforced on the Net and thus children cannot get into them. They might also believe that the U.S. Telecom law could actually have an effect upon what children will see on the Net. The truth is that all of these beliefs are inaccurate; the Net is full of stuff kids have no business seeing. Here are the kind of things you could find.

Sexual Material

Imagine, if you will, the kind of pictures and stories you would find in an adult bookstore or trinket shop in the middle of the red-light district in downtown Las Vegas. If you could find it in that bookstore, you can find it on the Net. Think also about the types of services you could hire in that same place. You can hire those same services on the Net.

Further, this material is presented in all the blaze of technicolor. While the quality may not always be up to the standards of a professional glossy magazine, what is depicted is just as graphic and just as easy to recognize.

If you find this hard to believe, then I suggest you tuck the children into bed one night, sneak off to the computer, and deliberately explore those steamy areas of the Net. All you have to do to find them is use your imagination and do a search in **Yahoo** (or any other search engine, for that matter).

Don't think that this material can only be found by actively searching it out, that is not *always* the case. Let me tell you a story…

A Story

The 17-year-old daughter of a friend of mine was using the Net to do some research for a paper on the death penalty. She did a search on "Cruel and Unusual Punishment" and started looking through the sites returned by the search. Innocently opening the fourth one down she was greeted with a site that specialized in cruel and unusual punishment of the S & M variety. Full-color pictures with accompanying leather items were featured as well. Being a reasonable girl she simply laughed and went on with her research.

The point of the story is that it is not always possible to know when you will encounter material that you don't want your children to see. While most of this stuff is found in places you would expect, every once in a while something slips through.

Bad Thoughts and Speech

But can I yell "FIRE" in a crowded virtual theater?

The virtue of a democracy is that you and I are entitled to think anything we want and to say most of those things out loud. Indeed, free speech is so precious, that we tolerate people advocating things that make our skin crawl or our blood boil with outrage. That is what free speech allows, and that is what you will find on the Net. I can guarantee you that there are many people saying things on the Net that you would strongly disagree with and not want your children to read.

While this material is less glitzy than the sexual material it is still very troubling and not something that children should see without guidance and some help from you about why people believe and say such things.

Bad People

As much as I wish I could tell you that everyone on the Net is good and kind and wouldn't dream of hurting or exploiting children, that simply isn't true. Just like the real world, the Net has its share of bad and good people. And just like the Wild West, you are what stands between the bad guys and your kids.

I don't want to scare you too much, however. Look, you could spend years online and never encounter a overly rude, mean, or bad person. Remember, you are not preparing your children for what they *will* encounter but for what they *might* encounter. And you are doing so because they will need tools to deal with such situations if they do occur. So let's talk first about the types of people they might meet and then about what to do about them.

The Rude Ones

The majority of these "bad" people on the Net are just rude. They might make snotty remarks to children in chat rooms, be overly impatient with new user questions, or just swear a lot. Maybe they don't like kids, maybe they don't like them cluttering up Net space with their toys; for whatever reason they say rude and insulting things even if they know it is a kid they are addressing. Certainly, children will see all types of profanity if they read many newsgroups or enter almost any chat room.

The Harassers

There is something about the anonymity of the Net that can bring out the harasser in some people. Particularly in chat rooms, kids can encounter people who will aggressively question them about personal issues, insult the kids' comments, and quite often go so far as to ask for sex (though how it is supposed to work over the phone lines I have no idea). While most of this is just a truth-or-dare kind of thing, you do have to seriously consider how much you want your kids exposed to that type of discussion.

The Very Bad People

Thankfully, only a very small number of people deliberately try to entice children into giving away personal information for nefarious purposes. Unfortunately, these adults may also try to talk children into doing inappropriate things and try to arrange real-world meetings.

The problem you as the parent have to face is twofold. Kids on the Net may get into long-term correspondence with one another and want to have face-to-face meetings (don't pen pals always want to meet?). So your first problem is whether you will allow such meetings and how they will be handled. The second problem is that you have absolutely no idea if the person on the other end of the correspondence is actually a kid. On the Net, a 30-year-old can pretend to be a 15-year-old and no one is the wiser. But if that 30-year-old keeps up the pretense long enough, do you really want him or her having anything to do with your child?

The crux of the problem is that you won't know if the person talking to your kid about meeting is another 15-year-old or a 30-year-old with lots of mental problems. Because of things like this, you will need to know some Net safety rules and live by them. These safety rules are for you the adults to enforce. Following them are the online rules of behavior, which are for kids.

Net Safety Rules

Here are some simple rules of thumb for you. They will help to ensure that your children will be safe on the Net.

Rule #1: If you don't have time to supervise your children on the Net, don't let them on it.

Regardless of what your kid might tell you, life will not stop if she or he is not on the Net. If things are very hectic in your life, then wait until they calm down before letting your child use either the Net or an online service.

It is important to remember that these places are adult environments that also have some sites for children. Because there are no walls between the kid areas and the ones for adults, however, you need to put up the boundaries yourself.

There are two things you need to do to keep children safe:

1. Supervise what your kids do on the Net.

2. Use some blocking software to keep them out of adult sites. (I discuss this software in Chapter 11.)

Let me explain what I mean by "supervise." Obviously, it will depend on the age of your kids, how much freedom you think they should have, and a lot of other factors. Let's talk about what to do with young children and move upward in age.

Rule #2: If your child is under 9, then he or she should only be on the Net with very close supervision.

That's right; you should know everything your children look at either by being right there beside them or by limiting that material beforehand. For example, it is perfectly reasonable to only allow kids of this age to look at a few places that you've already reviewed beforehand.

You could also view this as a great opportunity to spend some very interesting time with your child. You could explore the Net together. (After all, you watch television and movies together, don't you?)

Rule #3: Children under 13 should not be allowed in interactive areas and newsgroups.

Keep all younger children out of places on the Net where there are live conversations. Chat rooms and interactive areas are better suited to older teenage children (if at all). As for email, I would probably let a child under 13 correspond with a pen pal, but I would read the correspondence between the kids.

Note: *Hey, whatever happened to "A rule is a rule"?*

There is one exception I would make to this rule. I would allow children to participate in a strictly moderated forums/chat rooms such as the ones offered at certain times by educational groups, libraries, and the children's programs of commercial organizations like PBS.

These forums have an "official" adult online at the same time as the children. Profanity is not allowed, and rules of behavior are strictly enforced. Usually, there are set topics of conversation as well. In any case, the first time you allow your child to do this, sit right by the computer.

Rule #4: Children between 9 and 12 should have some supervision and stay in kid-rated sites.

Children 9 and above can wander a little farther afield. It will be enough to use some filtering software and occasionally review the sites your child visits. I would encourage children to take advantage of the research resources on the Net (such as Britannica Online) and visit sites intended for either children or families as a whole.

Rule #5: Children over 12 should only be allowed in interactive areas and newsgroups if they agree to *The online rules of behavior.*

The online rules of behavior are promises that you should have your children make before going on the Net. They involve their Net behavior and privileges (see page 257). I would also continue to use Internet filtering software with younger teenage children.

Rule #6: Spend a minimum of one month on the Internet yourself before you let an older teenage child have full access.

You know your child better than anyone else, so you will know when he or she is mature enough to deal with the Internet without restriction. Personally, I would be hard-pressed to believe that many teenagers under 15 are ready for this; on the other hand, I think most 17-year-olds are probably fine. Once again, it depends upon the kid.

What is more important than when you give full access to your child is *that you personally have a very clear idea of the types of things the kid will encounter.* The only way you will know that is by having the experience yourself. Spend some time surfing the Net, and do it before you let your child have unrestricted access. Having done this, you will be prepared to handle the kinds of issues and questions your child will have about the material and people he or she meets online.

Rule #7: Think carefully about whether a troubled child or one going through a difficult emotional period should be on the Net.

Listen, I know that this is a hard rule to follow. For some lonely or unsociable kids, the Net can be great and, in fact, something of a salvation. For kids with deeper emotional problems, however, it might not be such a good thing. Let me explain the problem and you can decide whether your child will benefit or not.

> *Note:* When done alone, surfing the Net is an isolating activity and disengages you from everyday life. Spending more time in a virtual world will only build up the distance a kid puts between himself and the people around him. If your child also has a hard time differentiating between fiction and reality, then lots of time on the Net will probably make it worse.

In either case, emotionally troubled children should not be allowed in chat rooms or other interactive areas on the Net. While I would not want any child to have an online encounter with one of *the very bad people*, can you imagine how much worse the result could be if the kid was already troubled?

Rule #8: Too much time on the Net is not good for children, so don't let them do it.

Think of this rule as more of a preference. Just as I would say that children should not spend all their time playing computer games or watching TV, neither should they spend all their time on the Net, unless something unusual is going on (like a big research project).

She just thinks that because she's a nerd.

Net surfing can be difficult to limit for some people and even more so for kids. Your job as the adult is to set the limits and then enforce them.

One proviso I would add is that the Net is more mentally challenging that either TV or video games. I would much rather see a child spend large amounts of time online than doing those other things. It also strengthens reading skills—something the other two activities do not do.

Online Rules of Behavior

These are rules that children should promise to follow as a condition of using the Net. If they break the rules, there's a clear consequence—no Net.

I have also repeated these promises in more compact form at the end of the book. I suggest you tear out that page and post it in a prominent location by the computer connected to the Net. Such a prominent display makes it harder for a kid to "forget" the rules. We all know that rules and promises are slippery little things that just seem to wriggle out of a kid's mind on certain occasions. Posting them by the computer is simply more practical than gluing them to the kid's head.

Note: The following promises are very similar to Larry Magid's set of online rules. You can find a copy of his rules at many Web sites, such as http://www.larrysworld.com/child_safety.html.

My Promises

I Promise: I will never give out personal information about myself without my parents' permission.

Personal information includes any of the following:

- Home address
- Telephone number

- Parents' work address or telephone number

- Name or location of school

- Town

- Last name

> *Note:* Town information depends entirely on where you live. If you live in New York City, then nobody could find you anyway. Towns of 500 people, on the other hand, are small enough for this to be treated as personal information.
>
> Same deal with last names. If your last name is Smith, who cares if you use it? If your last name is Smith-Carruthers, consider keeping the information to yourself. As a parent you need to decide whether this is information that can be shared or not.

I Promise: I will never meet someone from the Net without getting my parents' permission first.

Parents of younger children (approximately 16 or younger) should go to the meeting themselves. With an older teenager, you could moderate this a bit by only requiring that your teenager not go alone—a friend could go instead of you.

In either case, I would require that the meeting be in a well-lit public place (no exceptions). *Never, never, never let the first meeting take place in someone's home.*

Listen, these sorts of rules may seem overly paranoid to you, but you need to remember that you have no idea who will show up at the meeting. It could be any of the following:

- Another sweet kid just like your own child
- A messed-up whacked-out crazy kid
- An even more messed-up whacked-out crazy adult

I Promise: I will never send someone on the Net a picture of myself (or anything else) without my parents' permission.

This is the sort of promise that depends upon the child, the age, and the situation. Generally, sending pictures may be okay, but I would still have your children check with you first.

You should also go over the things you personally do not want your child to give out. These things might include credit card numbers, names of people in you family, pictures of the family, and so on.

I Promise: I will only give out my email address according to my parents' rules.

This is another one of those situations that will vary depending on the age of the child and who or what wants the email address. You, the parent, do need to remember that an email address is not like a home address and you can't find out where someone lives just by having one. Also, there are several harmless

Net sites you cannot get into without an email address (like Encyclopedia Britannica Online).

What you should do is set some concrete guidelines with your child about when it is okay to give out an email address. Certainly, older children should have far more latitude than younger ones.

> **I Promise: I will tell my parents immediately if someone scares me, or makes me feel uncomfortable or bad.**

The point of this promise is that you want your children to know that you expect to be told if a problem occurs. By making them promise to tell you about such unpleasant experiences, you will be able to help them deal with them in a constructive manner.

> **I Promise: I will follow my parents' rules for how I am supposed to use the Net.**

These rules should govern when your children are allowed on the Net, for how long, and what types of sites they may visit. You should also have your children promise not to mess with any blocking software that you have installed (it could really mess up your computer).

> **I Promise: I will be polite to other Net users.**

While "please" and "thank you" are not required (though nice), your child should offer at least a minimum of courtesy to other Net users. That means no flaming and no picking on other users.

This also gives your kid the perfect opportunity to complain to you with the tried-and-true whine, "but everybody else gets to flame on the Net, why can't I?"

Safe Web Sites for Kids

Some Web sites on the Net have been specifically made kid-safe. What this usually means is that the site creator has followed all the links in every direction to ensure that there is no offensive material anywhere.

If you want a quick method to keep your child reasonably safe, you can make one of these areas your child's home page. If you have your child stay within these sites, you can be reasonably confident that nothing inappropriate will be seen. You should expect to see more of these environments appearing over time, and they will certainly be places that are better for children than the Web as a whole.

Kid's Wave

http://www.safesurf.com/sskwave.html

Safe Surf, the organization dedicated to making the Net a safer place for children, is responsible for this site. Each of the sites that Kid's Wave has links to is also safe. Plus, all of the linked site creators have pledged that they will monitor their links. This level of commitment makes this one of the safest places on the WWW.

262   Chapter 10   Making the Net Safe

Figure 10.1
Kid's Wave Web Site.

There are great places to take your children online.

Here is a partial list of SafeSurf approved sites by category.

Favorite Site of the Month!
Elementary Ages | Older Kids / Parents | Space Stuff
Commercial Sites

IMPORTANT WARNING: Due to the present structure of the World Wide Web, parental supervision is highly recommended for children "surfing" the 'Net.

**SafeSurf is dedicated to correcting the situation.
We need your support in this effort.**

Kid's Wave is also fun. There are links to sites for parents, space, and fun commercial sites (see Figure 10.1). It also links to sites for children of different ages (see Figure 10.2 for an example).

Figure 10.2
Kid's Wave Older Kids Links.

Sites for Elementary Ages:

- Kid World-- is a fun filled place full of pictures, stories, jokes, riddles, and even a lesson on creating your own home page!

- Hickory & Dickory's Adventure Page -- is full of adventures both entertaining and educational. Children are sure to visit this site again and again.

- Alex's Scribbles-- is a collection of short stories for kids of all ages by Alex, a 5 year old surfer.

- Check out creative art from children around the world at Fridge Artz , a virtual fridge door filled with fun.

Safe Web Sites for Kids   263

Yahooligans

http://www.yahooligans.com/

Figure 10.3
Yahooligans Web Site.

Brought to you by those folks at **Yahoo**, this is a searchable, browsable index of Web sites specifically designed for kids ages 8 to 14 (see Figure 10.3). While Yahooligans does not guarantee that every link is safe, they do have a mechanism for reporting sites if you don't like them.

The sites that are part of this collection are nicely tailored to this age range. Kids can look through material on:

- School

- Art
- Computers
- Games, and more

Safe Links

http://www.safelinks.com/

Figure 10.4 Safe Links Web Site.

This is a company that has put together sites that are for the whole family and safe for children as well (see Figure 10.4). Their philosophy concerning sites includes a strong prohibition against any company or organization with any connection to alcohol, tobacco, firearms, or pornographic products.

Chapter 11
Security Software Compared

Covered in This Chapter
Security Software
My Recommendations
Quick Feature Comparison Chart

The good news is that there are several different types of security software available for filtering Net sites. The bad news is that none of them is 100% foolproof.

Let's start with the good news. First, I'll describe all the Internet blocking software that is available. I'll tell you how it works and what it can and can't do. After describing them:

I'll give you some recommendations on what I think you should use.

There are also demos of my two favorite packages on the CD-ROM at the back of the book. The chapter ends with a quick comparison chart of all the software.

Security Software

Each of these software packages uses some type of filtering principle to block out unwanted sites on the Net. Some allow you to customize by adding your own selection criteria and some do not. Some offer other features as well. Let's look at them in alphabetical order.

Free Advice: I have reviewed this software using my own criteria. In software, I tend to favor simple to use and stable over lots of features.

In any case, I want you to know that I have no financial interest in any of this software. You can buy any package or not and it won't make any difference to me. To that extent, my advice is free (of conflict of interest, that is).

Cyber Patrol

Cyber Patrol has a few unique features that make it especially useful to parents of teenagers. First, let's look at how **Cyber Patrol** works and how you determine what is blocked.

How It Works

Figure 11.1
Cyber Patrol's Filtering Categories.

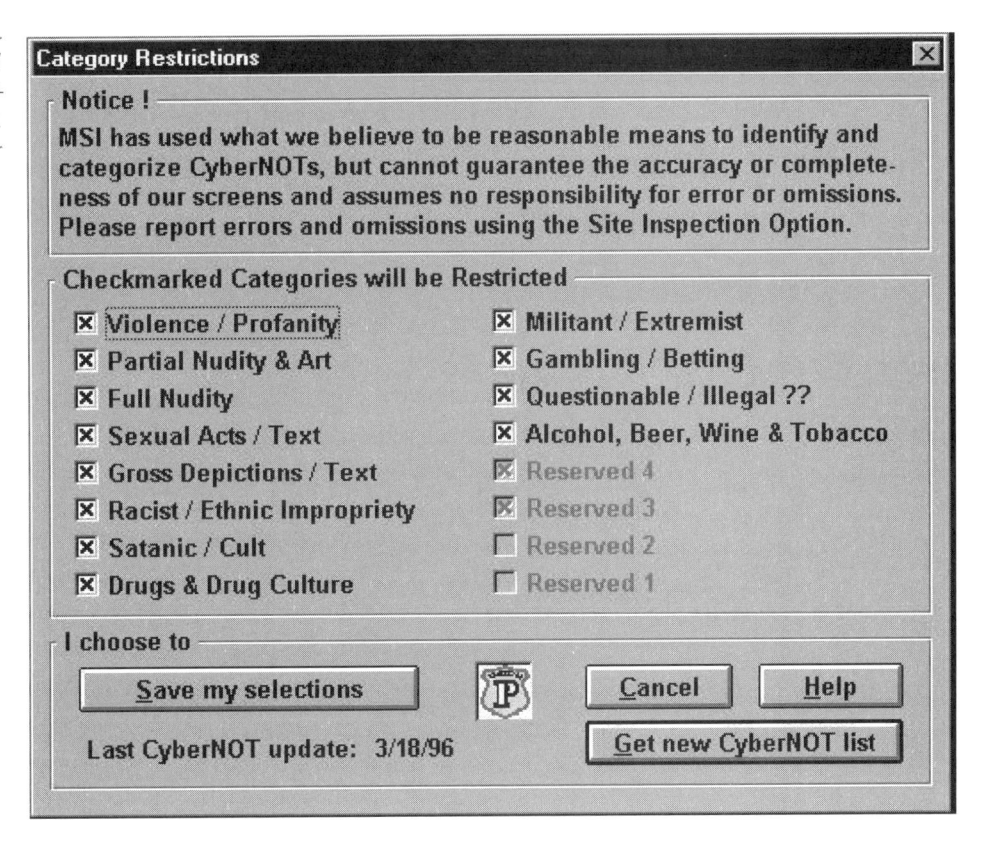

Cyber Patrol from Microsystems Software uses a filtering system to block sites based on a list. If a site contains material that fits in a category on this list, then it can't be viewed. This filter list is called the CyberNOT list and it works for Web sites and newsgroups. Figure 11.1 shows the wide range of categories you can restrict.

You download the CyberNOT list right after you install the **Cyber Patrol** demo or regular version of the software. You need to be connected to the Net to do this. After that is done you can update the CyberNOT list on a weekly basis for a standard fee.

What Cyber Patrol Blocks

One of the nicest things about **Cyber Patrol** is that it uses several categories in its blocking of material. You can choose to use or not use each one individually simply by checking or unchecking the box next to the item (see Figure 11.1).

Customizable Blocking

Cyber Patrol also lets you add your own material either to block or to specifically allow as you prefer. Such material includes:

- Web and FTP sites
- Chat groups
- Newsgroups

Setting up Time Periods

Another very nice feature that **Cyber Patrol** offers is the ability to limit access to either the Net or any computer program based upon time criteria:

- You specify what times during the day a child can be on the Net.
- You specify the total of daily and weekly time allowed.

Everything starts at **Cyber Patrol** Headquarters (see Figure 11.2).

Security Software 269

Figure 11.2
Cyber Patrol Headquarters.

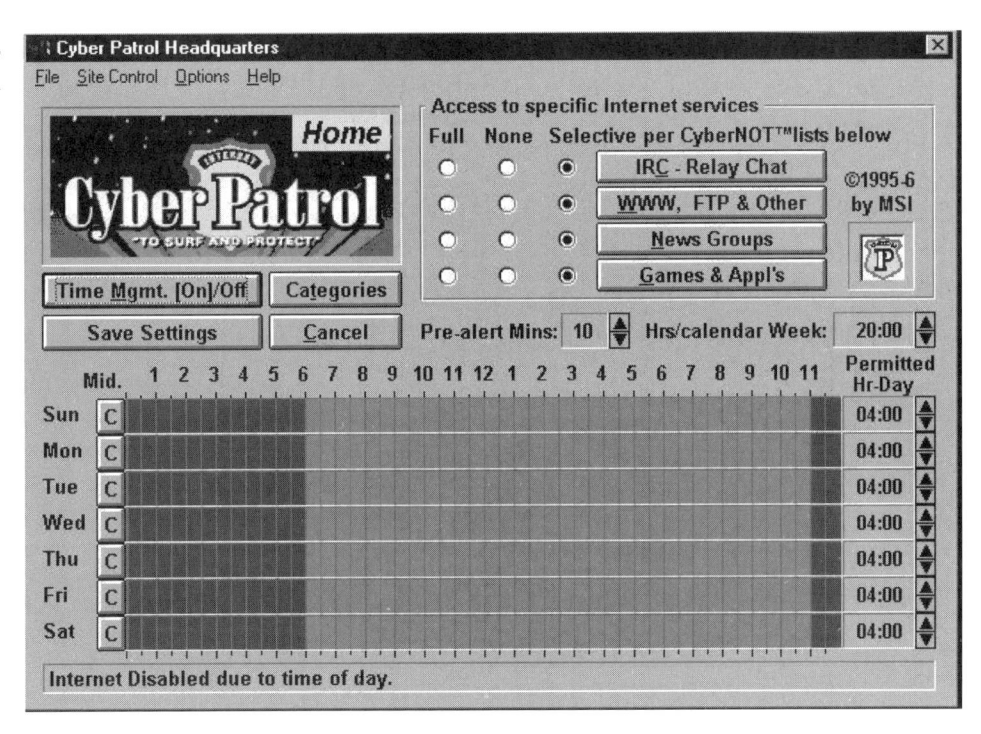

Alternate Blocking System

Cyber Patrol is the only program that allows you to use an alternate blocking system. Developed by SafeSurf, this blocking system allows you to fine tune the category restrictions even more (see Figure 11.3). For more information about the SafeSurf rating system see "The SafeSurf Rating Standard" on page 304.

Password Protection

Cyber Patrol offers password protection. In fact, there are two password types. One is the Administrator's password that allows you to determine what will be blocked and takes you to the Headquarters screen. The other gives full Net access for that session (called a Deputy Bypass). Nicely enough, this feature allows older children to have full Net access while still blocking younger children's use.

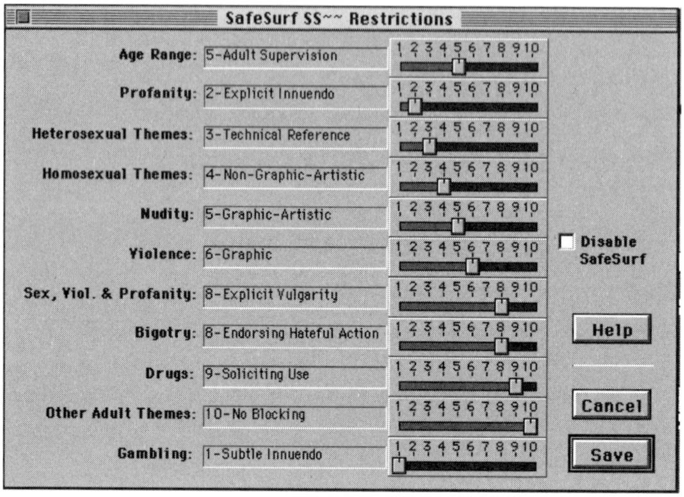

Figure 11.3
Cyber Patrol's Safe-Surf Rating System.

Platforms

There are two versions of **Cyber Patrol:**

- Windows (Windows 3.1 and Windows 95)
- Macintosh

Internet and Online Filtering Software

Cyber Patrol works with either an ISP or online services. CompuServe and Prodigy provide a free special version of **Cyber Patrol** to their members. America Online users do not have this option.

Best and Worst Features

The best features of **Cyber Patrol** are:

- You can limit when and how much time is spent online.

- A free version is available to home users.

- You can use and modify different filters.

- You can add to or ignore certain items on the filter list (the CyberNOT list).

The worst features are:

- It has a somewhat confusing interface for adding or exempting items from the CyberNOT list.

- If you don't install and uninstall it perfectly, it can cause big problems with your operating system.

Cyber Patrol's best features are unique. No other package lets you limit time periods of use on your computer, and no other company offers a free home-use version. These points alone make this a product worth considering.

Still, you need to balance those good points against the problems that you may encounter when running the demo version. (I assume that since I had problems, you might as well). You also need to have a certain amount of computer and Net experience to actually amend the CyberNOT list.

Where to Get a Demo Version

There are demo versions of **Cyber Patrol** in two places:

- on the CD-ROM at the back of the book.
- At Microsystems Web site:
     http://www.microsys.com

Where to Get a Regular Version

If you decide to order the regular version of **Cyber Patrol**, you can do it in one of two ways. Over-the-phone registration is available by calling:

(800) 828-2608

You can also order a complete copy of **Cyber Patrol** online by using the registration screen that is in the **Cyber Patrol** demo menu (see Figure 11.4).

Note: You can only use the online registration form when you are actually connected to the Net. You fill out the form on your computer in the Cyber Patrol program and then upload that form to Microsystems' Web site. Don't try to fill out the form at the Web site—that is just a picture and not a true form.

What It Costs

Microsystems offers a couple of pricing plans depending on what type of **Cyber Patrol** you want.

Figure 11.4
Cyber Patrol Online Registration Form

The Home Version

A wonderful option Microsystems provides is a "home version" of **Cyber Patrol** that families can use for free. The catch is that you have to look at ads whenever you encounter a blocked site, as shown in Figure 11.5. This version is also limited in other ways:

- You cannot customize the blocking.

- Only the sex-related sites are blocked.

- You can't limit when and how much time is spent online.

- Applications can't be blocked.

That is not much to put up with for getting a free piece of software, so this is a great deal. You can use the home version and subscribe to the filter list for a monthly fee:

$19.95   6-month fee for the CyberNOT list

Figure 11.5
Commercial at a Blocked Site Using Cyber Patrol.

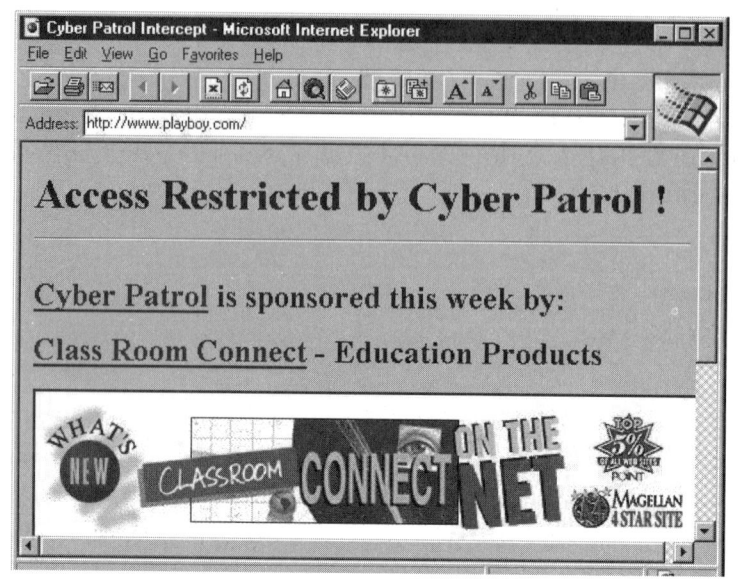

The Complete Version

If you don't like looking at commercials or you want the features that are left out of the home version you can upgrade to the complete version and subscribe to the monthly list:

$49.95   for the complete version of Cyber Patrol

$19.95   6-month fee for the CyberNOT list

Technical Support

Microsystems' technical support staff does get overloaded at times, so it can take a while before someone gets back to you with answers to questions. This can be crucial because you might encounter some problems using the software. Be patient—they do eventually call back.

CYBERsitter

This product works along lines similar to **Cyber Patrol,** but offers far more customizing capabilities, including the ability to block personal information from being sent out on the Net.

How It Works

Sites are matched against a list, and if they contain inappropriate material they are blocked. Or, you can choose to have the software provide a warning about sites rather than blocking them.

When a site is blocked the user just sees a standard Windows error message saying that the operation cannot proceed.

Customizable Blocking

CYBERsitter also lets you custom-block sites. Other types of restrictions that can be customized include:

- Common graphic image types (so that pictures cannot be accessed)
- Web and FTP sites
- Various electronic video and movie formats
- Other programs totally separate from the Internet that are on the computer (like games)

You do most of this restricting from this screen in **CYBERsitter** (see Figure 11.6).

Figure 11.6 CYBERsitter's Restrictions.

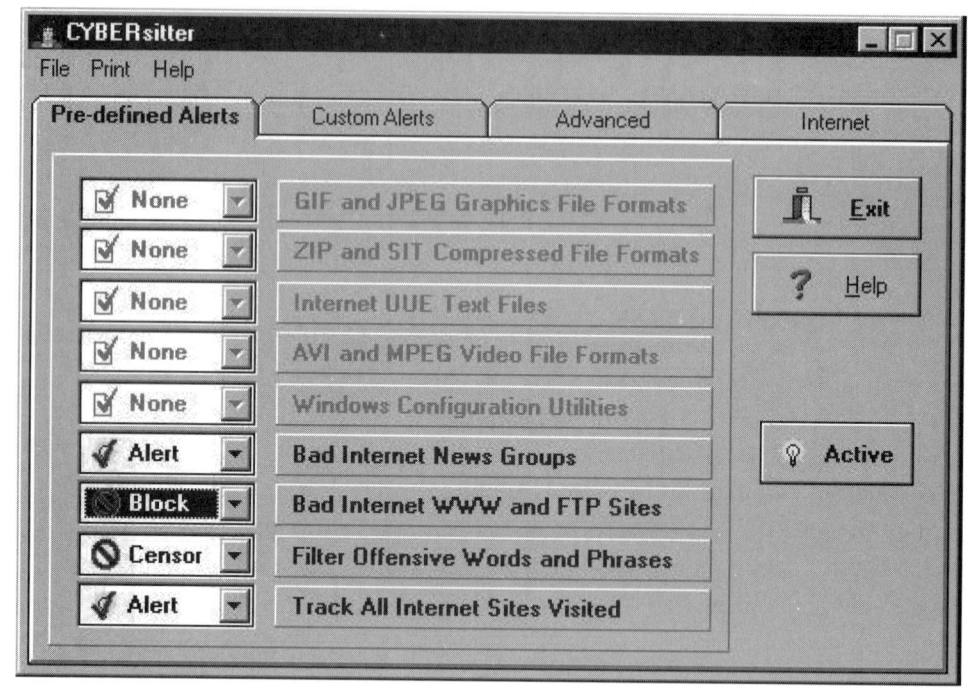

Password Protection

CYBERsitter offers optional password protection. You can have passwords or bypass restrictions with a particular password, or not have password protection at all.

Platforms

This is a Windows-only product. There are versions available for:

- Windows 3.1

- Windows 95 (did not work well at press time)

Internet and Online Filtering Software

CYBERsitter works with a direct-access internet account or an online service.

Best and Worst Features

The best features of **CYBERsitter** are:

- Its free list gets updated often.
- It works with either the Net or online services.
- Sites can be blocked or warnings given.

The worst features are:

- The Windows 95 version doesn't work with all browsers.
- It is difficult to diagnose problems.
- It has very difficult to use features and interface.

Let me explain a feature that may be useful but is very difficult to use. When **CYBERsitter** is on and someone tries to access a blocked site, only a standard error message shows up—there is no mention of **CYBERsitter**. This is both good and bad. Some people may think it is good because it makes **CYBERsitter** virtually undetectable to the user who is trying to access forbidden material. I think it is bad because it makes your job of setting up the software and ensuring that it works correctly enormously difficult—how do you know what is causing an error (it could be the browser, it could be **CYBERsitter**). The assumption of the creator of **CYBERsitter** seems to be that you need software that is as tamper-proof as possible.

I think this is a bad assumption to build into the software. If I had a kid who was going to constantly tamper with, thwart, and otherwise try to get around the software—I simply wouldn't let him or her on the Internet at all.

Another example of a difficult feature is the dialog you see when you attempt to uninstall the software (see Figure 11.7). How are you supposed to remember the original state of the program options? Looking in online help doesn't tell you; there are no listings under "uninstall" or "settings" to guide you in what to do. Eventually, you will just have to say "Yes" and hope for the best.

Figure 11.7 CYBERsitter Warning Dialog.

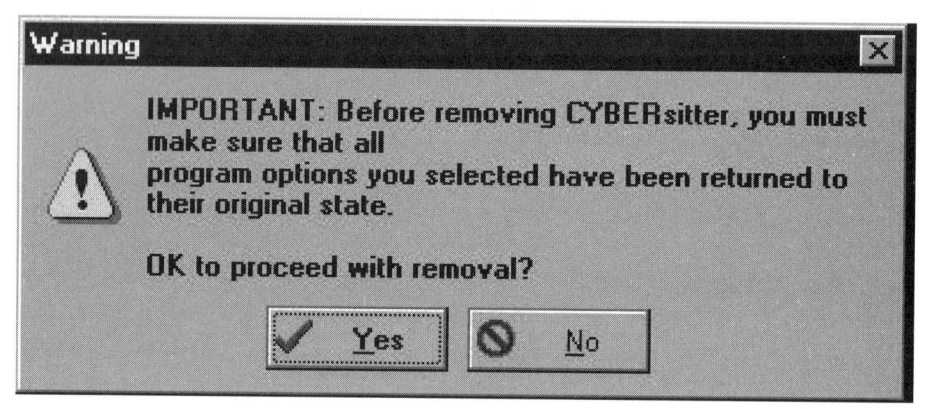

This product does have some nice points. It is commendable that **CYBERsitter**'s filter list is free and updated quite often. I also like that you can either block a site or just be warned about it. Plus, the online help is quite useful (see Figure 11.8).

Where to Get a Demo Version

You can download a demo version from the **CYBERsitter** Web site of Solid Oak software:

http://www.solidoak.com

Figure 11.8
CYBERsitter's Online Help.

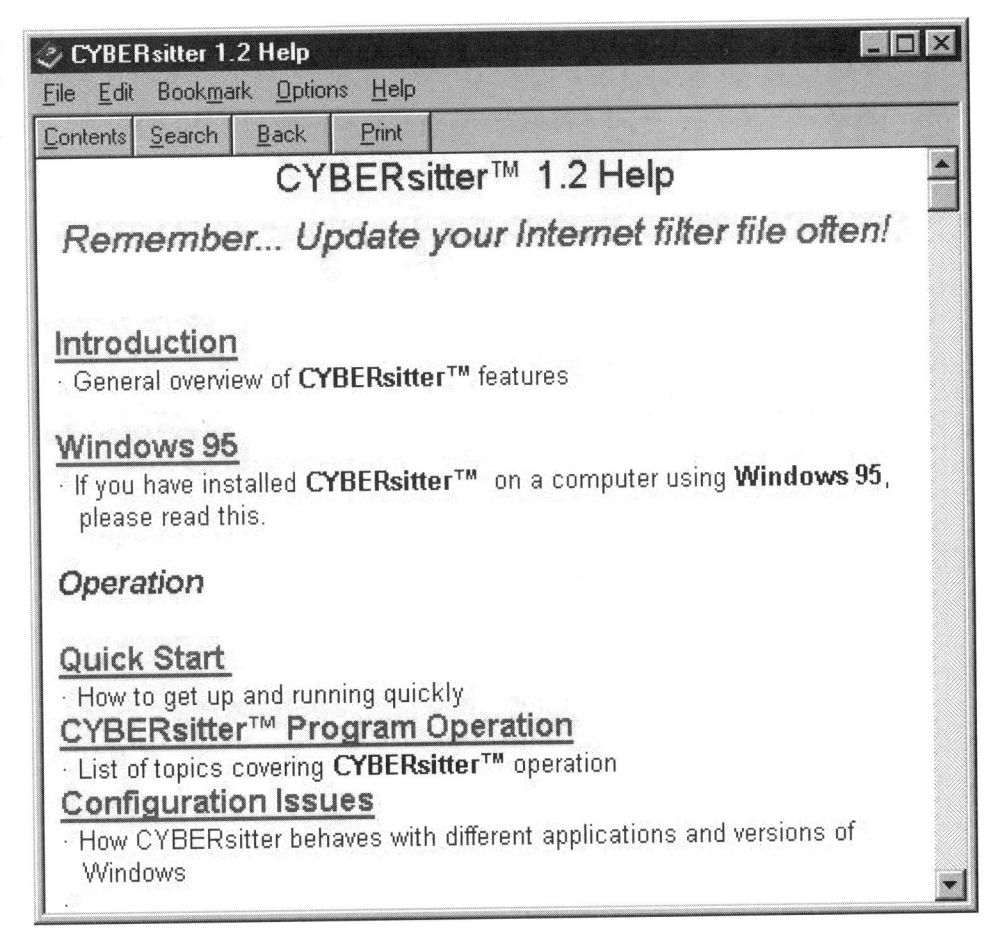

```
CYBERsitter 1.2 Help
File  Edit  Bookmark  Options  Help
Contents  Search  Back  Print

                CYBERsitter™ 1.2 Help
        Remember... Update your Internet filter file often!

Introduction
 · General overview of CYBERsitter™ features

Windows 95
 · If you have installed CYBERsitter™ on a computer using Windows 95,
   please read this.

Operation

Quick Start
 · How to get up and running quickly
CYBERsitter™ Program Operation
 · List of topics covering CYBERsitter™ operation
Configuration Issues
 · How CYBERsitter behaves with different applications and versions of
   Windows
```

Caution: If you are running Windows 95 you should wait until they have a version of CYBERsitter that works correctly with all browsers. If you are running a browser specifically designed for Windows 95 (32-bit), and you use CYBERsitter, it will look like it is on but do absolutely no blocking. Look at the Web site for the status of the Windows 95 version.

Where to Get a Complete Version

If you decide to order **CYBERsitter** you can do it online or over the phone at the following number.

(800) 388-2761

What it Costs

If you are ready to order a complete version, it will cost you:

$39.95	for CYBERsitter
no charge	for updates to the filter list

Net Nanny

This software uses a different approach to blocking things. It gives the parent absolute control over what is blocked. It also works for the entire computer, and not just for Internet filtering. In fact, it is probably better to think of **Net Nanny** as a filtering shell that you fill in with contents.

Everything that you do within **Net Nanny** is done within a DOS-based administration screen (see Figure 11.9).

How It Works

Net Nanny compares *everything* it sees against a list to which you can add words or phrases. Using a combination of keywords and phrases, **Net Nanny**

Figure 11.9
Net Nanny's Administration Screen.

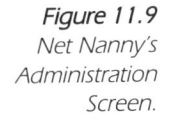

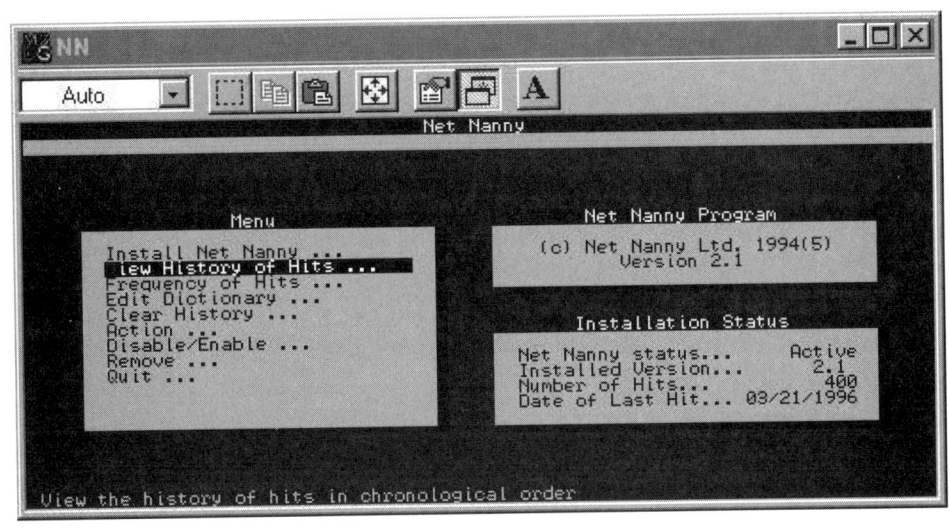

scans words as they occur in every program on the computer (that's right, every program you run on the computer and not just the Internet stuff). If it finds a match, two things occur:

- A log entry (application and time) is made showing what word triggered the entry.

- Net Nanny may do a shutdown. (This is an on/off option.)

What **Net Nanny** means by a shutdown depends on the operating system you are running on your computer (see Figure 11.10). Here are the possibilities.

- Windows 3.1—the application quits.

- Windows 95—the application tries to quit, but you can stop this from happening.

- DOS—the computer shuts down.

Figure 11.10
Net Nanny's Options for Accessing Blocked Sites.

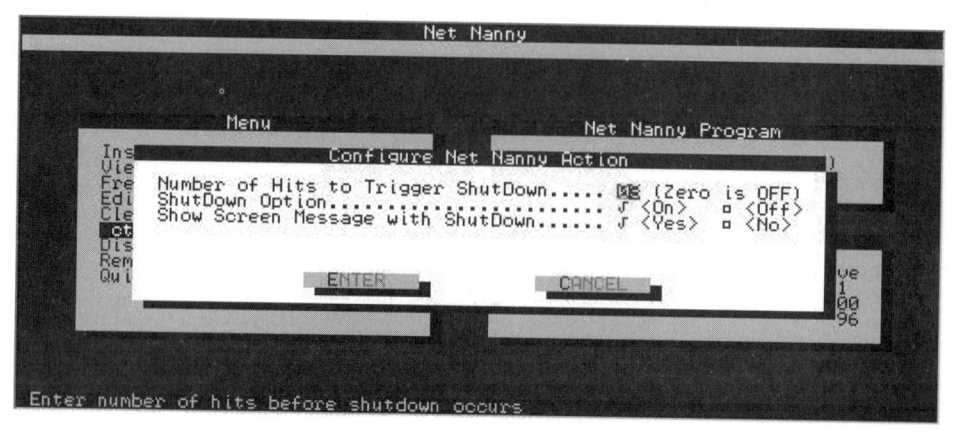

Customizable Blocking

Net Nanny is the ultimate in customizable blocking. It can block virtually anything and is only limited by the extent of your imagination.

Platforms

Net Nanny works with the following:

- DOS

- Windows 3.1

- Windows 95

It is worth noting that you go through a DOS installation first, even if you are running Windows.

Internet and Online Filtering Software

Net Nanny will work with online services, direct Internet access, and anything else on your machine for that matter.

Best and Worst Features

The best features of **Net Nanny** are:

- You can run it as a log (you don't have to block sites).
- It blocks personal information such as home addresses from being sent.
- It works with both online services and direct access.

The worst features are:

- It takes a lot of work to set it up correctly.
- It does not allow simple blocking, but instead shuts down when it encounters blocked phrases.
- Blocked phrases can come back to haunt you.
- You have to restart the computer every time you make a change to Net Nanny.

Net Nanny can be used in two ways: as a watching application that will simply report back to you about activities, or as a blocking application. If what you want is a watching-only application then **Net Nanny** can be quite useful.

Net Nanny can monitor what your kids get into by showing you in log form what types of words they tried to access and when.

As a blocking application, however, **Net Nanny** goes too far for my taste. **Net Nanny**'s approach is like using a sledge hammer when a fly swatter would do. It seems a bit punitive to me to pull the plug on an application or the whole computer when the kid could have been just surfing around (not really intending mischief).

In either case, if you want to be the sole determiner of what your child can view, this is the only program that will allow you to do that.

Where to Get a Demo Version

You can download a demo version from the **Net Nanny** Web site:

http://www.netnanny.com/netnanny

Where to Get A Complete Version

If you decide to order **Net Nanny,** you can do so online or over the phone at the following number.

(800) 340-7177

What It Costs

If you are ready to order a complete version, it will cost you this:

$49.95   for Net Nanny

no charge   for the list of words

SurfWatch

SurfWatch from SurfWatch Software uses the same approach to blocking as **Cyber Patrol** and **CYBERsitter**. It is one of the products that has been around the longest, and it is by far the easiest to use. It is also very painless to turn on and off because **SurfWatch** is a control panel.

How It Works

SurfWatch uses a filter list to figure out what to block. Sites are compared against this filter list of Web, FTP, and newsgroup sites. If the site matches a phrase or word on the list, it is blocked and can't be viewed. Users who try to access a blocked site are shown the dialog in Figure 11.11.

Figure 11.11
Surf Watch Warning Dialog.

As **SurfWatch** gets installed you are walked through several different dialogs, including the one telling you that it's time to get the latest version of the filter list and that you need to be connected to the Net to do so (see Figure 11.12). You will also receive a warning message on how to properly uninstall **SurfWatch**.

*Figure 11.12
Prompts for Updating the Filter List.*

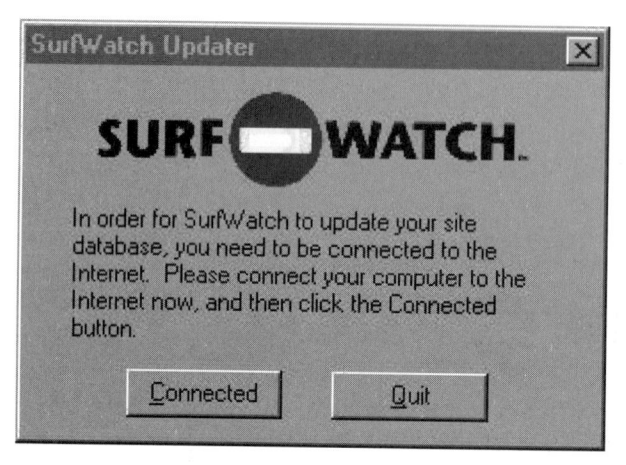

Once you have a current list, you are ready to go. You can update the list on a monthly basis for an extra fee. If you decide to subscribe to the monthly list, it is downloaded automatically when it's time; you don't have anything else to do or remember.

Customizable Blocking

SurfWatch does not currently let you add or remove categories, words, or sites of your own.

> *Note:* As of April, 1996, SurfWatch was working on a new companion program that will allow parents to customize blocking. By the time you read this book, the new program may be ready. Check at SurfWatch's Web site (http:/www.surfwatch.com). Surfwatch has also said that the update will be free to its current subscribers.

Password Protection

SurfWatch offers password protection. You simply type your password into the dialog whenever you want to turn **SurfWatch** off. On the Macintosh, **SurfWatch** will warn you that it needs to quit all open applications and then do so (see Figure 11.13). On Windows, you need to do it yourself.

*Figure 11.13
SurfWatch Warning.*

Caution: You should quit out of the browser you use to surf the Net every time you turn blocking on or off. This is true of all of the blocking packages and it has to do with something called caching.

Here's the deal. When a Web browser loads a site it makes a copy of it on your hard disk, so the next time you go back to that site it redraws on the screen a lot quicker. This is called *caching*.

You need to do two things: (1) make sure that your browser only caches by the session; (2) you need to quit from the browser when you have looked at sites that you do not want children to see. If you do not, then a child could go back to that blocked site (remember, it's on the hard disk) and there is no way to stop him or her. By quitting, you flush the cache of stored copies, and then there is no site trail to follow.

Platforms

There are versions of **SurfWatch** for the standard three platforms:

- Windows 3.1
- Windows 95
- Macintosh

Internet-Only Filtering Software

SurfWatch works only with direct access internet accounts. If you connect to the Internet via an online service, you will need to use different software.

Best and Worst Features

The best features of **SurfWatch** are:

- It is extremely easy to use.
- It is very stable on all platforms.
- It blocks sexual material very well.

The worst features are:

- It offers no customizable blocking.

This program is very straightforward. It is easy to install, easy to use, and easy to turn off. It does a pretty good job of blocking sites, as well. For a parent who does not know a lot about computers or the Net or who wants a hassle-free solution, this is the only choice. **SurfWatch** is also the only product that did not produce some type of problem during its use. Each of the other programs either did not work well on some platform, had problems when installing or uninstalling, or caused system problems in some situations.

Where to Get a Demo Version

There are demo versions of **SurfWatch** for all three platforms:

- On the CD-ROM at the back of the book.

Where to Get a Regular Version

If you decide to order **SurfWatch**, you can do so over the telephone:

(800) 458-6660

What It Costs

SurfWatch charges for both the program and updates to the filter list:

$49.95	for the complete version of SurfWatch
$5.95	monthly fee for the filter list

You can subscribe on a month-to-month basis or for a whole year at a time. You decide this at the time you first set up your subscription plan.

Note: SurfWatch has arranged a special price for readers of this book: $24.95 for SurfWatch and a $3.95 monthly fee (or $40 yearly fee) for the filter list. See the CD-ROM for complete details.

Technical Support

During the course of reviewing all this software I had an opportunity to talk with many of the technical support people at each company. While all the companies had competent people who answered my questions, I was extraordinarily impressed with the technical support offered by **SurfWatch**. They gave competent, honest, and easy-to-understand answers to all my questions (even when they didn't know who I was).

My Recommendations

Before I tell you what I think you should use, I want to explain what influences my opinion. Here is what I look for in a computer program:

- Does it crash or mess up my computer?

- It is easy to use?

- Does it do what it says it can do?

Only after I satisfy myself about these things will I even look at a program for nice features that differentiate it from other programs.

Now, I'm sure you realize that not everybody rates computer programs this way. Many people rate the number of features a product has as the most important criterion; others might use its price. Each group of people will end up giving you different recommendations.

How I Used the Software

I used the demo and regular versions of each product, and on both Windows and Macintosh computers where there were versions available. I called up technical support departments without saying who I was and surfed around on the Net trying to get into trouble and also just for fun. I turned blocking off and on and tried out any other features the product offered.

Monkeying around with each package like this, I had a clear favorite when I was done–**SurfWatch**. Other packages look more promising only when specific features are needed.

Best All Around Experience–SurfWatch

Most of you will be happiest with **SurfWatch**. Here is why:

- It's the easiest to use and has the best price.
- It's the most stable.
- It does a reasonable job of blocking sexual material.

Easiest to Use

SurfWatch was by far the easiest to use of any of the programs. The installation process was almost painless and went pretty quickly. There is no struggling over manuals, trying to figure out what to do and when. In fact, you don't ever have to use a manual or read any help files to use **SurfWatch**. Because there is only one little dialog in which you type your password, there is really nothing to master in using it. You just have to remember your password.

Most Stable

Not only did it install painlessly, it ran painlessly. On both Windows and Macintosh computers it ran well without causing mischief.

I cannot say that about the other programs. Each one caused me some grief either in the installation, the removal, or the running of the program. Since I don't like computer programs that cause me grief, and I tend to get annoyed when they do, I was all the more surprised by how well behaved **SurfWatch** was. I actually enjoyed using it.

SurfWatch is also the easiest to use on a computer that belongs to the whole family. Turning blocking off for adults and on for children is a one-step task that works right every time.

Reasonable Blocking

As I told you at the beginning of this chapter, no software-blocking product is fool proof. Every one of them will either not block everything you want blocked or block too much. **SurfWatch** does a reasonable job of blocking most of the sexual sites. You should also know that sexual material represents the majority of the content on the Net that you might want to keep children from seeing. Other material (such as violence, drugs, and illegal activities, hate literature) is much harder to find and is rare compared to the sexual subject matters.

No Customizable Blocking

People's major complaint about **SurfWatch** is that it does not allow you to add to or modify its filter list. (Something the company is working on.)

Having thought a lot about this, I must tell you I think this is less important than it seems. Once you add in the flexibility to modify what is blocked, you also add in complexity. My assumption is that people would rather have a product that took five minutes to learn than one that took several hours. If that is the case, then **SurfWatch** is the ideal product.

Further, none of the other products have found a way to make the customization process anything close to easy. I had to muddle through online help, and it took me a while to figure it out. I assume that it will take most people just as long. So, the question I think, you should ask yourself is:

> *"Do I really want to spend all that time fussing with a piece of software?"*

If your answer to that question is "Yes" or something like

> *"But, I really like having all those additional features."*

Then you should go with my backup recommendation, which is **Cyber Patrol**.

Best All Around Features—Cyber Patrol

Cyber Patrol is also a very good blocking product. And while it is much more difficult to use than **SurfWatch**, it is still much easier to use than the other choices. There are three really nice things about **Cyber Patrol**.

- You can specify times of day or total amounts of time on the Net.

- You can block more than sex sites and can choose which type of blocking to use.

- There is a free home version.

Specifying Times and Amounts

A friend of mine pointed out that **Cyber Patrol** would be just great for her sister who has teenage kids. The kids are home after school well before their parents. With **Cyber Patrol** the parents would be able to limit how much the kids can mess around on the computer (30 minutes or 1 hour, for example). Plus, parents can do this with more than just online time. They can use **Cyber Patrol** to limit how much a kid can use any program on the computer (even "Doom" and "Dark Forces").

My Yes-But-Be-Careful Point

You should be careful how you implement time restrictions, however. I frequently found myself logging on to the Net during a time I had restricted with **Cyber Patrol**. Here is what happened:

1. I could not get on the Net (the behavior you would expect).
2. My browser would give me the message I sometimes get when the network is overloaded (see Figure 11.14).
3. Sometimes, but not always, I would notice that my phone line was connected and my connection was live. (If I didn't notice I would stay connected until somebody else noticed or my connection timed out.)
4. If I was lucky, I'd remember, "Oh, its Cyber Patrol."
5. I would quit my browser.
6. Then I would put Cyber Patrol in bypass mode.
7. Finally, I would re-launch my browser.

*Figure 11.14
Message You Get When the Network is Busy, or When Cyber Patrol Won't Let You On.*

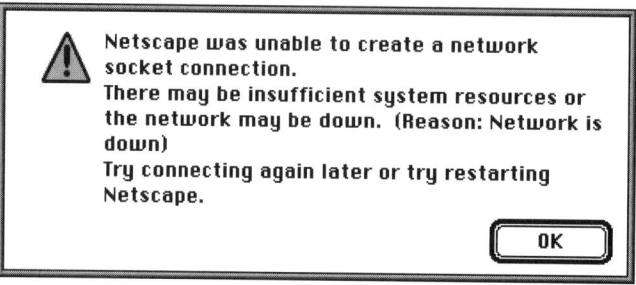

> ⚠ Netscape was unable to create a network socket connection.
> There may be insufficient system resources or the network may be down. (Reason: Network is down)
> Try connecting again later or try restarting Netscape.
>
> [OK]

If this doesn't bother you, then **Cyber Patrol** will be fine. I kept wanting **Cyber Patrol** to tell me it was interfering with my computer and ask me if I wanted to do a bypass. I also wanted it to put up the password screen and let me be on my way. I didn't like being trapped in an in-between state, with my computer actually connected to the Net, but unable to see it. (If I were charged by the hour for my Net access, I would especially dislike this.)

> *Note:* Microsystems has said they will address this problem in the next release of Cyber Patrol. They say that parents will be able to adjust blocking so that the Internet connection is broken. They are also adding some warning messages to remind users to check the modem.

Custom Blocking

Cyber Patrol's blocking categories are very extensive and cover most anything that would be of concern to most parents. By going through the check list of items you should be able to filter out everything you find offensive. Because **Cyber Patrol** also offers SafeSurf's filtering system (see Chapter 12), it gives you even more flexibility.

Indeed, **Cyber Patrol** does handle the categories of material much better than any of the other products. If it is flexibility and choice plus ease of use you want, then this is clearly the right product for you. If you want to block other types of materials besides sexual ones, then **Cyber Patrol** is the best choice.

The Free Version

Cyber Patrol also comes in a free, home use only version. Even though some of the features are disabled and you have to look at commercials, this is still a wonderful thing for Microsystems to do. They deserve praise for making this cost effective alternative for consumers.

Other Comments

Even though I think you will be happy if you go with either **SurfWatch** or **Cyber Patrol**, you may want to make this decision for yourself. Download the demos from their Web sites (or on the CD-ROM) and try them out. You may find that one of the other programs is what you want. In certain cases, it might be your only choice (for example, if you are running DOS).

I have two final warnings about all of this demo software. Please tape these warnings to your computer when you are using the software so that you don't forget them:

- Follow the directions exactly when Installing and uninstalling the software.
- Use only one blocking product at a time.

Very bad things happen when you ignore these warnings. A perfect recipe for disaster would be to throw the demo software away without uninstalling first. (You could end up reinstalling your entire system from scratch.) Strange things also happen when you have more than one blocking program going at once. You get all sorts of warnings and program problems, as well as crashes.

Don't Forget About Bess

The Real Bess

Remember that you do have one other alternative which is to go with Bess, my other favorite choice. Bess will block material at the level of your ISP and so is different from the commercial products I have talked about here. Bess is so simple it doesn't need any attention at all (no lists to update and that sort of thing). To read about Bess see "Bess, a Family ISP" on page 113.

Quick Feature Comparison Chart

Here is an almost exhaustive run through of all of the features of each product.

Feature	Cyber Patrol	CYBERsitter	Net Nanny	SurfWatch
Price	$49.95	$39.95	$49.95	$24.95 (special book price)
Time period for free filter list updates w/purchase	Six months	Forever	Forever	Two months
Filter list cost	$19.95 (6 mo.)	Free	Free	$3.95 (per mo.)
Platforms supported	Windows 3.1 Windows 95 Macintosh	Windows 3.1 Windows 95?	DOS Windows 3.1 Windows 95	Windows 3.1 Windows 95 Macintosh
Company name	Microsystems Software, Inc.	Solid Oak Software	Net Nanny	SurfWatch Software
Phone	(800) 828-2608	(800) 388-2761	(800) 340-7177	(800) 458-6600
Web site (URL address)	http://www.microsys.com	http://www.solidoak.com	http://www.netnanny.com	http://www.surfwatch.com
Types of Blocked Sites				
Blocks for sexual material and acts or nudity	Yes	Yes	You decide	Yes
Blocks for violence, profanity, drugs, or hate literature	Yes	Yes	You decide	No
GENERAL FEATURES				
Customizable list	Yes	Yes	Yes	No
Blocking filter choice	Yes	No	No	No
Ability to ignore blocking for particular sites	Yes	Yes	No	No

Chapter 11 Security Software Compared

Feature	Cyber Patrol	CYBERsitter	Net Nanny	SurfWatch
GENERAL FEATURES (continued)			
Blocks images	Yes	Yes	Yes	Yes
Image downloads blocked	Yes	Yes	Yes	Yes
FTP downloads blocked	Yes	No	Yes	Yes
Blocks newsgroups	Yes	Yes	Yes	Yes
Blocks chat rooms	Yes	Yes	Yes	Yes
Limits access time	Yes	No	No	No
Filters profanity	No	Yes	Yes	No
Blocks personal information from being sent	No	Yes	Yes	No
Blocks use of other software	Yes	No	Yes	No
Works with online services	Yes (free versions for members)	Yes (not AOL)	Yes	No
Password protection	Yes	Yes	No	Yes
Monitors access attempts	No	Yes	Yes	No
Gives choice between blocking and warning	No	Yes	No	No
Technical/computer knowledge required	Some	Moderate	Moderate	None
Difficulty to install and uninstall	Some	Moderate	Moderate	None
Built-in help	Yes	Yes	Yes	No
Phone technical support	Yes (508)879-9000	Yes (805)892-2557	Yes (604)662-8522	Yes (415)948-9505
Email technical support	Yes cybersup@microsys.com	Yes support@solid-oak.com	Yes netnanny@net-nanny.com	Yes support@surf-watch.com

Chapter 12
The Future of Net Safety

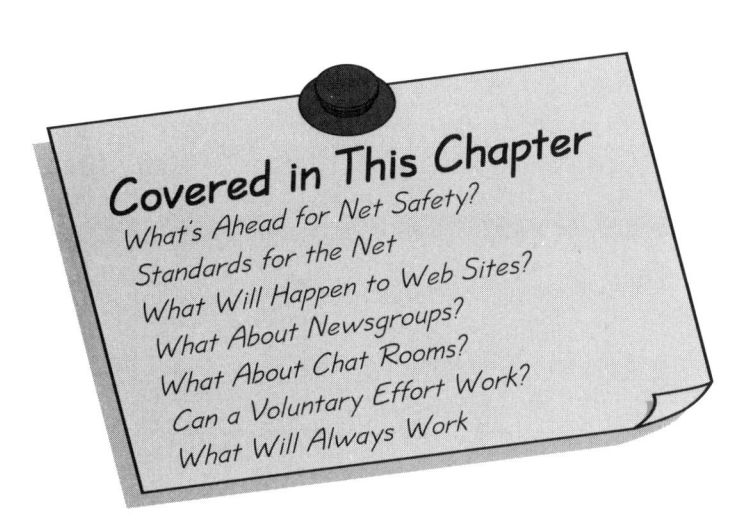

Covered in This Chapter
What's Ahead for Net Safety?
Standards for the Net
What Will Happen to Web Sites?
What About Newsgroups?
What About Chat Rooms?
Can a Voluntary Effort Work?
What Will Always Work

What's Ahead for Net Safety?

I'm going to play fortune teller for you now. I'll tell you where things are heading for children's safety on the Net, what will change, and what will not. For some of that future material to make sense, however, I will need to talk about things that are happening in the present.

Many of you may know that after a great deal of fussing and moaning in Washington, D.C., Congress and the President passed a law that contained a provision on the Internet. The gist of that provision was:

"No one may knowingly put anything indecent on the Internet that may be seen by children.

I wish I could tell you that this is a good law or even that it was constitutional. I can't even tell you that it is useful. The fact of the matter is that the United States does not control the Internet and cannot say how it will be used. Every single one of those members of Congress and the President knew it and still passed an unenforceable law.

So, you might ask:

"Why did they pass a law with a provision that is unenforceable as well as unconstitutional?"

So they could tell voters they are tough on smut.

Here Is the Answer

My best guess is *fear*. They were afraid that if they said, "Hey, that's stupid, we can't enforce that provision, get it out of there," some reporter or political opponent would have said, "So you are in favor of exposing children to all sorts of foul indecency and warping their impressionable young minds." Perhaps the thought of having to defend themselves against that charge was what brought about this foolishness.

> *Note:* The CD-ROM has the full text of the Telecommunications bill on it for your reading pleasure. Better yet go to
> http://www.yahoo.com/Society_and_Culture/Civil_Rights/Censorship/Censorship_and_the_Net/
> for a lively discussion of all of the relevant issues.

The Good Things

I can tell you that several good things have occurred as a result of this foolishness. It has really annoyed and irritated users of the Net—so much so that they have actually gotten themselves to agree on a few things. First, they have brought suit against the U.S. Government for infringing upon their constitutional right to freedom of speech.

> *Note:* Lest you think that only radicals care about such things, one of the groups that helped bring the suit was the American Library Association. I, for one, have never thought of librarians as being wacko radicals out to smash all that is good and decent in the world. How about you?

Second, Web pages are adorning themselves with the blue ribbon you see in Figure 12.1 as a sign of protest against this law.

Third, Net users and groups are coming up with some real solutions that just might fix the problem.

302   Chapter 12 The Future of Net Safety

Figure 12.1
SafeSurf Web Site.

Blue ribbon

Standards for the Net

Most of the solutions revolve around developing standards that Web page designers will use to rate the content of their pages. I want to tell you about the more important groups working on this issue.

The PICs Protocol

The PICS group (Platform for Internet Content Selection) has come up with a set of standards that will allow three things to happen

- **Sites can rate themselves**—a site creator will be able to voluntarily label the content of the site.

- **Third-Party Rating Services**—various services will be able to label the content of sites according to all sorts of categories (like sex, violence, and so on).

- **The rating systems will be easy to use**—parents and teachers will be able to use the rating and labels to control what children see.

The goal of this group is to provide these tools to everybody on the Net. They believe that this is the best way to both protect children and maintain the diversity that exists on the Net. For all of this to happen, a couple of things need to work together. But first let me describe two of the third-party rating services that you are likely to encounter in the future.

The RSAC Rating Service

RSAC (Recreational Software Advisory Council) is an organization that will be rating sites for three different categories: violence, nudity/sex, and language. Here is how it will work. RSAC will provide site creators with a detailed questionnaire about the site as it relates to the three categories. The site creator answers the questions and receives a rating from RSAC. The site creator then displays the rating as a label on the site. *(I call the rating labels "stickers".)*

The SafeSurf Rating Standard

SafeSurf, another rating system that site creators can use, has a lot more categories and ways to rate. All a site creator has to do is go to SafeSurf's Web site and fill out the form you see in Figure 12.2.

*Figure 12.2
Part of SafeSurf's Site Rating Form.*

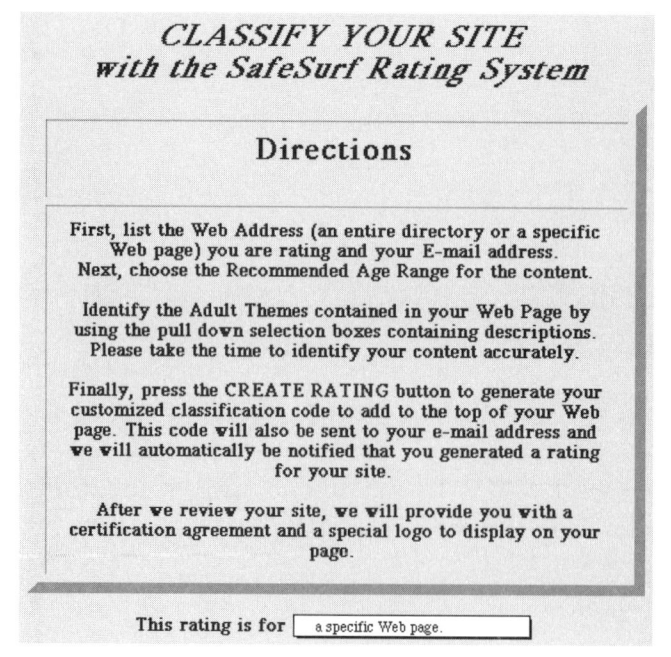

CLASSIFY YOUR SITE with the SafeSurf Rating System

Directions

First, list the Web Address (an entire directory or a specific Web page) you are rating and your E-mail address. Next, choose the Recommended Age Range for the content.

Identify the Adult Themes contained in your Web Page by using the pull down selection boxes containing descriptions. Please take the time to identify your content accurately.

Finally, press the CREATE RATING button to generate your customized classification code to add to the top of your Web page. This code will also be sent to your e-mail address and we will automatically be notified that you generated a rating for your site.

After we review your site, we will provide you with a certification agreement and a special logo to display on your page.

This rating is for [a specific Web page.]

Site creators rate various aspects of the site, including what age ranges it is appropriate for. Here are the age categories:

- All ages

- Older children

- Teens

- Older teens

- Adult supervision recommended

- Adults

- Limited to adults

- Adults only

- Explicitly for adults

A site creator places a value for each category (like profanity) on the site, as you can see in Figure 12.3. SafeSurf then generates a sticker for the site. SafeSurf also reviews sites to see if it agrees with the self-ratings and, if so, certifies the site.

With a system this detailed it becomes possible to differentiate between a site that holds a picture of Botticelli's Venus de Milo and one that holds a poster of Playboy's playmate of the month. This is information that can be used to determine what content will be presented under what circumstances. It also means that which sites are blocked becomes much easier for a parent to determine.

Figure 12.3
SafeSurf's Profanity Values.

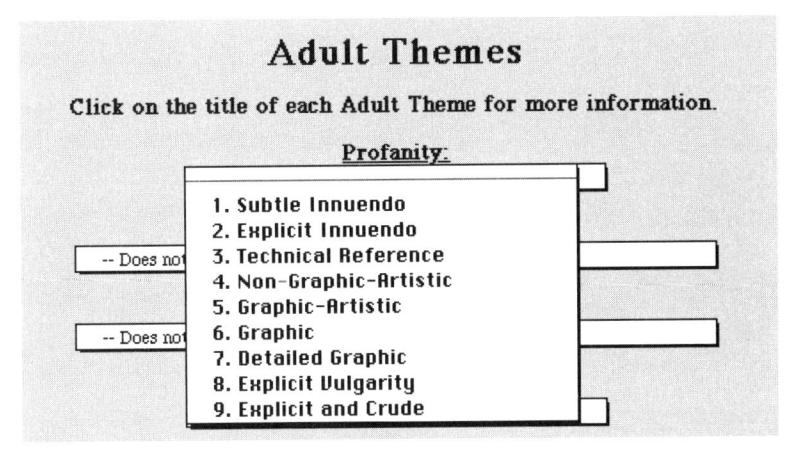

Adult Themes

Click on the title of each Adult Theme for more information.

Profanity:

1. Subtle Innuendo
2. Explicit Innuendo
3. Technical Reference
4. Non-Graphic-Artistic
5. Graphic-Artistic
6. Graphic
7. Detailed Graphic
8. Explicit Vulgarity
9. Explicit and Crude

306   Chapter 12   The Future of Net Safety

What Will Happen to Web Sites

The next piece in the puzzle is the Web browser. Several of the biggest browsers have already announced their intention to support these various rating systems. As soon as they do, you will have the ability to use the browser to filter Net sites based on the ratings.

In this future browser/software package, you set up a rating system you want for your children. Perhaps you choose the "Movie" rating system and determine that the kids can look at all PG and milder sites. When the child tries to go to a site (see Figure 12.4) several things happen.

*Figure 12.4
A Child Following a New Link.*

Child clicks here to go to Silly Billy's Site

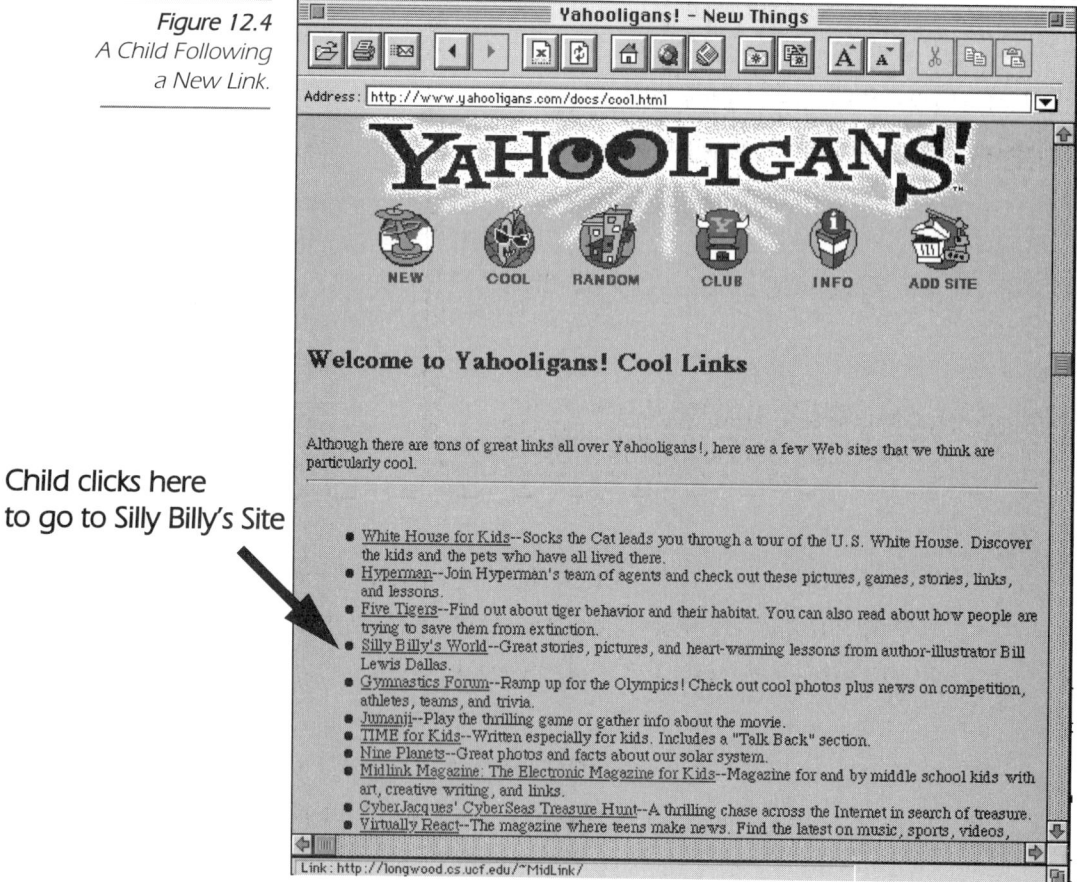

What Will Happen to Web Sites   307

- The browser looks ahead at the new site's rating sticker.

- If the site is PG or milder, the child can view it, as shown in Figure 12.5.

Figure 12.5
A site with an Acceptable Rating.

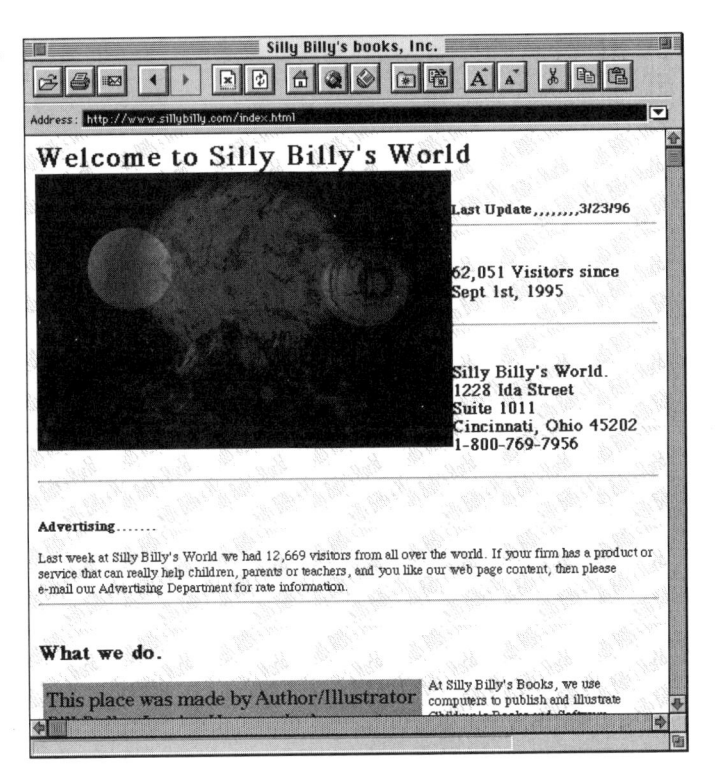

- If the site does not have an acceptable rating the browser blocks access with some sort of comment, as shown in Figure 12.6.

- If the site has no rating at all, the browser blocks access and makes some comment about that as well (see Figure 12.7).

308   Chapter 12 The Future of Net Safety

Figure 12.6
A Browser Indicating the Site Can't Be Viewed.

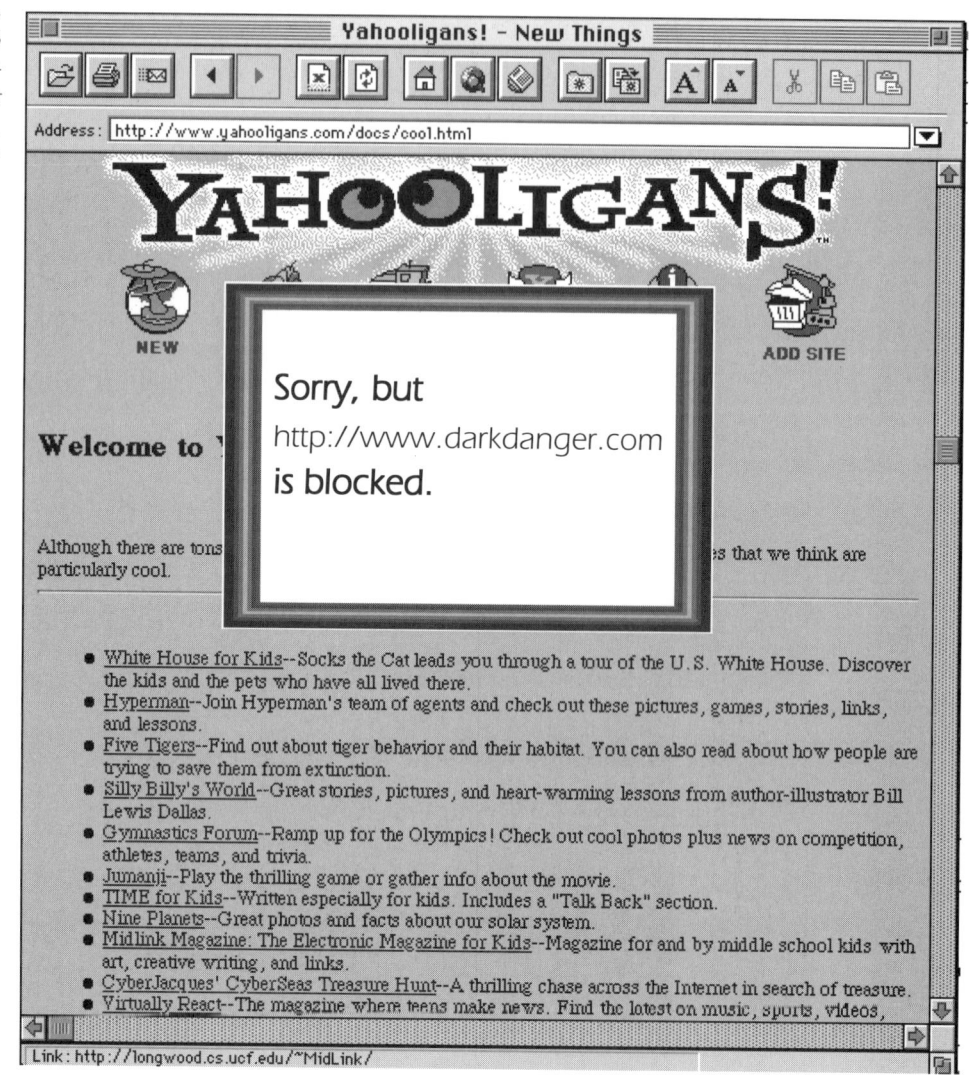

Remember, **Cyber Patrol** is already supporting the SafeSurf rating system. So it makes sense that you will see filtering software and browsers create versions specifically to work with such rating systems as well.

What Will Happen to Web Sites   309

Figure 12.7
Blocking a Site with No Rating.

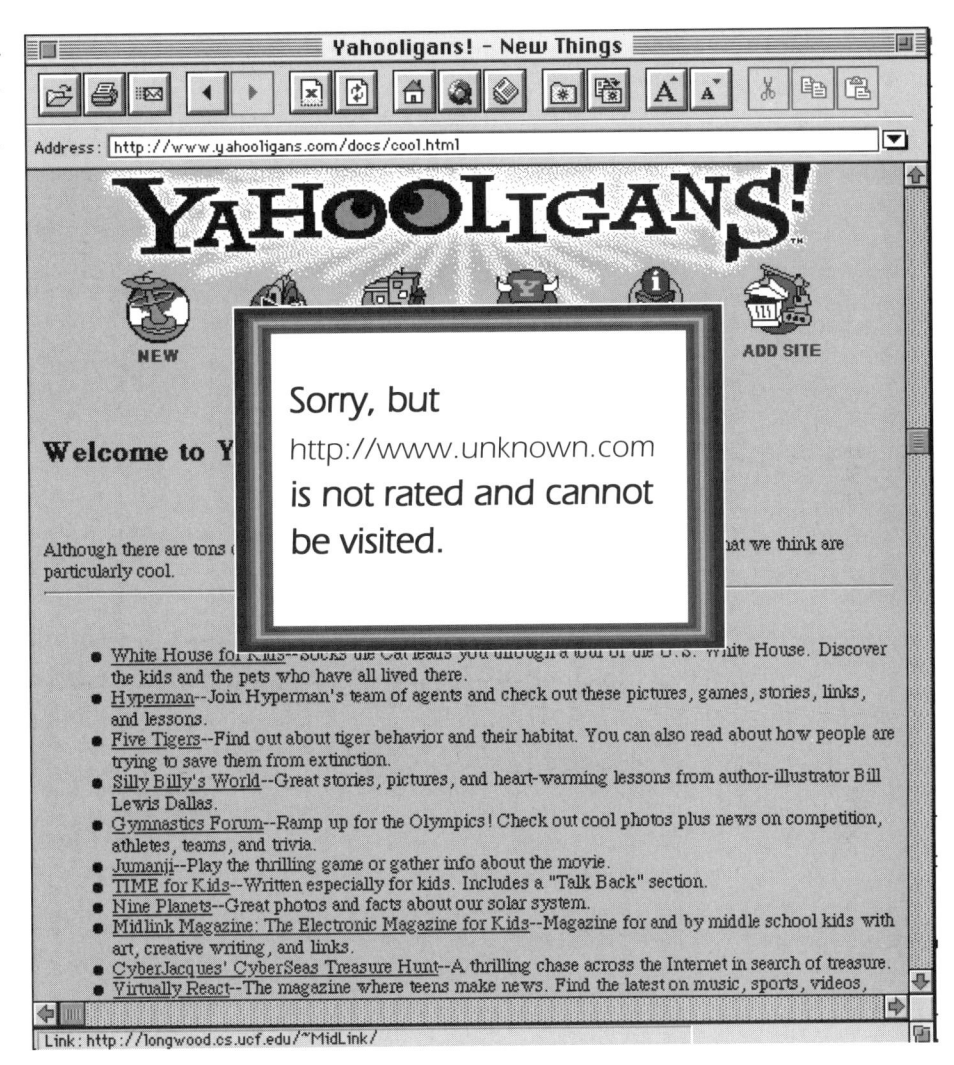

> Sorry, but http://www.unknown.com is not rated and cannot be visited.

How Soon Will This Happen?

Now it is truly crystal ball time. First, the major browsers like *Netscape*, *Mosaic*, and *Internet Explorer* will support ratings-based filtering. You might expect to see these new versions by early 1997 (crossing my fingers here).

Once that is done, site creators will rate their sites in droves. They will do so for several reasons:

- The software to do it will be free.
- It will be easy to do (it takes just a few minutes for a simple Web site).
- Nobody will want to be blocked for the wrong reasons.
- Most people will want to keep out people who don't want to be there.

For the system to work, however, most Web sites have to be willing to do this. If you ask me whether web site creators from all over the world will do it, my answer is "probably."

What about Newsgroups?

Newsgroups are not as easy to rate because the content can come from anywhere or anyone. It is also in newsgroups that the most notorious "adult material" can be found.

In reality, however, I think only one type of newsgroup will have a problem with a rating system and that is an issue newsgroup. Issue newsgroups deal with things like politics, religion, and so forth. The problem is that one commentator in that group could write so tamely that no one would be offended, while the next writer might make comments that would make a politician blush. Newsgroups like this will be difficult to rate using any rating system.

This leaves a majority of newsgroups which could be rated fairly easily. Many of the hobbyist newsgroups (like rec.gardening or rec.books.children) can and will rate themselves. Many newsgroups that have explicit adult material will also rate themselves. I think they will do so because it is easy and to avoid the wrath of the Net community.

What about Chat Rooms?

While I do believe that rating systems will be used on Web sites and newsgroups, I hold out no hope for chat rooms. They will continue to be places that children should not go.

Can a Voluntary Effort Work?

I imagine that a few of you might be skeptical as to whether this sort of thing can be done as a voluntary effort. You probably believe that it won't work unless somebody makes people behave.

For all our sakes, I hope that's wrong. If it can't be done voluntarily, it won't be done at all. Because the Net does not belong to any one country, it cannot be controlled by any one nation's laws. It is not the iron hand of force that will make the Net safe for children, but the sweet hand of reason.

What Will Always Work

Remember, however, you still have final control over what your children see and experience on the Net. If you think the Net contains material unsuitable for your children, then you, and you alone, have the perfect tool to protect them. You have your wisdom, your values, and your strong and capable hands that can reach out and turn the computer off.

Glossary

access time

The time you are connected to a network such as an online service or the Internet.

address

Either an email address of a person, such as julie@pobox.com, or a Web site address such as http://www.pbs.com. An email address always has a "@" in it.

alt

The newsgroups that start with this abbreviation (for "alternative") are the ones with the most bizarre, perverse, and entertaining content. Unlike other newsgroups, alt newsgroups don't need to be voted on in order to exist.

Archie

A type of search on the Internet. It is the Internet's basic system for finding files. An Archie server on the Internet is a computer that has lists of available archived files found on the rest of the Internet.

archive

A collection of files on the Internet. There is usually someone responsible for updating files and maintaining such archives.

ARPA

Advanced Research Projects Agency, the U.S. government agency that funded ARPANET, a precursor to the Internet.

ASCII

American Standard Code for Information Interchange. An ASCII file is a text file of characters.

binary

Non-text data files that can be downloaded.

blocking

The act of denying access to an address. Blocking and filtering mean the same thing.

browser

The software program that you use on your computer to view WWW, FTP, and Gopher sites on the Internet. The most popular browsers are *Netscape, Mosaic,* and *Internet Explorer.*

chat rooms
Messages sent between some users in real time.

cyberspace
A term created by the science fiction writer William Gibson in his novel, *Neuromancer*. It refers to the Internet and more generally to the digital world created by computers.

download
The act of copying or getting a file from a network to your personal computer.

email
A text message you create on your computer and then send to someone else on his or her computer. You send the email from one address to another over an electronic network.

Eudora
A commercial program for reading and sending email. A shareware version also exists.

FAQ
Frequently Asked Questions. Questions and answers regarding basic information on a particular subject. FAQs are commonly associated with newsgroups.

filtering
The blocking of certain Internet sites based on some criteria.

firewall

A method of restricting the data sent between an internal network of computers and computers on the Internet. It is used by companies to keep their internal network secure and yet still provide Internet access.

flame

A very rude remark. The flame is usually directed at another person and is almost certainly so rude that the person writing it would never dare utter it in person.

forum

An online discussion group where network users gather to discuss particular topics.

freeware

Software that can be used free of charge.

Gopher

A file search system. It is one of the older ways to search for a particular file that you want on the Internet.

home page

(1) The site from which you start each Web exploration. It is the site that you specify to your browser and to which you log on. (2) The top-level pages that people create for themselves on the Web.

HTML

Hypertext Markup Language. This is the language used in Web page design and it is what allows you to click on a spot in a page and thereby go to another Web page.

Information Superhighway

Another term for the Internet. Other terms include: Cyberspace, and the Net.

Internet

A world-wide collection of computers connected together and filled with interesting stuff. Slang expressions for this include: the Information Superhighway, Cyberspace, the Net.

ISP

Internet Service Provider. This is a company that provides access to the Internet via a phone number that you dial up from your computer.

JPEG

A compressed file format for images. Frequently, downloadable images on the Internet are JPEG images.

lurking

The act of reading a newsgroup but not taking part in the discussions yourself.

mirror site

A site that holds a copy of material from another site.

modem

A device that you attach to your computer so that it can call other computers.

moderated

A newsgroup or chat room that has some sort of guiding hand. The usual job of a moderator is to keep out offensive material and flames and keep discussions from wandering off the topic.

network

Any set of computers connected together that can communicate directly with each other.

newsgroups

A global network of Internet discussion groups on various subjects. "Newsgroups" is short for Usenet Newsgroups.

online service

Private networks that contain collections of discussion groups, topical information, and downloadable material. All of the online services offer "trapdoor" access to the Internet.

page

A WWW site. Pages refer to one another, and these connections are called links or hot spots.

PPP

Point to Point Protocol, an alternative to a SLIP account. You either have a PPP or SLIP account through your ISP.

shareware

Software that the author charges a fee for using. Usually, the author uses the honor system for collecting the money.

SLIP

Serial Line Internet Protocol. You either have a SLIP or PPP account through your ISP. A PPP account is better.

smilies (shorthands, or strange things you see in newsgroups)

A variety of shorthand abbreviations with longer meanings. For the complete list of these terms go to http://yahoo.com/Arts/Computer_Generated/ASCII_Art/Smilies. The more common ones that you might encounter are:

:-)	smile	:-(	Frown
;-)	Wink	:-D	Big Smile
8-)	Smile (user wears glasses)	:-Q	Tongue hanging out in disgust
:-O	Mouth open in amazement	<G>	Grin
<BG>	Big Grin	BTW	By the way
FWIW	For what it's worth	FYI	For your information
IMO	In my opinion	IMHO	In my humble opinion
OTOH	On the other hand	ROFL	Rolling on the floor, laughing
TIA	Thanks in advance	TTFN	Ta-ta for now.

surfing

The activity of moving from one Internet site to another in an unstructured manner.

TCP/IP

The set of communication protocols that specifies how data is transmitted on the Internet. TCP (*Transmission Control Protocol*) controls the sending of data, ensuring that it is delivered. IP (*Internet Protocol*) determines the structure of the data and the addressing used to deliver it to its destination.

thread

A group of connected messages in a newsgroup.

URL

Uniform Resource Locator. This is someone's or some site's address on the Internet.

World Wide Web

The graphic collection of material on the Internet that organizes material through hypertext links. WWW material is viewed using a browser.

Index

A

access time, definition of 40–41, 313
addresses on Internet 313
    definition of 36–38
Alta Vista search engine 218
America Online 59–67
    best features 59
    cost of 65
    homework, help with 63
    Internet access in 64
    parent controls 64
    telephone number 65
AOL. *See* America Online.
Apple Internet Connection Kit 103
archive, definition of 314
ARPANET 314
ASCII 314
The At-Home Dad Newsletter 211

B

Berit's Best Sites for Children 148
Bess, a family ISP 113–120
    cost of 117
    definition of 113
    recommendation of 118, 296
    telephone number 118

binary 314
blocking software
    in America Online 64
    in CompuServe 73
    Cyber Patrol 266–274
    CYBERsitter 275–280
    definition of 314, 315
    in Microsoft Network 92
    Net Nanny 280–285
    in Prodigy 83
    SurfWatch 285–290
books, online 33
Bps, definition of 48
browser
    definition of 49, 314
    implementing child safe standards 306
    Internet Explorer 314
    Mosaic 314
    Netscape 314

C

Captain Kirk Web site 179
CD-ROM, contents of 10
chat rooms
    child safety in 311
    definition of 29, 315
    moderated 318
    in online services 45–46

child safety
    chat rooms 311
    future of 306–311
    on the Internet
        rudeness 251
        sexual requests 251
    keeping children out of
        chat rooms 253
        newsgroups 253
    lack of supervision 252, 253
    meeting online people 251
    moderated forums 254
    newsgroup standards 310
    online rules of behavior 257–261, 323
    parental Net experience 255
    perverts 251
    rules for 252–256
    safe Web sites
        Kid's Wave 261
        Safe Links 264
        Yahooligans 263
    sexual material on the Internet 249
    software. *See* blocking software.
    troubled children 255
    unsafeness of Internet 248
    what will always work 312
childcare advice 208
Christmas site, Uncle Bob's 197
CIA World Fact Book 173
CNN Web site 157, 160
Cockroach World 178
commercial online service. *See* online service.
CompuServe 67–76
    cost of 74
    Cyber Patrol's use in 72
    best features 68
    Internet access in 73
    parent controls 73
    telephone number 74
Cool Site of the Day 151

Cyber Patrol 266–274
    used in CompuServe 72
    computers supported 270
    cost of 274
    features 271
    used in Prodigy 83
    recommendation of 293
    telephone number 272
CyberKids Web site 144
CYBERsitter 275–280
    computers supported 276
    cost of 280
    features 277
    telephone number 280
cyberspace, definition of 315

D

dialer, definition of 49
dinosaurs, Museum of Paleontology 191
Disney Web site 182
doctor's advice 204–205
download, definition of 315

E

Electric Library 229–231
email 315
    definition of 20–21
    program for 315
    understanding addresses 37
Encyclopaedia Britannica 225–229
encyclopedia
    Electric Library 229–231
    Encyclopaedia Britannica 225–229
    Free Internet Encyclopedia 232–234
ESPN Web site 169
Exploratorium Web site 185

F

family home page Web sites 213–216
Family Planet Web site 209
Family World Web site 149
FAQ
    definition of 26, 315
    on Internet connectivity 107
filtering software. *See* blocking software.
firewall, definition of 316
flaming
    definition of 27, 316
    rule against 260
Free Internet Encyclopedia 232–234
freeware 316
FTP
    definition of 32–33
    software sites 34
    understanding addresses 37

G

Galaxy Web site 133
Global Village Web site 124
Gopher 316

H

home page, definition of 316
homework, help with
    CIA World Fact Book 173
    Electric Library 229–231
    Encyclopaedia Britannica 225–229
    Free Internet Encyclopedia 232–234
    in America Online 63
    in Prodigy 82
    on the Internet 225–235
hot, WWW definition of 30

I

Information Super Highway. *See* Internet.
Inter-Links Web site 130
Internet
    atmosphere of 247
    censorship of 301
    child safety rules 252–256
    compared to online services 43–44
    connecting to, what you need 46–48
    contents of 19–36
    cost compared to online service 57
    definition of 14–19, 317
    equipment required 4
    hate literature on 250
    indecency provision in Telecom law 300
    physical components of 15
    sexual material on 249
    slang expressions for 317
    standards for 302–305
        future of 306–311
        PICS Protocol 303
        RSAC rating system 303
        SafeSurf rating system 304
    surfing 30–32
        definition of 18, 31
    types of computers on 16
    unsafeness of 248
    number of users 17
Internet account
    how to get 101
Internet Explorer 314
Internet in a Box 2.0 103
Internet Public Library 241
Internet service provider
    compared with online service 53
    definition of 44–45, 317
    how to get 101
    local ISP
        definition of 109
        where to find 48, 111
    quiz 52

Internet Starter Kit 102
ISP. *See* Internet service provider.

J

JPEG file format 317

K

Kbps, definition of 48
Kid's Wave Web site 261
Kids Web 146

L

Launchpad Web site 145
Dave Letterman's Top Ten List 192
libraries on the Net
    Internet Public Library 241
    National Library of Medicine 241
    Smithsonian 240
    WWW Virtual Library 136
links, definition of 30
lurking 317
    definition of 26

M

Julie McKeehan, email address xiv
MetaCrawler 237
Microsoft Network 87–95
    best features 87
    cost of 94
    Internet access in 93
    parent controls 92
    telephone number 94
mirror site 317
modem 4, 318
    type to buy 47
moderated forums
    child participation in 254

Mosaic 314
MovieLink Web site 184
movies 2
    reviews 210
MSN. *See* Microsoft Network.

N

NBC Intellicast Web site 166
Net Nanny 280–285
    best features 283
    computers supported 282
    cost of 285
    Internet access in 283
    telephone number 284
Net. *See* Internet.
Netscape 314
The New York Times Web site 163
newsgroups
    abbreviations in 319
    alt, definition of 313
    alt.parenting.solutions 202
    definition of 21–27, 318
    FAQ, definition of 26
    flaming, definition of 27
    keeping children out 253
    lurking, definition of 26, 317
    misc.education 203
    misc.education.home-school.misc 204
    misc.kids 201
    misc.kids.computers 202
    misc.kids.health 201
    moderated 318
    number of 21
    parenting ones 200–204
    posting, definition of 23
    rudeness in 24–25
    rules for 26–27
    standards for 310
    threads 320
    understanding addresses 37

O

online rules of behavior 257–261,
online service
    America Online 59–67
    best features of 56
    chat rooms 45–46
    comparisons
        costs of each 97
        to cost of Internet 57
        to each other 96
        to the Internet 43–44
        with ISP 53
    CompuServe 67–76
    definition of 42, 318
    forum, definition of 316
    free offers 58
    access to Internet 43
    Microsoft Network 87–95
    Prodigy 77–87
    quiz 50
    recommendation of 95

P

page, definition of 318
Museum of Paleontology Web site 191
parental controls. *See* blocking software.
parenting
    book reviews 208, 210
    childcare advice 208
    custody advice 208
    doctor's advice 204–205
    Internet safety advice 252–256
    legal advice 208
    movie reviews 210
    newsgroups 200–204
    newsletters 208
ParentSoup Web site 209
ParentsPlace Web site 207
PBS Web site 153
pen pals, finding 223

Pick of the day sites
    InfiNet's Cool Site of the Day 151
    Spider's Pick 195
PICS Protocol 303
Planet Earth Home Page 189
pornography on Internet 249
posting, definition of 23
PPP 318
Prodigy 77–87
    best features 77
    cost of 85
    Cyber Patrol's use in 83
    homework, help with 82
    Internet access in 84
    parent controls 83
    telephone number 85
Project Gutenberg 33

R

RSAC rating system 303

S

Safe Links Web site 264
SafeSurf xii
    home page 302
    internet address xii
    Kid's Wave 261
    rating system 304
Savvy Search 236
searching
    Alta Vista search engine 218
    using capital letters 221
    by country 238
    in foreign languages 236
    MetaCrawler, using 237
    for pen pals 223
    proper names 220
    Savvy Search, using 236
    search engine, how to use 219–223

sexual material on the Internet 249
shareware 319
SLIP 319
Smithsonian Library Web site 240
software, FTP sites to download from 34
The Spider's Web site 194
Sports World Web site 170
Sprynet 104
standards for the Internet 302–305
Star Trek Web sites 179
Star Wars Web sites 187
surfing 30–32
    definition of 18, 31, 319
SurfWatch 285–290
    computers supported 288
    cost of 289
    features 288
    recommendation of 291
    telephone number 289

T

TCP/IP 319
    definition of 49
telephone lines, necessary number of 41
text files, where they are found 32
thread, definition of 320

U

Ultimate Children's Internet Sites 139
Uncle Bob's Kids' Page 140
URL
    definition of 36–38, 320
    way to avoid typing 38

W

WeatherNet Web site 164
World Wide Web
    definition of 30–32, 320
    home page, definition of 316
    hot, definition of 30
    links, definition of 30
    standards for 306
    understanding addresses 37
WWW Virtual Library 136
    sports 168
WWW. *See* World Wide Web.

Y

Yahoo
    description of 126–129
    dictionary section 234
    Disney section 183
    family home page section 216
    local ISP list 111
    pen pal section 223
    searching in 127
    Star Wars section 187
    version for children 263
Yahooligans Web site 263

Using Internet Explorer to Get to a Web Site

If you are using an ISP, you can connect to the Internet and then click on the display or the URL on the CD-ROM. Internet Explorer will then open that *actual* Web page without your having to type in a URL at all.

Microsoft Internet Explorer

Versions of Microsoft Internet Explorer for Windows 3.1, Windows 95, and Macintosh can be found on the disk. Look on the CD-ROM to find information on how to install it.

Demo Blocking Software

There are demo versions of both Cyber Patrol and Safe Surf. Make sure that you read the installation file associated with whichever demo you choose.

There is also a set of pages demonstrating how Bess, the Family ISP works.

Demo Internet Software

You'll find useful freeware and shareware Internet software.

Miscellaneous Files

You'll find other files I mention in the book, such as Frank Hecker's article on the Internet.

What's on the CD

Any computer running Windows 3.1, Windows 95, or Macintosh OS can read the CD-ROM in the back of the book. Before doing anything else, read the "Read Me First" file on the CD-ROM for any last minute information.

Information about Web Sites in the Book

This book describes many different Web sites, usually with an address and a figure showing what it looks like. There are two ways to actually get to those sites once you are connected to the Internet:

- You can type the URL (the address) into your Internet browser.

- You can use Internet Explorer, the Internet browser on this CD-ROM, to see the same displays from the book on your computer.